THE AUTHOR

Irving L. Horowitz was born in Harlem, New York, where his parents had settled after emigrating from Europe. He was educated at the City College of New York, Columbia University, and Brandeis University. Following a year spent as Teaching Fellow in the Social Sciences at Brandeis University, he served as Visiting Professor of Sociology at the University of Buenos Aires, Faculty of Philosophy and Letters, and has since returned there on several occasions. Later he became Assistant Professor of Sociology at Bard College. He is at present Chairman of the department of Anthropology and Sociology at Hobart & William Smith Colleges.

Professor Horowitz is the author of *The Idea of War and Peace in Contemporary Philosophy; Philosophy, Science and the Sociology of Knowledge;* and earlier studies in the history of social and philosophic ideas. Brief essays of his have appeared in *The Journal of Politics; The Political Quarterly; History and Theory; Philosophy and Phenomenological Research; Philosophy: Journal of the Royal Institute; Diogenes; Hispanic American Historical Review; Dissent; Studium;* and other English-language and foreign-language periodicals.

RADICALISM AND THE REVOLT
AGAINST REASON

RADICALISM AND THE REVOLT AGAINST REASON

The Social Theories of Georges Sorel
With a translation
of his essay on
THE DECOMPOSITION OF MARXISM

---

by

IRVING LOUIS HOROWITZ

Chairman, Department of Anthropology and Sociology
Hobart and William Smith Colleges

Routledge and Kegan Paul
LONDON

First published 1961
by Routledge & Kegan Paul Ltd
Broadway House, 68–74 Carter Lane
London, E.C.4

Printed in Great Britain
by Richard Clay and Company Ltd
Bungay, Suffolk

CONTENTS

v

CONTENTS

ACKNOWLEDGEMENTS

EVEN a modest intellectual enterprise tends to make immodest demands on the time and energies of many people. This is, at any rate, true of this work. It would not be possible to detail the extent of my indebtedness to co-workers in the social sciences, except to confess that it is undoubtedly larger than I am capable of assessing. So with apologies to those whom I have not mentioned, let me offer my deepest appreciation to the following: Robert S. Cohen of Boston University, whose critical scientific perspective saw the shortcomings in the manuscript and offered constant guidance to help correct them. Abraham Edel, of the City College of New York, read an earlier draft of the manuscript and made suggestions for improvement which are, I hope, adequately reflected in the finished product. Lewis A. Coser, of Brandeis University, placed his enormous reserve of knowledge about western European socialism which can only partially be reflected in a work of such special scope.

The late Paul Radin, with whom I discussed the themes and times my book covers on many occasions, gave unstintingly of his time and unhesitatingly of his first-hand wisdom. His incisive comments on European sociology and philosophy at the turn of the century were genuinely inspiring. The loss of this humane scholar will be felt by those who knew him.

The technical assistance received was of the first quality. My wife, Ruth Horowitz, who by this time is a tried and tested collaborator on all of my ventures, gave the book its critical first and last look. Yvette Cameron and Eli Schleifer of the Brandeis University Library, and Marion Vosburgh of the Bard College Library, offered every assistance in procuring the necessary documents from the far-flung

ACKNOWLEDGEMENTS

empire of books, wherever they may have been housed. Bobbye Suckle Ortiz of New York City placed her rich knowledge of the romance languages at my disposal and aided me with the translation in all its stages. Mrs. Ortiz stoically shared in the chores of typing with Arlynne Turitz of Middletown, Connecticut.

In sum, the generous counsel of these friends and colleagues saved me from all types of error. For remaining shortcomings I am, of course, solely responsible.

IRVING LOUIS HOROWITZ

Geneva, New York
January 10, 1961

I

PRELIMINARY OBSERVATIONS ON THE REVOLT AGAINST REASON

'We owe to Sorel the rediscovery of the relationship between democracy in general and absolutism, and their point of intersection in civilization.'
Roberto Michels, POLITICAL PARTIES

THE work of Georges Sorel is a forthright attempt to convince people that the most significant statement of political philosophy is one which candidly admits that questions of philosophy involve some comprehension of the politics of philosophy. Statements about human nature and conduct, the State and Society, can be seriously entertained and utilized in human affairs only if they at some point connect up with the concrete experiences and abstract fantasies of mankind. Vilfredo Pareto, writing at the death of Sorel, indicates that it was Sorel's unyielding devotion to the ideals of social science, rather than his unconscious flirtations with metaphysical generalities that really marks Sorel as a man apart.[1]

Sorel sensed that philosophy is neither fiction nor science. This peculiar amalgam of the true and the false, the empirical and the ideological, the practical and the utopian, are the everyday paradoxes of ordinary existence.

[1] Vilfredo Pareto, 'Georges Sorel', *La Ronda* (1922), pp. 547–8.

1

It is in this sense that while Everyman cannot be a novelist or a social scientist, he can yet function philosophically. But since common sense is not yet the critical sense, man is a philosopher only in a fragmented and not completely rational form. Ordinary men still philosophize in much the same way as their primitive ancestors. It is theorizing about the unknown rather than over the known. It is an intellectual compensation for the manifold fears modern man shares about present and future existence. Sorel aimed to translate these fears and the myths they generate into a general theory of action.

The special attraction of Sorel for many has been his intuitive recognition of the primitivist, non-rational basis of thought in general, and political perspectives in particular. He framed a political philosophy of active radicalism based on the assumptions of irrationalism— on the superiority of the myth of projective impressions over critical judgment. When we consider how few prophets of socialism have been willing to test the soundness of their views in the cloudy waters of individual psychology, we can begin to surmise Sorel's place in the history of social ideas.

It is now over a half century since publication of Sorel's three most intellectually durable contributions to political sociology: *Réflexions sur la violence*, *Les illusions du progrès*, and *La décomposition du marxisme*. Their importance is perhaps best illustrated by the unfailing interest shown in his work by social scientists. Sorel grew to manhood in a restless society that witnessed the betrayal of one beautifully phrased social ideal after another, one violent political revolution after another, a society that could move from the Paris Commune to the infamy of the Dreyfus affair within a quarter of a century. This represented a decisive departure from Enlightenment rationalism of the eighteenth century and French utopianism of the nineteenth century. The supposition of an eternal *progrès de l'esprit humain* was in need of serious re-evaluation.

Sorel was in the forefront of a broad counter-rationalism and counter-utopianism that incuded representatives in every area: from Bergson in metaphysics to Baudelaire in poetry. Intellectual epochs have distinctive features by which they are known to all. Just as the second half of the eighteenth century put forth the idea of consciousness as a correlate to the notion of progress, and as the first half of the nineteenth century presented the idea of sensuousness as the highest reality; *fin de siècle* France initiated the contemporary effort to establish the unconscious as the motor force of human existence. It was Sorel's primary aim to employ scientific rationalism to go beyond both the rational and the utopian for an explanation of the motion and structure of human society. When we enter the realm of production, Sorel maintained, we leave behind us the dross of the abstract, idealist critique of society dominant in prior ages.[1] Likewise, when we enter the realm of the State we must perforce leave utopian fantasy behind.[2]

The task of moving beyond political rationalism and utopian radicalism is a major part of Sorel's work. His philosophy of history and his psychology of action were both forged in the crucible of this attempt to fuse socialism and irrationalism.

Although a certain fascination exists in tracing the influence of Sorel on modern political movements, he is of unquestionable interest intrinsically; for the fund of his political and philosophical ideas, and for the wide and paradoxical use of his leading tenets. Yet the sober fact remains that Sorel is essentially a minor figure in the history of ideas. He offers neither a consistent nor a unique standpoint in political theory. He is always responding to the immediate. All of his works have the characteristic of being a reply or a rejoinder to the writings of others. And as is usual with the less than great, Sorel's treatment of large themes is often ambiguous, crudely phrased and even logically specious. To paraphrase a remark that Freud once made in talking of Jung, our Sorel was nonetheless an excellent historian before deciding to become the prophet of syndical socialism. But it remains the prophecies of Sorel rather than his earlier historical studies of antiquity that command our attention and respect. Indeed, his historical studies are of concern now precisely for the way in which his political sociology is illumined by them.

The real importance of Sorel is, to use a much burdened word, symbolic. He represents an ideal type in the history of political ideas of the modern period.

This brings me to three lines of enquiry which seem particularly fruitful in the analysis of Sorel.

[1] *Introduction à l'économie moderne* (Paris, 1922, second edition), p. 246.
[2] *Réflexions sur la violence* (Paris, 1925, sixth edition), pp. 35–8 (50–2). The bracketed reference is to the corresponding pages in the most easily available English language edition; that published by the Free Press, Glencoe, Illinois, in 1950 with an introductory essay by Edward A. Shils. In all references to the *Réflexions*, the same form will be used; with references to the French text always immediately preceding the bracketed references to the English edition.

The first is his standpoint on the Enlightenment, with its attendant features of belief in the inviolability and invariability of human progress; in the possibilities of an illumination of the spirit through advanced legislative, juridical and educative techniques; and in the democratic credo of liberty, equality and a brotherhood in which each individual is to count as one. It is also the case that France has been the home of the sharpest critiques of Enlightenment—from the Social Catholicism of Dom Deschamps and the critical moralism of Jean-Jaques Rousseau in the eighteenth century to the subjective evolutionism of Bergson in the *fin de siècle*. The survival of this antithesis in French letters is manifested in philosophy proper by the conflict between the radical existentialism of Merleau-Ponty and Jean-Paul Sartre, and die-hard advocates of revolutionary rationalism like Auguste Cornu and Henri Lefebvre.

What made Sorel's contribution to this historical debate particularly notable was his insistence on a theory of socialism based on an anti-Enlightenment position no less absolute than that of the German mystic Hamann. Sorel set out to overcome and destroy the apparent incongruity of radical doctrine and an intuitionist psychology. In so doing, he achieved a special niche in the agonizing efforts to evaluate the meaning of Enlightenment and its practical uses to modern men.

A second and no less distinctive element in Sorel's social doctrine relates to the theoretical and pragmatic issues involved in a comprehension of the necessity of conflict and the worth of violence. Most sociologists and philosophers have dealt only in a cursory way with objections to the possibility of an integrated theory of social harmony that have their principal sources in thinkers like Marx, Nietzsche, Sorel and Freud.[1] The unconscious sources of spontaneous mass action, the irrational behaviour of a crowd composed of 'rational' men and the apocalyptic vision of historical transformation, continue to represent a clear challenge to locating common elements in different approaches to problems of peace and war, pacifism and

[1] A recent compilation, *The Nature of Conflict: Studies on the sociological aspects of International tensions* (Paris, 1957) held under the auspices of both The International Sociological Association and the United Nations Educational, Scientific and Cultural Organization, had done a great deal to catalogue the confusions on the issue of conflict, but very little to eliminate them. The factors in a conflict situation are carefully recorded; but since there is an absence of any causal primacy of these factors, the work avoids an examination of the central thing to be known, the nature of conflict.

violence. Sorel's objections to doctrines of consensus and eternal progress helped focus on the total problem of human conflict more incisively than any previous writer adopting a socialist position.

A third level at which Sorel can be understood concerns the question of politics itself; that is, the place of coercion and persuasion in modern political structures, the function and limits of State authority in modern societies, and the relation of political power elites to the masses at all stages of social intercourse. Sorel presents us with one of the most forceful critiques of the existing political order of industrial society to be found in the literature of power analysis. Just what a *realpolitik* having eclectic roots in Machiavelli, Vico, Marx and Bergson can achieve, and likewise what it fails to accomplish, can be largely uncovered in the examination of Georges Sorel's political sociology and philosophy.

The general antagonism to Sorel's social teachings is grounded in well intentioned sentiments and dangerous reasoning. It stems not simply from a loathing for authoritarian political philosophies, but also from an unwillingness to accept the challenge of such philosophies. The fact that European fascism has been vanquished as an immediate political threat, and that fascism claimed Sorel as a major theoretical prop, neither does away with the spectre of authoritarian political doctrines, nor with the case made against traditional liberal political aspirations. Indeed, the shattering experience of national socialism and fascism makes a study of the sources of authoritarian political theory of greater urgency than ever. Either the principles of economic and political democracy are constantly re-defined to meet the problems of a changing world, or these principles will become the euphoric platitudes of yesteryear. The type of outlook represented by Sorel is a potential antiseptic to the worst infections of present day democratic credos. To make believe that these infections can be washed away in noble sentiments is to run the grave risk of total disintegration.

Sorel moved counter to the mainstream of French intellectual life. His outlook was forged in defiance of sociological theory as it existed in the polite academic world of the *fin de siècle*. However, if he was violently opposed to the Fabian socialist sociology of Emile Vandervelde and Sidney Webb, he showed at the same time a sincere interest in the writings of Emile Durkheim, Frederic Le Play and Gustave Le Bon. Similarly, if he had a view of Diderot as a thorough-going philistine who was enamoured with phraseology, his regard for such

5

diverse figures as Karl Marx and Henri Bergson was both profound and authentic. In historical materials, Sorel never failed to reveal his indebtedness to Renan and Taine, while rarely missing an opportunity to disparage the studies of Jean Jaurès.

The frequently repeated charge of Sorel as anti-intellectualist tends to reduce itself to the factual statement that Sorel was emphatically opposed to the rationalist tendencies in French sociology and philosophy. However one wishes to gain entrance into Sorel, whether from an appraisal of his personal career as a man of letters, or through an investigation of his cultural milieu, or through an examination of the factual, logical and empirical foundations of his political thought, it is quite clear that we are dealing with a man of ideas and letters rather than a man of action. And Sorel was fully aware of this; for in describing the art of politics he never confused it with the science of political sociology.

If we distinguish between intellectualism in general and philosophic or scientific reasoning in particular, a more genuine source of Sorel's confusion can be uncovered. Sorel had a keen disrespect for systematic philosophy and metaphysics. Even in his last years we find him struggling with Croce against a view of truth resting on a teleological determinism.[1] However, since he also retained a lifelong contempt for a correspondence theory of truth, for a view of truth as anything more than the relation of statements to one another, he was cut off from any stance by which he could establish the superiority of his pragmatic method of *diremption*. By ruling out the long range worth of either empirical or dialectical methodologies, the search for truth became transformed into a demand for action. But this demand for action retained its intellectualist ends, since the truth of action somehow yields truth in general.

What gave Sorel's view such poor philosophic colour, what made him a constant target for the claim of anti-intellectualism, was the inability of his pragmatic method to reveal why exact scientific reasoning deserves any epistemological primacy. It is at this level that Sorel functioned most inadequately. Both Croce and Julian Benda insisted that Sorel was the arch metaphysician of socialism. The fact remains that he was quite clumsy in the realm of philosophic speculation. What can be said of European pragmatism in general, applies with even greater force to its chief proponent. Sorel makes knowledge part of the course of political action; not on rational grounds, but as

[1] Letter of May 6, 1907, *La Critica*, XXVI (1928), p. 101.

a requirement of ideology. Social science, which for Sorel stands apart from politics, does not stand apart from a doctrine of pure activity. In this sense, Sorel's *anti-politique* is a way of making amends, albeit in a partial and fractured way, to a social science methodology and not just a hatred for politicians.

The pragmatic view of reality held by Sorel does not admit of cognitive modes of establishing the truth or error of facts and propositions. He denies the function of ideas as intrinsically an antiseptic for social ills. To the extent that Sorel rests his case on a shaky pragmatic methodology, he can be justifiably considered antagonistic to intellectualism. However, there is a distinction to be made between the role of intellectuals as ideological defenders of political parties, and the place of intelligence in social life. This distinction was made with greater pungency by Sorel than by his crusaders. The view of Edouard Berth has incorrectly been attributed to Sorel. Whereas Sorel merely indicated that the proletariat can do without the rationalizing intellectual in forming its revolutionary policies, and that the intellectual might still perform useful, if subordinate work on behalf of the producer classes, Berth denies to this strata even this subordinate position. For Berth, the 'fact' that the intellectual sells himself to the highest bidder, suggests that business success and not principle must guide his every action. Berth's intellectual is the prostitute of the political world.[1] Sorel's position was more involved by virtue of the distinction between science and politics, intelligence and rationalization. It might be a position which, no less than Berth's, turns out to be self-refuting; but this has to be established on grounds other than the hue and cry of anti-intellectualism.

One cannot explain Sorel's position by grafting him on to a liberal tradition as if he were in 'the tradition of humanism.'[2] It is no less a blurring of intelligence to view him as 'consistent, rigorous, and thoroughly radical.'[3] The sources of Sorelian political philosophy are deep in the soil of western civilization. He stands as a continuing reminder that the rationalist tradition is not alone in claiming the loyalties of men. The tradition of rational philosophy has entailed a protracted battle against the dialectical mysticism of Heraclitus, the rational mysticism of Plato and Philo and the theological

[1] Edouard Berth, *Les méfaits des intellectuels* (Paris, 1914), pp. 233–4.

[2] Richard Humphrey, *Georges Sorel, Prophet Without Honor* (Cambridge, 1951), pp. 27, 218.

[3] Gorham B. Munson, 'Georges Sorel: Mythmaker for the Social Revolution', *The Modern Quarterly* (New York), VI, No. 1 (1931), p. 93.

subjectivism of Augustine. This contest between myth and logic continued unabated in the medieval period, with now one and then the other, first Averroes and then Eckhart, performing a socially revolutionizing function.

The downfall of the medieval scholastic synthesis resolved only the forms in which *logos* and *mythos* did battle. Against the formidable array of scientific rationalism and humanism, another counter-attack was launched, on three fronts. First came the domination and power theories of Machiavelli, Vico and Ibn Khaldun. Second was the institutionalization of *l'esprit* and *geist* carried out by Hegel, Meinecke and Ranke. Third was a schism within the ranks of *mythos*, with Pascal, Schopenhauer, Nietzsche and Bergson locating the source of energy in individuals rather than in history. Thus in terms of these three stages of the radical revolt against reason, as Cassirer has pointed out, rationalism continues to be but one pole of contemporary ideological interests rather than the universal or necessarily scientific expression of human experience.[1]

This conflict of intellectual loyalties has not been nearly as weighted and one-sided as rationalist spokesmen of *Aufklärung* and *Illuminismo* made it appear. The subsequent history of western thought reveals that no necessary correlation can be made between rationalism and political and social radicalism. There is a clear-cut sense in which the choice between rationalism and irrationalism is a moral choice and not one dictated by empirical evidence. It is by the concrete consequences in specifically determined situations that preferences on behalf of either rationalist or irrationalist perspectives can be made.[2] The type of viewpoint expounded and developed by Sorel, precisely because it came at a period of European history in which rationalism had been emptied of radical consequences, had the effect of separating sense from sentiment, deed from desire, thought from rhetoric; and above all, radicalism from romanticism.

To believe that this conflict between logical and mythological conceptions of the world has abated in the half century which separates us from Sorel's major writings is to perform a disservice to the democratic view of society. It is to deprive this view of the force of the historic conflict within the western tradition between democracy and

[1] Ernst Cassirer, *The Myth of the State* (New Haven, 1946), pp. 53–60.

[2] Karl R. Popper's *The Open Society and its Enemies* (Princeton, 1950), contains a full discussion of the moral choice involved in either rationalism or irrationalism. See in particular the chapter called 'Oracular Philosophy and the Revolt against Reason', pp. 410–42.

totalitarianism.[1] In order to settle one area of this conflict, and perhaps to further illumine the whole problem, it is important to reckon with the political sociology of Sorel. For the long-range significance of his work is the extent to which it aids in attaining a clearer insight into the empirical workings of society and its citizens.

Sorel's most famous work, *Reflections on Violence*, his only book that is widely known in the English-speaking world, typifies the worst and best aspects of Sorelian thought. His works, which are uniformly a response to the writings of others, reveal a poverty of formal organization, and involve an indiscriminate shifting of the basis of argument from fact to hypothesis to free speculation. An additional problem encountered is his tendentious style, combined with frequent repetition designed to bowl over the intransigent opposition. These structural and stylistic difficulties have often prevented a balanced appraisal at the hands of critics and crusaders alike.

Nor is the task of evaluating Sorel lightened by the fact that those in sympathy with his views have mainly been recruited from the backwaters of political and intellectual currents. In England, disillusioned poets and disengaged gentlemen have turned to him more for the comfort provided by the myth of violence and the vicarious heroism it entails than for an understanding of the political processes in modern life. In Italy, aristocratic *fasci* who made pretence at being experimentally inclined futurists, became both the main source and chief embarrassment for advocates of Sorel's syndical socialism. In France itself, a number of Sorel's younger devotees emerged as radical defenders of the sovereign rights of the German Army of Occupation during the Second World War. This is clearly not an easy legacy to overlook; nor should it be.[2] However, the legacy of reaction is deeper and more pervasive than any of Sorel's supporters have presented, and more paradoxical and complex than any of his critics have yet been willing to grant.

There is a compelling force of the Sorelian viewpoint in an age in which instrumental theories of knowledge, indeterminist attitudes in the physical sciences, voluntarist notions of historical change, pluralist theories of culture, and existentialist accounts of the human

[1] J. L. Talmon, *Origins of Totalitarian Democracy* (London, 1952). This extraordinary examination of the sources and content of modern democratic theory demonstrates that the supposed conflict between Russia and the West is, ideologically at least, largely a myth, disguising profound antagonisms within western political theory.

[2] See ch. VI, pt. 2.

abyss have become standard currency in western intellectual exchange. There is a contemporaneity in Sorel that bridges the years, overshadowing some of the lesser anomalies and annoyances encountered in his writings. The most general question of social philosophy and political sociology, power and its sources, dominates his writings, influencing a decade of European consciousness.

II

MEN AND MOVEMENTS IN
FIN DE SIÈCLE FRANCE

'Overwhelmed by his own works, contemporary man has seldom had less control over the environment into which he is plunged. Neither his concepts, nor his instruments, nor his feelings nor anything in himself is adapted to the world that surrounds him, or is capable of assuring its control. This, no doubt, explains the success of doctrines which proclaim that the world is absurd and picture man as a solitary, blown upon from all four corners of the earth, whose only possible greatness lies in accepting with iron courage a universe which requires nothing from him and has nothing to give. Powerful expression of impotence, virile witness of decadence, these fin de siècle *doctrines have at least the merit of all doctrines of crisis, of making us look at the drama of our condition.'*
Emmanuel Mounier, QU'EST-CE QUE LE PERSONNALISME?

EMILE ZOLA opened the founding of the Third French Republic with the ringing and familiar cry of evolution and progress: 'Oh! courage, mon siècle! Avance, avance encore.' But at the same time other voices from the world of culture announced a distinctly harsher future. Mallarmé, Baudelaire and Rimbaud spoke of the absurdity and rank sentimentality that lay at the core of Zola's outcry. The *mal de siècle* presented in a psychological dimension the doom of middle class civilization, and more generally, of all claims of the

11

priority of the social. The connected themes of alienation and irrationality coloured the French scene.

Rimbaud speaks of becoming a prophet 'through the calculated derangement of all the senses'. What was rational and noble for the bourgeoisie of the early nineteenth century was decried as a great hoax. The *mal de siècle* announced the death of the age of reason and its romantic aftermath. The *fin de siècle* threw all its resources into showing that the life of reason dwindles away to a life of sentimentality. Further, a universe all objectivity and progress stifles the subject and produces mechanism in place of humanism.

Sorel's intellectual biography begins before the *fin de siècle*. It is true that Sorel as a creative writer did not exist prior to this. Youth and early manhood were spent as a civil engineer official in government service, where he fulfilled such undertakings to the State as to receive a nomination for the Legion of Honour and a high pension upon his retirement from the government. He rejected both, proving that during this long period of intellectual hibernation, a number of crucial ideas on the ideal relation of citizen and the State had already crystallized.

From Renan and Marx, both of whom he read early in his life, he learned that real freedom could not come through dependence on a reactionary State machine, and especially not from the bourgeois Leviathan. At the point of retirement, when ordinary mortals consider their lives complete and deserving of State support, Sorel's life as an historic figure begins.

The suppression of the Paris Commune preserved a French bourgeoisie turned conservative, but it could not do the same for the political aristocracy. Monarchism and the cause of Divine Right were dead letters in the political arena. From the decay of the Empire arose the Third French Republic. France once more opened a window to the future conflicts of Europe. The issues of the *fin de siècle* became the great schisms of the twentieth century: republicanism versus authoritarianism, anti-semitism vying with religious liberalism, militarism against civil society, legal formalism versus direct action. Atop these concrete issues rode the socialist spectre which was to haunt the palaces of power far more than was imaginable even in the halycon days of 'forty-eight'. Such was the national turmoil created by the Dreyfus affair, the corruption in military and civil life, the growth of trade unionism, the numerical growth and legalization of socialist parties, Catholic divisions over the policy of *ralliement* to the Republic, that it swept into active participation even a comfortable, constitutionally passive civil servant like Sorel. Professionals abandoned their unwritten law that in political quietude resides material plenitude. As in the age of Enlightenment, they became ideologically committed to the policy of *engagement*.

1. Charles Péguy: The Unity of Revelation and Revolution

In order to resolve the problem we have set for ourselves, namely, under what conditions was Sorel's unique combination of radicalism and irrationalism moulded, we must define in specific terms the social and intellectual milieu of *fin de siècle* France. Whatever the starting point in such an investigation, Catholicism, Syndicalism, Nationalism and Socialism, and the forms of their interpenetration, all merit attention. The intellectual tasks were set for Sorel by this environment of life and letters. In this setting, perhaps the strongest element in an immediate sense was Catholicism. Sorel was born and raised a Catholic, lived his married life according to the rigid standards of the Testaments, advocated moral purification as the basis of proletarian regeneration and, above all, numbered among his very closest associates between 1895 and 1905 Charles Péguy—perhaps the most significant voice in French social Christianity since Proudhon.

The tone of French religious life has traditionally been sounded by the relationship between Catholicism and secularism. The virtual absence of Protestantism in its open and variegated forms created a more intense struggle for the minds of men than in nations where Protestantism had met with success. However, it should not be thought that Catholicism achieved the monolithic status it proclaimed as an ideal. Pope Pius IX defined in 1864 a *Syllabus of Errors*, which included a rejection of the separation of State and Church, similarly a rejection of toleration, a denial of the right of civil law to mediate civil conflicts, and a general rejection of religious and social liberalism, such 'errors' were no less present in France than in Protestant nations like England and Germany.[1] The Counter-Reformation, following centuries of Protestant departures from the Roman Church, suppressed open Protestantism only to expose the Catholic Church to a series of severe internal jolts.

[1] For some idea of the failure of the *Syllabus errorum* to achieve its ambitious ends in France, see Robert F. Byrnes, *Antisemitism in Modern France*, Vol. I (New Brunswick, 1950), pp. 28–9, 308–9.

The mass of Frenchmen remained loyal to the established Church, so that while Enlightenment currents may have swept professional and intellectual classes, they left untouched the large peasant mass. For the educated, the ruptures and fissures within the Church were causing religious doubt. Two reasons urged Sorel's response to this inner Church schism. First, as we shall see, his entire philosophy of history moved against the Enlightenment faith in reason and progress through education; and no less, against the *philosophes'* scantily hidden contempt for the peasantry. Secondly, he always retained a higher regard for the faith of peasant-artisans, with their mystical devotions to earth and hands, than for the rationalistic faith of the intellectuals. In this, Sorel was more akin to the Counter-Enlightenment critiques that wafted out of Germany through the writings of Herder and Hamann, than to the French romanticism of Zola and Hugo, which through all its broodings about the agonizing alienation of modern man kept faith with the principles of progress and liberty. The German religion of the oneness of people, Church and nation was better suited to Sorel's attempt to rationalize Catholic ideology.

The wordly debate in French Catholicism of the *fin de siècle* over participation or rejection of the Third French Republic, and of republican principles in general, illustrated how the Protestant ethos asserted itself in Catholic life. Autonomy of the State in worldly matters, the principle of toleration, ideas of religious privacy, in short, all of the things denounced in the *Syllabus of Error*, simply took different forms in French affairs.

From Joan of Arc in the fifteenth century, the ghost of religious revolution from within has haunted conservative Church elements. Her insistence on the supremacy of private judgment, and of the nationalistic symbols of France over the myths of the Church Universal, threatened to subordinate monolithic institutional authority. These qualities were shrewdly perceived by Bernard Shaw in his prefatory description of the condemnation and canonization of Joan as a 'protestant Saint.' Nor did the relative success of the Counter-Reformation in France quiet the issue for long. In the seventeenth century, disquieting, critical Protestantism is once more asserted, now emerging as the struggle of Jesuitism and Jansenism, Paris against Port-Royal.

Pascal, no less a dangerous mystic than Joan, took his standpoint against the dominant Jesuit team-spirit, its collective repression of individuality as a result of a monolithic point of view. Pascal's 'Protestantism' took the form of an emphatic defence of the concrete life of the thinking individual, the necessity of both choice and commitment at a personal level. This intensely personalistic, evangelical note struck by Pascal occurs repeatedly through the history of Catholicism during the Enlightenment. Personal salvation replaced the idea of institutional obligation as the main ideological instrument of Catholic opposition to the materialism and scientism of Enlightenment.

The insinuation of Protestant values into Catholic doctrine was a necessary paradox. For while it temporarily damaged the operational efficiency of the Church in France, it was the long range instrument of its preservation as the one and true religion of Frenchmen. A critical stage in this paradoxical history of the Church was reached in the *fin de siècle*. Social Catholicism, feeling the lagging influence of the Church in wordly matters, bitterly fought orthodox Catholic elements who expressed their conservative aims by advocating a return to monarchism and an inflexible opposition to the very idea of republicanism. Social Catholicism once more associated the image of Joan of Arc with the idea of a Church having popular mass support; nationalist and yet anti-monarchical.

Papers like *Justice sociale* and *Vie catholique*, begun by the younger Social Catholics, spread to the influential Church leaders. These underground elements coalesced around the student movement led by Marc Sangier, *Le Sillon*. This movement, which appealed to many young priests as well as lay Catholics, published a newspaper and later a journal, offered popular educational courses that linked workers and intellectuals, quickly spread from Paris to the provinces. *Le Sillon*, which began with the modest attempt to show working-men that the Church was deeply committed to progress no less than socialists who had forsaken Christianity, assumed increasingly larger proportions as parallel developments were taking place in the higher echelons of the Church.[1]

This conflict between reform and reactionary elements within the Church of France reached its culmination in a clear victory for those

[1] For further information on these various forerunners of left groups within Catholicism and on the worker-priest movement, see Joseph N. Moody, 'France From Old Regime to Democratic Society', in *Church and Society: Catholic Social and Political Thought and Movements, 1789–1950* (New York, 1953), p. 171; and Denis W. Brogan, *France Under The Republic: The Development of Modern France, 1870–1939* (New York, 1940), p. 370.

advocating republicanism and constitutionalism. Two elements were considered in Rome's decision: the apparent firmness of the Third Republic which only isolated the Church from the people, and the unwillingness of groups like *Action française* to give up inherited political ideas even if it meant subversion of Church authority. Thus, with one blow, Rome sought to revitalize the power of the Church among the people and insure Papal supremacy in doctrinal matters. In 1891, the first major decision was taken; Pope Leo XIII issued his famous *Rerum Novarum*, which specifically aimed at closing the rupture in French religious life. It had as a general effect, a recognition that the *Syllabus Errorum* was an historical dead-letter.[1] This document established the legitimacy of democratic and republican institutions in the eyes of the Church, while at the same time maintaining the providential origins of political power. The statement of the Pope directed the Church authorities to acknowledge the factual. The people of France had freely accepted and fervently supported the Third Republic, and thus the Church had no alternative but to adapt itself to this condition—and this adaptive process had always marked Catholic flexibility and tested its strength.[2]

While the clash of Church values did not cease, there was an outburst of Catholic activity in the political arena. Slogans of 'Christ, the People and Liberty' were raised. The popularity of this active political Catholicism, while limited and fractured into as many parts as the labour movement itself, gained steady force as the ideas of Enlightenment finally waned. The lack of any real progress for the masses, their continued economic plight in the midst of a growing bourgeois opulence, served to recreate an atmosphere in which the antinomy between material advance and moral decline was once more attentively heeded. This element was also to be found in the writings of the socialists, who transposed to the economic plane what Rousseau viewed as a moral issue. With Catholic politicians released from the fetters of the popular identification of monarchism with

---

[1] Pope Leo XIII, 'The Condition of the Working Classes', Encyclical Letter, *Rerum Novarum* (May 15, 1891), in *The Great Encyclical Letters of Pope Leo XIII* (New York, 1903), pp. 208–48. For a further explanation of the new Papal position, see *The Pope and the People, Select Letters and Addresses on Social Questions* (London, 1929).

[2] Compare, Edouard Lecanuet, *La vie de l'Eglise sous Leon XIII* (Paris 1930), pp. 610–18; and J. J. Chevallier, *Histoire des institutions politiques de la France moderne* (Paris, 1958), pp. 421–4.

Catholicism, their ability to fight on the same realistic terrain as socialists became manifest.

If socialism had to come, and not a few Catholic theorists were convinced that it would, then at least it should be infused with the spirit of historical Christianity. Pope Leo XIII, writing to the Bishop of Grenoble, expands on his encyclical in just such realistic terms. 'We do not seek to dabble in politics but where politics are closely bound to religious interests, as they are in France, the pope has a mission to determine the conduct which best safeguards the supreme interest —that of the Church.'[1] Increasingly, this was the posture taken by a social Catholicism which had in fact become a Christian socialism. Saint Joan, Pascal, and the father of French social Catholicism, Lamennais, became the heroic predecessors of a *fin de siècle* in search of tradition. In Charles Péguy, this tendency received its most eccentric and yet its most noble theoretical expression.

The early founders of the Third Republic were either Comtian positivists, like Ferry, Gambetta and Floquet, or avowed materialists like Clemenceau. They proclaimed the superiority of science in theory and application like their eighteenth century predecessors. But by the *fin de siècle*, Catholic voices had penetrated the political theatre. Political life became seasoned with an anti-Enlightenment flavour. Ferdinand Brunétiere, a man for whom Sorel retained a deep and abiding respect, was proclaiming the bankruptcy of objectivistic interpretations of science. In a series of articles published in 1895, Brunétiere presented a virtual declaration of war on the capacity of a social science to predict future events with any degree of accuracy. He held it impossible to solve problems about the origin and destiny of man, and further, that a worldly view is incapable of providing the foundations of a moral view.[2]

In the very process of republicanization, the image of Pascal appears once more, this time not as Protestantism and heresy, but as honest disillusionment with Enlightenment. In the writings of Mounier, friend, biographer and successor to Péguy, we can clearly see how the choice was posed between irrational radicalism and a rational conservatism. 'We also echo to its Pascalian note. [Mounier is here speaking of existentialism.] Just as materialism in all its forms,

---

[1] Pope Leo XIII. Letter to M. Fava, Bishop of Grenoble (June 22, 1892). Quoted in *French Royalist Doctrines Since the Revolution*, by Charlotte Touzalin Muret (New York, 1933), p. 191.

[2] See Alexandre Zévàes, *Histoire de la Troisième République* (Paris, 1938), p. 198. See also, Paul Bureau, *Quinze ans de séparation* (Paris, 1921).

scientific, economic, psychological, performed a useful service in disposing of a sterile, spiritualistic rhetoric, before relapsing itself into a new verbalism, so the philosophies of the abyss are a fortunate antidote to the various *Stimmung* of bourgeois thought, its foolish optimism, its specious idealism, and the positivistic levelling down of of the real. The vertigo of the abyss, one's own abyss, is a strong spiritual tonic against bourgeois self-satisfaction.'[1]

Péguy succeeded in tying together the threads of the *fin de siècle* revolt against reason. It emerged as a fighting credo and not just disillusionment as with Brunétiere. In his justifiably famous essay on Joan of Arc, Péguy expresses the militant Christianity befitting to a Luther discourse. 'I do not believe that I have ever spoken of the *Catholic World*. I have often spoken of the Church, of communion. I do not feel truly myself, I do not really touch the bottom of my thought save when I write Christendom. Only then do I fully see what I say.'[2] Sorel's enthusiasm for Péguy, and for this study of Joan in particular, reveals how intimate Sorel felt the causes of socialism and Christianity to be. This is the case not only in his early pre-Marxian stage, but at the height of his philosophical agnosticism in the period after he wrote *Reflections on Violence*. In a communication to Croce, Sorel is critical of his colleague Maurice Barrès for the latter's inability to come to terms with 'the mystery of lamentation, supplication and lyrical glorification' found in the pages of Péguy's essay.[3]

Sorel the socialist shared with Péguy the Catholic a remarkable congruence of opinions on the leading political figures of the age like Jean Jaurès, Waldeck-Rousseau and Clemenceau; and no less, on the great issues of Dreyfusism, Nationalism and socialist values. Just as Sorel never really became institutionally fused to any part of French socialist politics, so too, Péguy remained, as he himself knew, on the outskirts of respectable and even liberal Catholic opinion.[4] Both men pushed beyond the theoretical limits of their respective peasant origins; perhaps this common origin accounts for their independent arrival at similar conclusions. Another, more immediate reason, is that Péguy's *Cahiers de la quinzaine* provided a weekly meeting place for Sorel for nearly a decade. They shared a mutual

[1] Emmanuel Mounier, *Qu'est-ce-que le personnalisme?* (Translated as *Be Not Afraid: Studies in Personalist Sociology*) (New York, 1954), p. 147.
[2] Charles Péguy, *Men and Saints* (London, 1947), p. 179.
[3] Letter of February 28, 1910, *La Critica*, XXVI (1928), p. 337.
[4] Charles Péguy, *Note conjointe* (Paris, 1935), p. 276.

admiration for one another, in spite of distinct personality differences. Péguy had an apparatus and Sorel had the charisma.

Speaking on one of Sorel's favourite topics, the moral regeneration of the proletariat and the intrinsic conflict between morals and politics, Pèguy offers an interesting analysis of the components of this friendship. 'Our socialism was essentially, and officially moreover, a theory, a general theory, a doctrine and method, a philosophy of organization and of the re-organization of work, the *restoration* of work. Our socialism was essentially, and moreover officially, a restoration, a general and universal restoration. Nobody at the time contested the fact. But the politicians have been on the move for fifteen years. Two kinds of politicians, the politicians strictly speaking, and the anti-politicians. The politicians have passed on. What was at stake was a general restoration, beginning with the working class world; a total restoration founded on the previous restoration of the world of the worker. It was a matter of making the world of the worker in general healthy, of restoring the whole city to health, organically and atomically, beginning with the individual. That was the method and the ethics and the general philosophy of M. Sorel, himself a moralist and philosopher, which found its highest expression in his work.'[1] It was these words which helped inspire Sorel to tackle the question of French patriotism and pseudo-patriotism.[2]

At the turn of the century, Sorel was already employing Péguy's language of moral renovation and the mystique of the masses as an effective challenge to politics. In defence of this, Sorel cited the seeming incapacity of the learned world of rational intellectuals to penetrate to the deeper mysteries of social change that long ago was common knowledge to religion. 'It is by these processes that Catholicism continually revitalizes itself, benefiting from all the mystic evolutions, occultisms, that are being produced in the world. Protestantism and Judaism do not possess this power of regeneration and this capacity for sublimating the religious sentiment that Catholicism has by virtue of its transcendence of the conscious by a simple esthetic sentiment.'[3]

---

[1] Charles Péguy, *Notre Jeunesse* (translated as *Temporal and Eternal*), (London, 1958), pp. 62–3.

[2] 'Le mystère de la Charité de Jeanne d'Arc de Charles Péguy', *L'Action française* (April 14, 1910). Reference is made to another article of the same year in Pierre Andreu, *Notre Maitre, M. Sorel* (Paris, 1953), p. 280.

[3] *La ruine du monde antique* (Paris, 1925, 2nd edition), p. 165.

The ease of communication between the two men indicates the extent to which the Christian socialism of Péguy could become the socialized Christendom of Sorel. The mystique of the Church, the idea of eternal salvation, becomes the myth of socialism, the idea of salvation at the temporal plane. The transformation of the profane into the sacred, the politique into the mystique revealed a sublimity of human consciousness that became for both thinkers the true worth of a doctrine.[1]

Sorel had a 'rupture' with nearly every one of his associates. Yet his differences with Péguy in later years never led to acrimony and negative generalizations. Péguy always remained for Sorel the 'truthful representation of the old France that died.'[2] To be sure, one of Sorel's last reflections on Péguy indicated that he, Péguy, did not take his mystique and its humble peasant origins seriously enough, that he became too enamoured with middle class artistic contrivances to reach the masses with the early clarity and directness.[3] Sorel was disturbed by Péguy's apparent unwillingness to distinguish between the mystique as a human force and the Catholic mythology as a supernatural factor. This distinction was for Sorel precisely the division between his radicalism and Péguy's conservatism. Sorel's myth is a pragmatic and worldly concept.

Nonetheless, the weapon of revolution for both men was something quite apart from science or *realpolitik*. However admirable it might be for men to make decisions on the basis of rational foresight, the fact is that decisions to act are usually made impulsively. The channelization of these impulses required the myth for Sorel and the mystique for Péguy. The mystique had the advantage of being thoroughly spontaneous, distinctly motivated by the innermost desires and fantasies of alienated man. The mystique, in consequence, required no fabricator. Denying the value of Péguy's romantic vision of Catholicism, and operating within an agnostic psychology, Sorel was forced into a purely behaviouristic view of human motivation.

Therefore Sorel's myth unlike Péguy's mystique was an imposed entity. It was something men made, rather than divinely present. Three distinct levels are present in Sorel's theory of myths: the myth believer whose actions are totally oriented to wish-fulfilment, the

---

[1] For an analysis of the kinship in attitudes and ideals between Sorel and Péguy, see Daniel Halévy, *Péguy and Les Cahiers de la Quinzaine* (London, 1946).
[2] Sorel as cited in Pierre Andreu, *Notre Maitre, M. Sorel*, p. 269.
[3] 'Charles Péguy', *La Ronda* (1919), pp. 58–9.

myth-maker, whose charisma enables him to focus the energies of the masses without the necessity of full rational comprehension, and the rational élite, who occupies a unique position in the pyramid by virtue of their grasp of the social and psychic mechanisms of political action. What is entailed is more than a verbal distinction between mystique and myth. It is a transformation of irrationalism from an organic mass factor to an élitist tool for social domination.

Catholicism for Sorel was an expression of the organized myth and its value for mass action in an industrial age. To radical Catholics like Péguy, concerned with French rational development, Sorel offered a militant alternative to the relative stagnation and corruption of *politique*. That Sorel offered this solution without straying too far from the Catholic lexicon was a large factor in sharpening the conception of Péguy on the harmony of revelation and revolution. However, Carr has rightly pointed out that Péguy 'could not in the long run accommodate himself to a philosophy which enthusiastically hailed the dogmas of the Church as necessary myths. Nevertheless, when Péguy died on the Marne in September, 1914, it was in the firm faith in war as the means of salvation for a decadent French society which Sorel had held from the outset of his career.'[1] For Sorel this abstract alliance with Catholic action offered a way out of having to make an ultimate decision between *New Testament* revelation and *Communist Manifesto* revolution, while at the same time, making use of the emotional value of both.

It was the sacred knowledge that 'the modern world is an unchristian world, which has succeeded perfectly well in doing without Christianity' that finally separated the two men.[2] For Péguy, this fact only revealed an agonizing need to search out what went wrong and where. His interest was in correcting Church practices by bringing them into line with its own original inspirational sources and modern historical realities. For Sorel, this would be a utopian retreat, since the grounds for searching out and accomplishing a transvaluation of values had gone beyond conditions of Christian life. What was radical in Christianity is now represented in socialism. Evangelical prophecy had become absorbed by a prophetic radicalism.[3] Modern

---

[1] Edward Hallett Carr, *Studies in Revolution* (London, 1950), pp. 160–1. See also the analysis of Péguy's 'decision for war' in H. Stuart Hughes, *Consciousness and Society* (New York, 1958), pp. 350–6.

[2] Charles Péguy, Notre Jeunesse, *loc. cit.*, p. 137.

[3] *La ruine du monde antique*, pp. 310–11. See also his 'L'éthique du socialisme', *La Revue de Métaphysique et Morale* (May 1899), No. 124.

Socialism had to evolve its own set of symbols, its own rituals, and its own catechisms.

The personal rupture between Sorel and Péguy, which took place several years before the war—with Péguy charging Sorel with sabotaging the *Cahiers de la Quinzaine* and also with intrigue against Julien Benda. Sorel denied both allegations, claiming them to be the consequence of Péguy's theoretical embrace of the Church triumphant—is a plausible, though by no means exhaustive account of the polarized response to the same proletarian challenge.[1] The most likely explanation of the break between the two is that Péguy's literary and political sensibilities were outraged by Sorel's rapprochement with the royalist Charles Maurras and the *Cité française* and the *Indépendence*.[2] Nonetheless, the rupture declared by Péguy was not a declaration of war. They retained the dignity of admiring associates, and more important, an underlying unity in ideas and values.[3]

The lack of firm political allegiances spared Sorel the anguish that Péguy felt at the lack of support for his outlook within the Catholic social movement. Church power had too long sanctioned monarchist and anti-democratic currents to satisfactorily cope with the challenge of industrial economy and the proletarian entrance into politics. Sorel noted that 'the material interest of the Church so blinds Catholics that they are capable of every kind of stupidity.'[4] By the time the *ralliement* became reputable Church policy, the issue was no longer Republicanism versus Monarchism. Attention had shifted to forms of republican authority: socialist or capitalist control of the State; and ideologically, whether the State should be worshipped, tolerated as a necessary evil or constantly fought.

The worker-priest movement, which had its origins in the *fin de siècle*, collapsed under the weight of Church uncertainty. Anti-semitism, the force of a journalist like Drumont, became the binding element in Catholic social sectors. This unity through conservatism, to the chagrin of Péguy, once more caused the Church to be viewed suspiciously by contemporaries as a force for monarchism and militarism. With the ultimate vindication of Dreyfus, and the accom-

---

[1] Compare the accounts of the rupture of Sorel and Péguy in Jean Variot, *Propos de Georges Sorel* (Paris, 1935), pp. 254–59; and Daniel Halévy, *Péguy and Les Cahiers de la Quinzaine*, pp. 171–2.

[2] Pierre Andreu, *Notre Maitre, M. Sorel*, p. 280.

[3] Romain Rolland, *Péguy* (Paris 1944), Vol. I, p. 97.

[4] *Réflexions sur la violence*, p. 312 (229).

panying revelation of bureaucratic corruption in civil and military affairs, the Church lost its long battle to prevent the legal separation of the Church and State. By the time this separation took place in 1905, the movement of events had swamped Church attitudes. A new form of organization had arisen to obviate, if not eliminate, the necessity for Church organizational support. The mystique had gone out of the Church, replaced by the myth of the State.

In the minds of radicals like Sorel, the choice between State and Church authorities left little to choose from in so far as revolutionary mass sentiments were concerned. Neither Péguy's Christian socialism nor Jaurès' State socialism seemed an appropriately radical response to the world of industrial capitalism.[1] Something incorporating the elements of each, the mystique of religion and the organizational force of government, was needed to galvanize the producers into action. The answer was to be found in the *syndicats*.

2. Fernand Pelloutier: Irrational State against Rational Man

The ferment in the Church which produced both the *ralliement* and restorationism as an outlaw doctrine, was clearly something forced upon it—by external political factors. The Church admittedly moved to absorb a force that had become larger and more pervasive than itself—the ripening labour movement. Restorationists played upon the fears of the Catholic leadership, insisting that the Republic would move towards socialism and secularism with greater ease, and further away from the Papacy.[2] The most powerful anti-Semite of *fin de siècle* France, Edouard Drumont, inveighed against the Machiavellianism and cowardice of Pope Leo's surrender to republicanism.[3] This inner Church strife rendered the Church a spectator on the historical scene. The age of completely secular politics became a reality.

With all the furore over republicanism, the mood of French labour at the opening of the *fin de siècle* was both cautious and confused. The caution was brought on by the failure of either utopianism or terrorism to bring about the cherished aims of labour pre-eminence. The confusion was occasioned by the contradictory reactions of the

---

[1] *La ruine du monde antique*, p. 320.
[2] Charlotte Touzalin Muret, *French Royalist Doctrines Since The Revolution* (New York, 1933), pp. 193–9.
[3] Robert F. Byrnes, *Anti-Semitism in Modern France*, pp. 334–5.

State to labour demands. With each new thrust of labour into the flanks of French society, the bourgeoisie became increasingly conservative, expressing its fears through the ministries of the Republic. The notion of some radicals that the State had evolved into an instrument of bourgeois interests created increased pressures for a competing organization to offset State authority. However, reform socialists noted that the French State, quite unlike the German State, was offering conciliatory legal measures to ameliorate the condition of the working class. Thus, along with the multiplication in the number of legally sanctioned workers' groups, came an increase of unions hostile to one another in theoretical matters. The average size of the *syndicats* doubled in the *fin de siècle*, while the number of *syndicats* formed more than quadrupled.[1] The age realized a major socialist ambition, mass organization. But in the French manner, this was accompanied by mass doctrinal confusion expressed in intense factional disputes.[2]

This confusion was in part due to the State's failure to live up to its role as *bête noire*. The law of 1884, granting the liberty of working class association, carefully put into statutes what was already a social fact. Far from threatening the foundations of industrial capitalism, the growth of syndicalism, of organized producer associations,[3] only

[1] Francois Barret, *Histoire du travail* (Paris 1951), pp. 76–7.

[2] The term *syndicat* is usually translated to mean trade union. Now while the terms are approximately similar, the differences between French labour organizations and those in England and the United States are large enough to warrant attention. Among the outstanding differences we might mention the following: The *syndicat* is generally organized around craft lines rather than industry-wide. Its structural organization is much looser than in Anglo-American trade unions, with very few paid functionaries devoted to internal matters. The forms of strike led by *syndicats* were more in the nature of one-day vacations from work, rather than a protracted 'no contract, no work' strike such as is customary in the English-speaking nations. Also, the *syndicat* usually gave explicit expression to a political philosophy, and had direct association with the political and bureaucratic machinery of government. The literature of English or French syndical socialism as it functioned up to the First World War is relatively slender, given the importance of the subject. For some idea of the scope and appeal of syndicalism to workers, see Emile Pataud and Emile Pouget, *Syndicalism and the Co-Operative Commonwealth* (Oxford, 1913). The preface by Peter Kropotkin is particularly instructive. For some account of the philosophic basis of European syndicalism, particularly as it relates to the thought of Henri Bergson, see John W. Scott, *Syndicalism and Philosophical Realism* (London, 1919). James A. Estey, *Revolutionary Syndicalism: An Exposition and a Criticism* (London, 1913) offers a serious empirical investigation of the strengths and shortcomings of French syndicalism, with particular reference to its leaders.

[3] The terms producer and producer organization also offer semantical difficulties, since in English producer often denotes entreprenurial functions, that is, the

ncreased the voices urging political compromise. Reform spokesmen argued that if the State seems to respond most to bourgeois pressures, it was because of social imbalance rather than any intrinsically coercive features of the modern State. Thus, to make the State more responsive to labour pressures, what was needed was a more powerful and ideologically cohesive working class organization. The State being pliable, the task was to balance bourgeois ownership with working class numbers.

Reform socialism became the major political expression of a theory of countervailing power elements in the State. Reform syndicalism performed a similar role by viewing the class struggle as a present, but not necessarily perennial condition of industrial capitalism. It turned its gaze on the immediate conditions of life: the establishment of collective contracts and the suppression of arbitrary individual methods of fixing salaries. In the general political arena, reform syndicalism argued for the establishment of social legislation. The method for obtaining maximum reforms was held to be conciliation. Men of reason would always find common grounds. The strike was viewed as a last-ditch weapon to be used only when employer–employee relations deteriorated completely, and the gains of a strike action were manifest.[1]

Clemenceau's policies during the *fin de siècle* regime further increased the reform orientation of labour. The creation of a Ministry of Labour, the establishment of a retirement law, and the enforcement of an eight-hour work day, encouraged the *syndicats* to seek restitution through the State. Clemenceau's militant opposition to revolutionary socialism as an adjunct of labour ideology, reflected a bourgeois willingness to have a labour partner in running French society. Extremes were frowned upon. Neither the military super-democracy of a General Boulanger, nor a pure proletarian democracy brought on by terrorist groups, were to be tolerated. Paul-Boncour, in his reflections as minister in the Third Republic, notes how Clemenceau expressed the position of the State. 'Half-jokingly, half-seriously, to a delegation from the *Confédération Générale du Travail*, he

---

man who produces is contrasted to the man who works. As it is used in this book, and by Sorel, the word producer will simply mean the man who labours with his hands, which includes the work done by both factory workers and peasantry. Thus, the term producer is less ambiguous than worker, since a worker can be non-productive, and more inclusive than proletarian, since the proletarian refers strictly to factory labour, commodity production.

[1] François Barret, *Ibid.*, p. 78.

said as he pointed to his ministerial chair: You'll be sitting here soon.'[1]

Indeed, such leaders of the labourers like Jules Guesde, Jean Jaurès and Alexandre Millerand, vanguard socialists of the *mal de siècle*, became prime movers in reform State socialism during the *fin de siècle*. Before the century had ended, Millerand entered the government. Just before doing so, he formulated the guiding policies of 'national socialism'; that is, the specifically French character of the proletarian conflicts. Not the workers of the world, but those of France, were the critical element in labour progress. Millerand formulated the idea of a gradual emancipation of the workers through the transformation of capitalist monopoly into the public administration of industry. To Millerand's way of thinking, the State would be the caretaker of the proletariat, and eventually, undertaker for the bourgeoisie.[2]

What united Clemenceau and Millerand was not a simple fondness for reform, but a philosophical common ground. These were, after all, the men who still took Enlightenment ideology seriously. Education, legislation and a disposition to use the rational faculties wherever possible were seen as the basis of enduring progress. Reform tendencies came to completely dominate interpretations of the philosophy of progress developed by Helvetius and Diderot. The *philosophes* were no longer considered revolutionary dangers. They became part of the 'great French tradition' Millerand spoke of. His national socialism was closer in spiritual ancestry to the national capitalism of Waldeck–Rousseau than to Marxism. The antagonism of Sorel for the Enlightenment, his willingness to go along with Brunétiere in labelling Diderot a philistine, had at its core this transformation of Enlightenment into Statism. If rationalism were the intellectual weapon of reform, then by the same token, irrationalism had for Sorel become the *virtú* of revolutionary efforts to control *fortuna*.

The claim of *trahison* was at once sent up as a cry in the night: socialism betrayed. No sooner had Millerand pledged labour to the State, than Pelloutier offered a counter-pledge. The workers would not be 'corrupted' by its 'natural' class enemies. Self-defence meant

---

[1] Joseph Paul-Boncour, *Recollections of the Third Republic* (New York, 1957), pp. 154–5; also, A. Zévaès, *Histoire de la Troisième République*, pp. 247–59.

[2] See George Douglas Howard Cole, *A History of Socialist Thought*, Vol. III, Part I (*The Second International 1889–1914*) (London, 1956), pp. 350–3.

independence from and opposition to the State. Pelloutier threw down the gauntlet: the workers, without God, without country, without patriotism—honest men and implacable enemies of material and moral despotism—would never yield to a tepid reform policy sanctioned by the State.[1]

Parallel sentiments echoed from a different sector of society, the socialist intelligentsia—*le cercle Sorelienne*. Once the unifying force of the Dreyfus affair had been ended in decisive victory for the republic, radical socialists turned to more fundamental social considerations. We find Sorel accusing Millerand of betraying the principles of socialism to a reactionary government.[2] Jaurès is viewed as a babbling Fabian who means to get socialism by a 'humane' policy of giving annuities to bankrupt bourgeois to keep labour harmony.[3] Guesde fares no better. He is ridiculed as a perfect example of a decomposed Marxist who turns to the State for revolutionary salvation.[4] In their common hatred for reform of any kind as weakening the class struggle, the alliance of Pelloutier with Sorel was sealed. Pelloutier offered Sorel an uncomplicated and morally unsullied approach to problems of revolution that was to fulfil the prophetic role of the proletariat in a way that Péguy could only look for but never find.

The organizational apparatus preceded Pelloutier in the form of the *Bourses du Travail*. What Pelloutier was to term a 'State within a State' was created in 1892 as a sort of working class educational alliance. With the expansion of its branches it assumed wider functions. These functions had a typical craft flavour of guild organizations: mutual assistance in locating vacant positions for each of the members, propaganda services, economic and statistical data on the changing condition of labour in the country, assistance in the creation of *syndicats* and co-operatives, and services of resistance to employers in strike situations.

Despite its organizational looseness, the multiplicity of activities engaged in by the *Bourses du Travail* saved them from becoming Fabian centres of intellectual exchange and pamphleteering. This organization became, in Pelloutier's vision, the beginning of mass political awakening by virtue of its very emancipation from politics

[1] Fernand Pelloutier, 'Lettre aux anarchistes' in *Le Congrès du Parti socialiste français, 3–8 décembre 1899* (Paris, 1900), p. vii.
[2] Letter of August 21, 1901, *La Critica*, XXV (1927), p. 364.
[3] *Réflexions sur la violence*, p. 142 (120).
[4] Letter of October 29, 1898, *La Critica*, XXV (1927), p. 174.

as such.[1] In the hands of a political craftsman like Pelloutier, the *Bourses* became the concrete expression of the ties of anarchism and syndicalism.[2]

Sorel's immersion in French politics in the 'nineties was clearly shallow and tenuous, as it was throughout his life. Because of this, his whole-hearted positive response to the work of Pelloutier and the labour exchanges is of more than passing interest. Pelloutier seemed to offer a concrete manifestation of a pure radicalism, unsullied by the dogmas of Marxians from whom he was seeking intellectual escape, and the bare-faced reformism of socialist politicians. The *Bourses* gave practicality and operational validity to Sorel's vision of a dynamic and morally pure working class growing in revolutionary strength outside and against the State—rather than within the bureaucratic government apparatus as the reform socialists maintained. The *Bourses* were more; they showed Sorel the image of future socialist man. It was just this failure to produce a representative type of future man that characterized State socialism. When Sorel viewed the *Bourses*, he saw the contour of future society—'a thing of conscience, rather than an instrument of government.'[3]

Sorel's deep mistrust of the politics of orthodox socialism was reinforced by its fetish, the legal road to success. It seemed that before a strike was called it had to be cleared through the Ministry of Labour. In the *fin de siècle*, the word 'socialism' aroused suspicion more than it did fear. It seemed that membership in, or declaration of affection for, socialist ideals, was a sure sign of political success. Socialism gave every indication of reproducing the bureaucratic authority of the capitalist State. At approximately the same time that Sorel became disillusioned with official socialism, Daniel Halévy and Peter Kropotkin came forth with a theoretical examination of this seeming paradox of socialism without a humanist content. The great schism in socialism was held not to be that between utopian and scientific orientations, but between authoritarian and anarchist beliefs.[4] Halévy wrote that in 'the origins of the socialist move-

[1] Fernand Pelloutier, *Histoire des Bourses du Travail* (Paris 1902), pp. 70–1.

[2] Compare the accounts in Jean Maitron, *Histoire du Mouvement Anarchiste en France: 1880–1914* (Paris, 1951), pp. 286–90; and François Barret, *Histoire du travail*, pp. 76–7.

[3] Preface to *Histoire des Bourses du Travail*, p. 26; also *Matériaux d'une théorie du prolétariat*, p. 153.

[4] Much commentary on anarchist literature is both inadequate and incorrect; the following are generally reliable statements of the issues involved. For an appreciation of the nineteenth-century philosophical origins of anarchist doctrine,

ment, the general term which is applied to all its tendencies, there are two currents, the one authoritarian, the other libertarian.'[1] Kropotkin expressed the same theses as a fundamental distinction in socialist ideology. 'These ideas, to be precise, generate two principal currents, authoritarian communism and anarchistic communism; between there are also a certain number of intermediary schools.'[2]

These voicings had Sorel's deepest sympathies; saving him from a pessimistic attitude that was the consequence of rejecting both capitalist and socialist reform policies. The emphasis both Halévy and Kropotkin placed upon the revolutionary potential of the peasantry remained an enduring part of Sorel's thinking. Kropotkin's theory of the French Revolution as emanating from the countryside, his regard for the fundamental democracy of the land toiler, touched the rural Catholic origins of Sorel. This was to provide an important common ground with Péguy. But since the pronunciamentos of Halévy and Kropotkin were offered without suggestions for the practical implementation of a pure socialism of producers, Sorel remained sceptical. Pelloutier, temporarily at least, helped to dispel this doubt. The role of the *Bourses* during the *fin de siècle* was the basic empirical evidence Sorel required.

Pelloutier was by no means the founder of anarchism, integral socialism or libertarian socialism, as anarchism has been alternatively called. Its history in France had been long and bloody. Prior to 1894, it was a minority and partially secret society that published such flaming periodicals as *Le Dynamite*. Anarchism had every intention of bringing down the walls of the capitalist Jericho in the flames of terror. As long as this anarchist wish was confined to newspaper editorials, few serious problems arose. But with the putting into motion of a round of assassinations and institutional disruptions, the State legally smashed anarchist terrorism in the 'trial of the thirty'. The era of individual anarchism came to a quick halt. The

---

see Alain Sergent and Claude Harmel, *Histoire de l'anarchie* (Paris, 1949); and also Max Nettlau, *Der Vorfrühling der Anarchie: ihre Historische entwicklung von den anfängen bis zum jahre 1864* (Berlin, 1925). For sympathetic critical accounts, see, from the liberal position, Ernst V. Zenker, *Anarchism: A Criticism and History of the Anarchist Theory* (London, 1898); and from a Marxian position, George V. Plekhanov, *Anarchism and Socialism* (Chicago, 1918).

[1] Daniel Halévy, *Essais sur le mouvement ouvrier en France* (Paris, 1901), p. 271.

[2] Peter Kropotkin, *Communisme et Anarchie* (*Temps Noveaux*). (Paris, 1903), No. 27, p. 4.

long cherished Babeouvist notion of minority insurrection fell victim to its inherent isolation from social realities.[1]

Pelloutier functionally related socialist policies to the economic conditions of the producers by joining anarchism to syndicalism. The historic isolation of socialist thought from the workers was given a severe jolt. Sorel gives expression to this when he notes that 'Pelloutier saw clearly the need for basing present-day socialism on an absolute separation of classes and on the abandonment of all hope for political reconstruction of the old order. He saw in the labour exchanges (*Bourses du Travail*) the most complete organization of revolutionary tendencies of the proletariat.'[2]

Péguy's spiritualization of socialism found its counter in Pelloutier's activism. In addition, like Péguy, Pelloutier possessed the necessary mystique in his personality no less than in his approach to labour problems. Pelloutier came closest to Sorel's Homeric concept of proletarian self-sacrifice. A meteoric, one might say Byronic person, Pelloutier packed into thirty-four years of life a reappraisal and reorganization of the French labour movement. He was the earliest anarchist to define the limits of political and anti-political behaviour, as a relation between morality and immorality. This moral fervour with which Pelloutier approached socialism fitted in completely with Sorel's apocalyptic-mythological doctrine. What Jean Maitron has written is clearly pertinent: 'Pelloutier personified the new man who was also the militant worker, dedicated until death to the cause of the disenfranchised, a model worker, morally irreproachable, working unyieldingly in a tenacious effort to ceaselessly go beyond himself.[3] This comment simply paraphrases Pelloutier's own notion of the good worker-revolutionary.[4]

Pelloutier's affirmation of proletarian aims as calling into question human virtues played a decisive role in Sorel's philosophy of history. The ability of the producers to forge a system of values superior to any held by other groups or classes was considered proof that the *syndicats* could wield social authority which would not degenerate into coercive *bureaucracy*. Advanced workers would form

---

[1] Jean Maitron, *Histoire du Mouvement Anarchiste en France (1880–1914)*, pp. 231–41.

[2] *La décomposition du marxisme*, p. 62; also *Matériaux d'une théorie du prolétariat*, pp. 154–5.

[3] Jean Maitron, *Histoire du Mouvement Anarchiste en France*, p. 278.

[4] Fernand Pelloutier, 'Lettre aux anarchistes' in *Le Congrès du Parti socialiste Français*, p. vii.

an élite of a new type, informing the whole of society of the duties imposed by moral behaviour.[1] The missing link in socialist doctrine, the socialist man, had arrived full blown in the person of the charismatic Pelloutier.

By custom and definition anarchism has acquired a negative flavour. It involves a rejection of the State, of any authority invested in a legal person said to have greater rights to power than the human person. In view of the operational untenability thus involved, the kindest statement of anarchism is that it is a healthy philosophic posture for the individual. In the Anglo-American culture men like Sir Herbert Read and William Ernest Hocking have used it as an astringent to the infections of the bureaucratic mentality. The whole line of French anarchism from Proudhon to Halévy shared in this perspective and were content with its intellectual results.

Pelloutier came to anarchism with a distinctly different frame of mind. For the worker-intellectual despairing of rationalist poses, anarchism acquired a positive character. The labour federations offered a live option to the State. The *Bourses* were to become a 'State within a State.'[2] Pelloutier meant this slogan in a literal way. The *Bourses* were to assume all positive State functions, from the protection of proletarian rights to education in the possible forms of human emancipation.[3] Anarchy was to be made over into a social force first and an ideological force second. A backward proletariat was to replace an effete bourgeoisie.

This social perspective fed two ancillary streams, both crucial in Sorel's development and both widely circulated during the *fin de siècle*. The one was the anti-political nature of anarcho-syndicalism; the other the counter-ideological role of a pure movement of producing classes. In Pelloutier's zealous organizational hands, both were connected to revolution and not simply to personal revolt. The *Bourses* under his leadership expanded so as to include a membership culled from all segments of the socialist spectrum—Possibilists, Blanquists, Allemanists, Anarchists and independent, unaffiliated socialists. Pelloutier's idea that party affiliation was subsidiary to trade union association came to be regarded as a way out of the impasse of the multi-party system. Only the *Bourses* could link a divided

---

[1] *Matériaux d'une théorie du prolétariat*, p. 128.
[2] Fernand Pelloutier, *Histoire des Bourses du Travail* (Paris, 1902), p. 146.
[3] Fernand Pelloutier, *Ibid.*, pp. 184–5.

socialist movement with an equally fragmented syndicalist movement.[1]

The fusion of socialism and unionism was seen as functionally complete in the general strike. This was not conceived of as either a strike for wages and allied demands, nor as a widespread attempt to garner political concessions from the State. While the possibilities of immediate gains were not denied in the general strike, its essence was to evoke the deepest class allegiances and obligations of the workers. As economic strife between classes would become more intense, in accordance with Marxian theory, the meaning of the general strike would become wider in implications. The syndicalist strike would entail direct worker participation in a broad social and economic upheaval. It would become an instrument for compelling the State to abandon its place on the historical stage to the direct association of producers. For the most part, revolutionary syndicalism did not view the general strike as a replacement for the traditional economic strike. Rather, it was to replace all politically sponsored strikes. Keynoting this approach was an intense disdain for anything which the government or oppositional politicians desired of the workers. The general strike was anti-politique; conceived as part of the permanent social revolution, as such, it was part of the movement towards socialism.'[2]

The theoretical underpinning of the general strike is summed up in the much abused, but in this case accurate, concept that the goal sought in all cases justify the methods employed. Violence in all its forms was sanctioned. Realism became romanticized. For Sorel, the rules of war, which really came down to the absence of rules, were to govern the conduct and aims of the general strike.[3] The open hostility with which Guesde, Jaurès and Bernstein viewed the general strike perhaps did as much to convince Sorel of the efficacy of Pelloutier's approach as any abstract congruence it had to the Nietzschean theory of struggle. The Christian socialism of Péguy was fulfilled in the revolutionary syndicalism of a Pelloutier. This new Christ called for the destruction of the bourgeois world with the same passion that the historical Jesus envisioned the decline of paganism. Mysticism became concrete prophecy subject to human will and

---

[1] Maurice Pelloutier, *F. Pelloutier: Sa vie, son oeuvre, 1867–1901* (Paris, 1911), pp. 18–35.
[2] Victor Griffuelhes, *L'action syndicaliste* (Paris, 1908), pp. 33–7.
[3] *Matériaux d'une théorie du prolétariat*, pp. 61–2.

sacrifice. In this fashion, Pelloutier's moral syndicalism fed the main-stream of Sorel's vision; offering a way clear of the debris of legal Marxism and State socialism. 'Apocalypse—which represented a scandalous ancestry to socialists who wished to make Marxism compatible with the practice of politicians in a democracy—in reality corresponds perfectly to the general strike which, for revolutionary syndicalists, represents the advent of the new world to come.'[1]

The authority lodged in the State machinery was bitterly denounced by Pelloutier for its effects in grinding to dust the rights of labour. But unlike most theoretical anarchists, he thought in terms of attracting the lower echelons attached to the State. If the State was an artifact, grafted on to society by class needs, Pelloutier reasoned, this does not imply that each petty official or soldier was hostile to workers demands by definition. These lower sectors in the employ of the State were no less its victims than society as a whole. This shrewd separation of individual will and State function led him to conclude that the soldiers and other men armed by the State could definitely be included in a realizable scheme to sow the revolutionary seed.[2]

Pelloutier's common-sense definition of arms and men, his utter disregard for traditional socialist arguments and precepts—coupled as it was with a fervent apocryphal sense of socialism as the essence of human destiny—had a mighty attraction for Sorel, who by the mid-'nineties was already revising revisionist Marxism and scoffing at orthodox rebuttals. 'Words matter little to those who wish to get at the root of things' said Sorel in speaking of Pelloutier, and no doubt thinking also of himself. To both men, 'the veneration of labels is for parliamentarians.'[3] They urged the anarchists to forget the tactics of minority terror and enter the *Bourses* for a fundamental education in the social realities of proletarian life. Yielding to patronizing sociological theories of the tyranny or backwardness of the masses was considered an intellectualist abomination. Not only was the worker considered the physical equal of other social sectors, but he was the moral leader of society. Especially for Pelloutier, proletarian higher morality was rooted in the nature of a class struggle that was no less a total human struggle between good and evil. Pelloutier's innocent romanticism was probably a more direct

---

[1] *La décomposition du marxisme*, p. 64.
[2] Fernand and Maurice Pelloutier, *Lettre sur la guerre* (Nantes, 1919), p. 10.
[3] *La décomposition du marxisme*, p. 63.

and powerful influence on the development of Sorel's morality of violence than the more diffuse notions of Nietzsche.[1] Hubert Lagardelle, follower of Pelloutier and friend of Sorel, inherited the problems of the *Bourses*. He became a prime mover in the growth of the comprehensive trade union formed in 1895, the *Conféderation Générale du Travail*. In summing up the ideals of anarcho-syndicalism, he makes it quite plain that a new lower class élite is eventually to take over from the State. In contrast to politics in democracies was the true democracy of producers, in particular, the conscious producers organized along class lines. The decision-making unit is no longer the capricious individualist, but the group. The producers as a group are responsible for defending their own specific material and moral interests, seeking no rewards or gratuities from the State. The intellectual fares no better than the proletarian, since the revolt of producers is no less a rejection of abstract speculations on its own behalf than it is a denial of politics separated from economics. The scientific society needs technicians rather than intellectuals.[2]

The emphasis on organizational supremacy and the collectivity of decision-making that was integral to Pelloutier's vision did not conform in every detail to Sorel. Nonetheless, Sorel prefaced the *Histoire des Bourses*, and in it he contrasted Pelloutier's approach to the casuistry and compromising stance of official socialism.[3] Sorel's anti-politique took concrete form in his anarchist argument for the autonomous development of the producers. This theory of proletarian purity paralleled the activities of Pelloutier, but was formulated by Sorel independently.[4]

The broad legacy left by Pelloutier and *fin de siècle* syndicalism in general was to provide the foundations of a political movement alert to revolutionary potentials in each situation and unafraid of direct action. The general strike, sabotage, boycotts, were all grist to

---

[1] Although many references to the relation of Sorel and Nietzsche have been presented, most of the writing has been impressionistic, necessarily so, since Sorel had as late as 1890 made no mention of his German fellow irrationalist. Persistent ideas that Sorel derives his theory of violence from Nietzsche ignores the impulse to a theory of violence given from strictly French sources as diverse as Edouard Vaillant and Pierre Joseph Proudhon. It was only after the turn of the century that Nietzsche exterted a real force on Sorel's outlook.

[2] Hubert Lagardelle, *Le Socialisme, ouvrier*, in *Collection des doctrines politiques*, *IX* (Paris, 1911), pp. 57–9.

[3] Preface to *Histoire des Bourses du Travail*, pp. 14–17.

[4] *L'avenir socialiste des syndicats* (Paris, 1901), pp. 12–14.

the anarchist mill. However it was precisely Sorel's unwillingness to translate a doctrine of violence from a description into an activity, that separated him from the political currents Pelloutier died for. Sorel was very much under the sway of accepted sociological method, in so far as he accepted Durkheim's principle of the logical disjunction between fact and value.

The optimism of revolutionary syndicalism during the *fin de siècle* gave way to disillusionment during the next generation. The repeated failure of anarchism to define, much less reach its goals, led to disenchantment on the part of most workers, and their reversion to the realizable aims of the economic strike and even the political strike. As in the case of Christian socialism, the plague of minority conscience haunted the activity of a movement for which Sorel had the deepest hopes. Anarcho-syndicalism was on the horns of an ineluctable dilemma: either to become an educational alliance without hope of immediate success—a pressure group like English Fabianism, or to seek a real foothold in proletarian affairs by entering the mainstream of that accursed thing—politics. In either case, the end of pure anarcho-syndicalism was clearly forecast by the time of the last large gathering of revolutionary *syndicats* in Paris during 1907.[1] Sorel's disillusionment had become manifest while the copy of his speeches to the Congress still fed the presses. Why Sorel beat a 'retreat' and retired into his 'hole' is a complex matter.[2] What we shall concern ourselves with in this retirement from anarchist affairs is the limits and shortcomings of the movement rather than the men who led it.

Why did Pelloutier's integral socialism fare no better than Péguy's abstract religious socialism? This was a question that Sorel's policy of non-involvement in political affairs addressed itself to. His disillusion with syndicalism carried him into other political absurdities, such as faith in the restorationist nationalism of Maurras. However, at the theoretical level there is real justification for Sorel's separation from Pelloutier's vision.

The answers Sorel offered for the disintegration of anarcho-syndicalism ran along three pivotal paths. First, revolutionary syndicalism took its mission in a too literal sense. It approached socialism as a reality around the corner rather than a myth to which men must continually strive to attain. Second, the elemental democratic

[1] See my 'Historical Note on *The Decomposition of Marxism*,' pp. 202–3.
[2] Letter of June 24, 1908, *La Critica*, XXVI (1928), p. 108.

ideology governing Pelloutier and Lagardelle was inappropriate to the occasion. Revolutions are made by men; but men in turn are either leaders or followers, producers of myths or believers in them. The last point is that syndical socialism did not offer a psychology for getting men to act. It failed to distinguish between the ends of action and the stimuli to action.

Though these themes have been treated often in the literature of political philosophy from Plato to Machiavelli, a literature that Sorel was fully appraised of, it was the *fin de siècle* advocates of a revised *realpolitik* who stirred Sorel's imagination along new paths. We may take as a characteristic critique of rational politics the work of Gustave Le Bon. Sorel, who had favourably reviewed his work in 1895, offering only minor objections to Le Bon's belief that proletarian sympathies with their oppressors are greater than with their own leaders, was led to radical divergencies from Pelloutier. What is curious is that Sorel's polyglot mind could harbour both a faith in syndical socialism and a series of objections to the possibility of such a social structure realizing itself. Indeed, when the break with syndicalism does take place, the echo of Le Bon remains audible.[1]

Pelloutier saw the irrationality of the State, but continued, as did so many radicals of the *fin de siècle*, to retain a firm belief in the rationality of men—particularly the individual producer. Pelloutier's moral socialism and sense of craft organization was framed as a rational alternative to the insane State. What Le Bon did, and Sorel after him, was to complete the analysis of irrationality. The masses in whom Pelloutier placed the burden of his faith is compared by Le Bon to 'those microbes which hasten the dissolution of enfeebled or dead bodies.'[2] This Kafka-like imagery is used to explore the darker shades of human nature that increasingly came to occupy Sorel's attention. The intense disdain Sorel manifested for the 'dismal' sciences like sociology and economics stemmed in no small part from their imagined disregard for deviant behaviour patterns.

Le Bon's 'collective hallucinations' upon which men act[3] is per-

[1] Compare Sorel's review, of Le Bon's *Psychologie des foules* in *Le Devenir Social* (November 1895) with comments made a decade later in the *Réflexions sur la violence*, pp. 192–5 (150–3). If anything, his appreciation of Le Bon increased with time.

[2] Gustave Le Bon, *Psychologie des foules* (translated as *The Crowd: A Study of the Popular Mind*). (London, 1896), p. 19.

[3] Gustave Le Bon, *Ibid.*, pp. 46–7.

haps not as romantic a vision as Péguy's mystique and not quite as morally worthy as Sorel's myth, yet in psychological content they parallel one another. 'A crowd thinks in images, and the image itself immediately calls up a series of other images, having no logical connection with the first.'[1] But anarcho-syndicalism did not provide these images. Every aim was considered by Pelloutier as politically feasible. Thus every setback the movement suffered had to be considered a real setback. Defeat in steady dosages is not recommended for either advocates or followers of a *realpolitik*. To use Le Bon's phraseology, if the masses were 'suggestive' to revolutionary syndicalist propaganda, the other side of the proletarian *bête machine*, its 'irritability' with a fumbling leadership, became manifest with each failure of deeds.

While Le Bon superficially stands at the opposite pole from Machiavelli in his conviction that mass psychology in the *fin de siècle* was the 'last resource of the statesman who wishes not to govern crowds . . . but at any rate not to be too much governed by them,'[2] it is clear that the same referential points—the ruled and the ruler, the myth-maker and myth-follower—are used by them both.

It is just this sense of a theory of élites that is absent in Pelloutier's vision, and central to Sorel. The separation of chiefs and braves is instinctively grounded for Le Bon.[3] A particular idea grips the political leader in such a way that all other opinions appear as mistakes and superstitions. The myth instilled, the leader who is above all a man who can act and can stimulate others to action, must infuse the masses with his particular idea. The leader instils the myth by arousing mass faith. This is done through 'affirmation, repetition and contagion.' Prestige, not the acquisition of truth, is the real mark of leadership.[4] The belief that the rationality of the individual man carries over into mass man was for both Le Bon and Sorel a misplaced regard for reason. The purely rational involves a constant questioning of assumptions; and in so doing breaks down the faith in leadership, thereby seriously curtailing the ability to take action.

This rationalist faith of syndical socialism in human perfectability, when coupled with a thinly veiled form of hedonist psychology of self-interest, was for Sorel the fatal blunder of Pelloutier's followers.

---

[1] Gustave Le Bon, *Psychologie des foules* (translated as *The Crowd: A Study of the Popular Mind*) (London, 1896), pp. 45–6.
[2] Gustave Le Bon, *Ibid.*, p. 21.   [3] Gustave Le Bon, *Ibid.*, p. 134.
[4] Gustave Le Bon, *Ibid.*, pp. 147–59.

Radical syndicalism advocated socialism as a social system that harmonized with the self-interest of workers. Yet, as Le Bon persuasively indicates, and Sorel so much agrees, 'it is assuredly not self-interest that has guided crowds in so many wars, incomprehensible as a rule to their intelligence—wars in which they have allowed themselves to be massacred as easily as the larks hypnotized by the mirror of the hunter.'[1] Elsewhere, Le Bon adds that if self-interest does not guide the crowd in war, neither does it guide the masses in their social struggles. Instinctually, the crowd is conservative and Caesarist, responding to the human appeal of élitism and not the utopian appeal of anarchist society. Le Bon shared with Sorel a keen interest in the historical role of irrational mass behaviour. He was particularly concerned with showing the motivation of crowds in revolutionary situations, and devoted most of his later writings to empirical studies to support his contentions.[2]

It is clear that these ideas are offered by Le Bon as a scientific account of mass behaviour. As such, an implication is carried between knowledge of how to propel men into action and the myth supporting action. What Le Bon sought to do was not simply criticize democratic institutions, but uncover the mainspring of political sociology. It is a basis of wisdom, however, that no political party, or anti-political grouping as the case may be, could seriously be expected to incorporate into a party programme. Inherent in the dichotomy of Le Bon and Pelloutier is the gap between science and action, between thoughts about action and action as a stimulant to thought. There is no doubt that Sorel preferred Le Bon's vision over Pelloutier's. Political sophistication was clearly on the side of the theorist. And as sectarianism and factional disputes developed in the *Bourses*, Sorel came closer to Le Bon's psychology of the act. Sorel did qualify Le Bon to the extent that his ideas were considered valid only for societies lacking a mass dedicated to the ideal of class warfare. However, since for Sorel class conflict is itself an ordered myth that could easily be translated into Le Bon's language, this qualification is more an endorsement than a substantive critique.[3]

Élitism is in its nature contrary to democratic doctrine. In view

[1] Gustave Le Bon, *Psychologie des foules* (translated as *The Crowd: A Study of the Popular Mind*), p. 65.
[2] Gustave Le Bon, *La révolution française et la psychologie des révolutions* (translated as *The Psychology of Revolution*) (New York, 1913), especially pp. 102–12 on 'The Psychology of Revolutionary Crowds.'
[3] *Réflexions sur la violence*, pp. 192–3 (152–3).

of this we might have imagined Sorel's unwillingness to support radical syndicalism could have come at any time. That his support for it, as well as for any other movement he attached his name to, never extended beyond the written word, was a consequence of his commitment to the *intellectual* ideal of uncovering the sources and causes of action wherever they may lead. The ambivalence of Sorel was directly linked to the attempt to find a political home that could accept the scientific spirit. Here was a man who believed that political action was based on mythology, while never ceasing a personal search for a political alliance true to the canons of scholarship. The paradox of such an attempt made Sorel as absurd as the figures and ideas of *fin de siècle* he castigated.

Rather than characterize Sorel as an anti-intellectual, it might be more prudent to note that he simply expanded the intellectualist ideal to a rational study of irrational factors in human behaviour. It is certain that to the extent Sorel took and applied Le Bon's work seriously, he could no longer remain affiliated with any mass move-ment—even one professing the collective emancipation from politics. Le Bon's character sketches of irrational man complemented Pel-loutier's critique of the irrational State. What remained for Sorel was to discover a general motor force in the social structure which could complete a philosophical picture of the way men behave.

3. Henri Bergson: The Liberation of Will From Intelligence

After a usually hectic week of writing on the rise and fall of ancient civilizations, polemicizing against official Marxism in France and Italy, inveighing against legal socialism in Germany and England, dashing off correspondence to Croce and Delesalle, planning the theoretical rejuvenation of anarchism-syndicalism, flaying into the bourgeois State with glowing adjectives, and participating in the formation of periodicals and journals, we find Sorel in a different guise entirely. On Friday afternoons he would drop by Péguy's office, and together the two men proceeded to the *Collège de France*, where along with the Parisian *literati* and intellectuals from other shores, they would listen in rapt attention to Henri Bergson.

This involved a blithe abandon of his contempt for intellectuals, particularly those of Jewish ancestry.[1] Sorel would silently absorb

[1] Sorel's anti-semitism, which has been the subject of intense debate, cannot be dismissed without some explanation of its multi-fold character. At the

39

Bergson's explanation of how a theory of consciousness becomes transformed into an enervating principle of life, and how the principles of mechanics are subordinated to a more general principle of energy. Bergson, the talk of the stylish cafés, became the toast of the pre-War disenchanted and self-styled alienated intelligentsia. Sorel, who joined Berth and Benda in the chorus of those shouting about the treason of the intellectual, was nonetheless not averse to poring over Bergson's treasonous texts on the 'mysteries of life.' No stronger evidence than his regard for Bergson and later James can be mustered to show that Sorel employed the notion of a treasonous intelligentsia to disguise a repugnance for rationalism. Bergson replaced the neo-Malthusian and Spencerian visions of the principle of struggle. For Sorel, the myth of a vital force transcending material evolution was a

---

economic level, the parallel with Marx is noteworthy. It was not primarily the Jew as a religious or cultural force that drew Sorel's fire, his appreciation of Renan's *Histoire du peuple d'Israel* prevented this for a time, but the Jew as an economic entity. His contact with the Jew was largely confined to West European Jewry, those who had taken the road to the Enlightenment he so much despised. The contradiction between capitalism and radicalism was so firmly etched in Sorel's mind that he neither appreciated nor countenanced the co-existence of these two factors in the Jews. This attempt to square what, for Sorel, was a circle, is his chief blast at the Jews of Paris, Milan or Berlin. The added element of seeing the professional segments of Jewish origin absorbed in socialist politics only confirmed his image of the *clerc* as treasonous—a statist cancer on socialist radicalism. In this way, the Jew was identified by Sorel with both the economic decomposition of capitalism and the political reformism characteristic of orthodox socialism. On this primary level, see his essays: 'A propos de l'anticléricalisme' and 'Léon XIII,' both in *Études socialistes* (1903), pp. 239–56, 257–82.

At the political level, Sorel's approach clouds up considerably. The Dreyfus affair centred his contradictions and anxieties. At the level of defending the Republic against monarchist counter-revolution, military corruption and Church opposition to the reopening of the Dreyfus case, Sorel stood firm with republicanism. The Jews come in for attack not because of the juridical issues, but in terms of the long range consequences. It was not the separation of State and Church that so much troubled Sorel as the separation of the French from their heroic and essentially Catholic mythos. The Dreyfus case put an end to social homogeneity said Sorel. He held the Jews responsible for sundering the claims of French nationalism from the Catholic vision. The Joan of Arc legend died with the victory of Dreyfus and the Republic. The Jew was envisioned as the myth-destroyer, the antithesis of Sorel's myth-maker. His early views of the Church and State are to be found in the pamphlet, *Essai sur l'état et l'église* (Paris, 1901). His later views, which spell out in detail his conception of Church institutions to Catholicism as a religious force, and both to the Jewish question are to be found in another pamphlet, *La révolution dreyfusienne* (Paris 1909).

Sorel's attitude to the Church became increasingly negative as he became convinced of its revolutionary impotence. On the other hand, his regard for the Catholic ethos remained intact. Catholicism was held to be capable of eternal duration. It was not a synthesis of the Judaic-Graeco tradition, but a new revela-

better way to consider the motor-force of struggle than gloomy predictions on the catastrophe of over-population, or on the predatory
nature of man as a biological entity.[1]

Bergson's role in the formation of Sorel's outlook is tinged with
ambiguity. Whether Sorel took only fragments from Bergson, applying them in patchwork fashion to meet his own intellectual needs,
or simply viewed Bergson's doctrine of the unconscious as a necessary
pre-condition of a rounded political philosophy is a critical issue only
if a causalist sequence of moving from idea to idea is considered a
completely valid criterion. Whether Sorel was a Bergsonian prior to
sifting through Bergson's doctrine, or whether he saw in Bergson an
intellectually respectable buffer, seems to be the argument of a partisan, and is not necessarily germane to understanding the inter-
relations and kinship in the ideas of the two men.[2]

As a matter of historical record there was intellectual indebtedness and embarrassment on both sides, albeit in unequal doses.
Bergson appreciated how Sorel's revolutionary morality could indirectly intersect with his own on the plane of action, but chafed at

tion with an integrity of its own. He came to contrast the mystical economy of the
Catholic with the rationalist faith of the Jew. Hatred of the Jew, a negative force,
bound the Church together; this was doomed to failure. But the revolutionary,
warrior spirit of the Catholic faith is that positive, eternal force that Sorel sets up
against the pietistic rationalism of Judaism. This 'theoretical' appraisal led him to
the conclusion that Catholicism represents the uncompromising radical spirit,
while Judaism represents the compromising spirit. Therefore, radicalism at some
point along the way required a critique of Judaism as such. Sorel's theoretical
appraisal of the historic Church and the divine religion is formulated in *De l'église
et de l'état. Cahiers de la Quinzaine*, No. 3, Vol. 3, (Oct. 1901).

Sorel's later associations with the royalist, anti-semitic papers, *L'Indépéndence*
and *Action Française*, intensified his anti-Jewish attitudes. Indeed, if his theoretical opposition to the Jews can be explained on non-anti-semitic grounds, his pre-
War emotive bleatings against the Jews *qua* Jews, puts an end to speculation on
this point. The tangled web of interpersonal relations with Jewish intellectuals,
particularly Benda's role in bringing the rupture of Sorel and Péguy to a head,
remains a problem in biography. From a theoretical position, it must be said in
fairness to Sorel that anti-semitism remains a private, minor motif, existing in
large measure apart from the foundations of his philosophy or sociology. For an
idea of the personal animosities Sorel felt for Jewish associates, see his letters to
Croce between August and November of 1912, in *La Critica*, Vol. XXVI (1928),
pp. 437–40.

[1] The most complete exposition of the relation of Bergson and Sorel is Pierre
Andreu, *Bergson et Sorel* (*Les Études bergsoniennes*) (Paris, 1952), Vol. III. A
compressed version of this material is in Andreu's *Notre Maitre, M. Sorel*,
pp. 239–68.

[2] For a comparison of how partisan analysis tends to come to the same fundamental core of agreement, see Agostino Lanzillo, *Giorgio Sorel* (Rome, 1910),
p. 93; with Paul Perrin, *Les idées sociales de Georges Sorel* (Alger, 1925), p. 24.

the anti-democratic content of Sorel's position.[1] For his part, Sorel early admired the systematic qualities of Bergson's biological philosophy of the unconscious. The appearance of the *Essai sur les données immédaites de la conscience* signified to Sorel 'a vigorous tree that is planted in the milieu of the desolate plains of contemporary philosophy.'[2] Yet he was hostile to biologism as a generalized expression of man's fate, and took steady exception to Bergson's continual argument by analogies to biology, psychology and the arts. Above all, Bergson's position was evolutionary in a fashion intrinsically inimical to revolutionary social action.[3]

The comments of Sorel and Bergson upon one another are, after all, in the nature of afterthoughts. They are reflections of mature men upon each other's past. Perhaps the similarities of their positions, if not their sentiments, prevented an open embrace. What Maritain says of Bergsonism is assuredly no less the case for Sorel. 'An anti-intellectualist philosophy cannot form *disciples* properly speaking, for a disciple is one whose *intellect*, set in action by a doctrine received, thinks it anew on its own account; *ideas* alone are communicated; impressions, sensations and intuitive sympathies can only be individual. Bergsonism can therefore have only propagators more or less faithful to the "current of thought" of their master and who repeat more or less well the metaphors they have learned.'[4] The subsequent use and abuse of Bergson and Sorel, the spate of books on each offering the one and true explanation, bears out Maritian in almost prophetic fashion. Seers of the *fin de siècle*, Sorel and Bergson were not even witnesses to events of later decades. Although both men lived far into the twentieth century, neither really gave up the old battles and the old allegiances. This is I think particularly true in the case of Bergson.

The political thought of Sorel falls into two distinct parts: an objective analysis of the structure of power, coercion and authority as they manifest themselves in the concrete life of the State; and second, an analytic study of the subjective impact of propaganda, mass action, ideology and mythology on the lives of ordinary men. Bridg-

[1] See Gaetan Pirou, *Georges Sorel: 1847–1922* (Paris, 1927), pp. 56–7; and Pierre Andreu, *Notre Maitre, M. Sorel*, p. 244.

[2] *D'Aristote à Marx* (*L'ancienne et la nouvelle métaphysique*) (Paris, 1935), pp. 167–8.

[3] *De l'utilité du pragmatisme* (Paris, 1921), pp. 415–16, 444–51.

[4] Jacques Maritain, *La Philosophie Bergsonienne* (translated as *Bergsonian Philosophy and Thomism*) (New York, 1955), pp. 278–9.

ing the objective and subjective, the will of the State and the counter will of society, is an attempt to evolve a doctrine of the political–psychological complex as a movement in time, as a philosophy of history.

In the development of the psychological and historical aspects of this political theory, the full force of Bergson's outlook came into focus. The Nietzschean influence on Sorel is nebulous, and rested in large part on an unclear notion of what the German 'anti-Christ' is all about. The Jamesian impact came at a late stage in Sorel's life. *De l'utilité du pragmatisme* is a statement of staunch support for James at the expense of Bergson. However, like so many of the men that Sorel came upon around the World War period, James functions as a booster of the alter-ego that had all but been destroyed by events. Look! The man from America takes the same philosophic position; it must be so.

If we accept a criterion of immediacy and availability, then one must upgrade the importance of Bergson in relation to Sorel. Whether Sorel would have developed his political sociology in quite the same way independent of Bergson is an issue of little portent. It is enough to say that both were responding to a cultural milieu, and both did a great deal to shape the specifics of this milieu while drawing sustenance from each other. What I shall therefore concentrate on is a brief statement of Bergson's theory of general psychology particularly as it bears on considerations directly relevant to Sorel's work.

If we take as the starting point a shared regard for the need to re-cast the theory of progress and evolution, and a common chafing at the over-simplifications in mechanistic and deterministic extensions of science, then we shall be close to the unifying elements in the work of Bergson and Sorel. It is no less true that these were the binding themes of *fin de siècle* thought generally. Both men sought to stretch consciousness beyond the confining limits of reason and intelligence; on this major substantive issue they joined hands with the age. The intensity of a turning inward for answers to general problems, to a view of life in which reason is confined to recording the operations of an unreasoning life force, so succinctly expressed by Bergson as early as 1889,[1] and Sorel in

---

[1] Henri Bergson, *Essai sur les donées immédiates de la conscience* (translated as *Time and Free Will: An Essay on the Immediate Data of Consciousness*) (London, 1910), pp. 161–2, 186–7.

1890,[1] reflected a crisis in culture that sliced through socio-economic ties.

If the old slogans of education and legislation for progress had become a last gasp of the bourgeois mind of the *fin de siècle*, the proletarian inheritance of progress through struggle and self-reliance had become no less platitudinous. What Bergson and Sorel were doing in effect was giving notice to their respective audiences that neither Clemenceau's nor Jaurès' repeated insistence on the ultimate triumph of humanism, intelligence and the good will could stand against the evidence of either common or sublime sense.

The spirit of voluntarism, where the individual will is held superior to all external controlling factors, found many reflections in the philosophic arena. Bergson was in many respects an inheritor of *fin de siècle* culture in which vitalism was the leit-motif of even the second echelon theorists like Alfred Fouillée. The clearly negative tone of the revolt against positivism, and, more heatedly, mechanism, found its completion in the critique of reason itself. If reason does not yield truth in as primary a discipline as physics, what give us the presumption to believe it can fare better in the innermost regions of conscience? Relativism, probabilism and possibilism admittedly satisfied the operational needs of natural science, but could they satisfy the seemingly insatiable demand for truth and meaning? The very posing of the question in this form indicated that voluntarism, while critical of past attempts at philosophic synthesis, was ready to give the synthetic method one more fling before yielding up its claims to empirical disciplines. The quest for certainty informed the spirit of the age no less than any other activity of the decade. The old physics and academic sociology were held no longer useful, but the desire for absoluteness was as central in irrational, negative philosophies, not one whit less than in its rationalist foil.

'We have let ourselves be duped by the imagination, which never considers anything but ready-made and principally verbal images,' writes Fouillée in righteous indignation. He warns us 'not to be duped similarly by pure intelligence, which can not easily apply itself

---

[1] *Contributions psycho-physiques à l'étude esthetique*; and, *Esthétique et psychophysique*. Communications to *Revue philosophique*, vols. XXIX and XXX (1890–91). These two pieces give the first indication that Sorel could not find a home in epistemological materialism, and would clash on more than one occasion with Marxians on this score. This does not mean, however, that Sorel took the same philosophical stance as Bergson. Physics just as assuredly informed Sorel's outlook, as evolutionary biology was the early scientific inspiration for Bergson.

except to ideas of definite contour, expressed by definite and immutable words.'[1] Certainty was not surrendered; it simply became transformed from a material realm to individual psychology. It was this same Fouillée who inspired Sorel to write his study and critique of Socrates.[2] Nonetheless, Sorel was no follower of Fouillée, any more so than he can properly be classed an adherent of the Bergsonian metaphysic. What is clear is that the climate of opinion was such that irrationalism, whatever its source, found a responsive chord in Sorel; whether that source was a syndicalist radical suspicious of ideas, or a metaphysician dubious of action.

It was not simply the germination of psychoanalysis in Paris that provoked Bergson's reappraisal of the roots of metaphysical thinking.[3] Paris was also the home of a stream of consciousness literature in which symbolism was employed to uncover the mainsprings of the human animal. Edouard Dujardi and Jules Laforgue had by the close of the *mal de siècle* already indicated a growing discontent with literature and art as representations of a mechanical universe. The drama of life was no longer seen in terms of man against man, but as internalized perspective of man against himself. Nor was this a strictly Parisian event. Vienna, where Freud was already well at work on the study of the personal unconscious, also witnessed a parallel effort to render in a literary way the torment of the inner man. The work of Arthur Schnitzler, Richard Beer-Hofmann and Hugo von Hofmannsthal had well prepared the cultural soil for a positive reception of psychiatry and psychoanalysis. It should be remembered that if Freud's ideas were greeted with scepticism among his medical colleagues in both Vienna and Paris, this was not the case with the large *kultur*-centred middle classes of both cities.[4]

[1] Alfred Fouillée, *La Psychologie des idées-forces* (Paris, 1893), Vol. II, p. 85.
[2] James H. Meisel, *The Genesis of Georges Sorel* (Ann Arbor, 1951), p. 51.
[3] The description of France as the home of psychoanalysis is based on the development of abnormal psychology in the two great research centres at Paris under Charcot and later Janet, and at Nancy, under the leadership of Bernheim and Liébault. It was under Charcot that the first major studies were made in the psychoanalytic theory of hysteria, and the relation of hypnosis to the dream materials. Freud's respect for Charcot is well known. The French psychiatrist was responsible for clearing much of the ground for Freud's discoveries. See J. C. Flugel, *A Hundred Years of Psychology, 1833–1933* (London, 1951), second edition, pp. 216–18. For the extent of Freud's regard for Charcot's work, see Martin Freud, *Sigmund Freud: Man and Father* (New York, 1958), p. 21.
[4] I am indebted to Carl Schorske for a first appreciation of the similarities of Paris and Vienna during the *fin de siècle*. The biography of Freud by Ernest Jones, *The Life and Work of Sigmund Freud* (New York, 1953–7), particularly the

If the intuitionism of Bergson is not particularly original, it was systematic in a fashion quite alien to the writings of Guyau, Lachelier, Tarde and Fouillée. And if philosophic virtue extends not only to novelty of expression, but to summarizing the novel tendencies of others, then Bergson's real value to the *fin de siècle* can be gauged. In point of fact, Bergson never left the 'nineties intellectually. Even in his later works, like *Les deux sources de la Morale et de la Religion*, where some attempt at a social philosophy is offered, the enemies are still the French nineteenth century positivists and the English social Darwinists like Herbert Spencer. The age formed Bergson; and unfortunately it also chained him. If he is all but forgotten outside of philosophic circles, it is because the intellectual monsters he did battle with have become fossilized.[1]

Like Freud and Vienna, Bergson and Paris were concerned with the underground elements in existence, the basic morphology of the unconscious. Bergson came into a prominence denied his colleagues because he was able to fashion something resembling an ethic and an epistemology grounded in what Sorel appropriately termed 'the psychology of the deeper life.' The transformation of philosophy into psychology is both Bergson's weakness and strength. For while the novelty of his system captured the imagination on both sides of the Atlantic civilization, the simple fact that psychology is subject to constant empirical scrutiny and alteration dated Bergson's outlook more quickly than is ordinarily the case with philosophical systems.

Nonetheless, it was as a psychologist of real merit that Bergson acquired his appreciative audience. The work of Pierre Janet, Charcot, and Alfred Binet was available to him. Their work on hysteria, mystical insights and unconscious motivation, which prefigured the Freudian school in Vienna, was a critical element in Bergson's more

---

first volume, contains much illuminating material on the interconnection of medical circles in Paris and Vienna. In a different sphere, Erich Kahler's brilliant speculative enquiry, *The Tower and the Abyss* (New York, 1957), confirms the belief that a cultural transformation accompanied the changed political reorientation of the age.

[1] This point is emphasized because in my discussion of Bergson I employ the range of his writings, including some of those which appeared after the turn of the century. The minor shifts towards psychology and away from biology in demonstrating the existence of a stream of consciousness, or the increased emphasis on the role of Christianity as the message-bearer of a higher religious synthesis, do not, in my opinion, provide a sufficient basis for speaking of any substantive development in Bergson's philosophy. In any event, the more technical aspects in Bergson's thought, where even the minor shifts take place, are not germane to this discussion.

generalized statements.[1] In his earliest work, Bergson wrote that 'not all our ideas are thus incorporated in the fluid mass of our conscious states. Many float on the surface, like dead leaves on the water of a pond; the mind, when it thinks them over and over again, finds them ever the same, as if they were external to it.'[2] The idea that consciousness is only that marginal portion of the mind that gets to the surface is plainly stated by Bergson. 'Just in proportion as we dig below the surface and get down to the real self, do its states of consciousness cease to stand in juxtaposition and begin to permeate and melt into one another, and each to be tinged with the colouring of all the others. Thus each of us has his own way of loving and hating; and this love or this hatred reflects his whole personality.'[3]

This psychology of the unconscious is more than an explanation, even in broad terms, of the mechanisms of the human mind. It is a clear call to arms against materialism; against the human will allowing itself to be pushed about by external factors. Self-awareness becomes a proof of the inner basis of action. And freedom is defined by Bergson as the measure in which such self-awareness can replace mechanical causality as the reason for action. 'The moments at which we thus grasp ourselves are rare, and that is just why we are rarely free. The greater part of the time we live outside ourselves, hardly perceiving anything of ourselves but our own ghost, a colourless shadow which pure duration projects into homogeneous space. Hence our life unfolds in space rather than in time; we live for the external world rather than for ourselves; we speak rather than think; we are acted upon rather than act ourselves.'[4] Philosophy is converted into self-realization. Here is a view clearly suited to an activist social doctrine, and Sorel was quick to seize the point. The doctrine of socialism was not so much important unto itself as it was a means to achieve the goal of a healthy personality.

[1] In a useful introduction to Bergson's psychology of the dream, Wade Baskin has indicated some of the secondary sources of Bergsonian thought. Most important of these were Tissie's *Les rêves, physiologie et pathologie*; articles by Delage on repressed materials as the main source of dreams, in *Revue Scientifique*, II, July 1891; and Krauss' essays on the origin of dream images, in *Allgemeine Zeitschrift für Psychologie*, XV, XVI, 1858–9. Baskin's preface is to the English language edition of Bergson's *World of Dreams* (New York, 1958), first offered as a lecture to the *Institut Psychologique* in 1901, and published in June of that year in the *Revue Scientifique*.
[2] Henri, Bergson, *Time and Free Will*, p. 135.
[3] Henri Bergson, *Ibid.*, p. 164.
[4] Henri Bergson, *Ibid.*, p. 231.

Consciousness is not so much a fact of mind as it is a moral virtue. It is, in Bergson's words: 'the light that plays around the zone of possible actions or potential activity which surrounds the action really performed by the living being.'[1] Consciousness makes possible creation; and creation in turn calls into operation the whole gamut of emotions to gain its ends.[2] Sorel cites approvingly Bergson's belief that 'to act freely is to recover possession of oneself, and to get back into pure duration.'[3] Seizing upon the social potential of this idea, Sorel goes on to equate action to the creation of a world of imagination. Freedom becomes the ability to create 'artificial constructions' of 'movements which depend entirely on us.'[4] Just as most of the activities of the imagination disappear from our minds like Bergson's 'dead leaves,' the few imaginings which take root in the mass mind form the basis of useful social myths. Sorel's social myth is, on inspection, like Bergson's mysticism in that both are at the basis of great social and moral transformations.

It is significant that Sorel saw in Bergson not the extension of a utopian vision, but its very suppression. The social myth makes no claim to project present relations into the future. It simply takes consciousness as the summation of past events retained in present memories. To Bergson, 'the idea of reading in a present state of the material universe the future of living forms, and of unfolding now their history yet to come, involves a veritable absurdity.'[5] Sorel nods in vigorous affirmation, citing this absurdity as 'one of the greatest illusions of the utopians.'[6] Both men saw in action its own reason for being, requiring no philosophic rationalization or utopian projection to demonstrate its value. It was just this philosophical manipulation of science that Sorel felt to be the ultimate sin of the rationalist tradition. It wanted knowledge and truth as a precondition to acting, and ended up by gaining neither knowledge nor action.

To maintain that action is its own excuse for being carries with it deep implications for everything else. The *fin de siècle* generation was reacting to a sentimentalized expression of emotions; to an inner turmoil that never sets itself free from mechanistic psychology.

[1] Henri Bergson, *Creative Evolution* (New York, 1911), p. 159.
[2] Henri Bergson, *The Two Sources of Morality and Religion* (New York, 1935), p. 37.
[3] Henri Bergson, *Time and Free Will*, p. 232.
[4] *Réflexions sur la violence*, p. 43 (56).
[5] Henri Bergson, *Creative Evolution*, p. 371.
[6] *La décomposition du marxisme*, pp. 66 f.

Inner turmoil was a necessity, but it was the translation of such feelings into directed action that ultimately counted. Turmoil is material necessity; the capacity to act spiritual liberation. 'To reply to an action received by an immediate reaction, which adopts the rhythm of the first and continues it in the same duration, to be in the present and in a present which is always beginning again—this is the fundamental law of matter.' Herein consists the realm of Bergsonian necessity. But the really free act of the free will is indeterminate. The free man alone 'can fix, at long intervals, that becoming to which their own becoming clings, able to solidify it into distinct moments.'[1] Although Bergson tries mightily to prevent his thoughts on freedom from becoming an *imperium in imperio*, an object apart from material necessity, the logic of his philosophy moves precisely in the direction of sundering freedom and necessity from its traditional Spinozistic shell. James and Sorel were simply more rigorous in carrying through the implications of a philosophy of time as consciousness, and freedom as the will to act.

Sorel stood closer to Bergson than to James on at least one major point: a reluctance to surrender the stable claims of science to the instability of a pure pragmatic universe. The difficulty in their affirmation of science was that it was an act of piety, without any but a pragmatic anchor. Indeed, it was to Sorel's way of thinking, Bergson's highest achievement that philosophic speculation was not confused with empirical science.[2] Nonetheless, both were willing to employ science to slaughter the demons of an abandoned mechanism and a precariously perched positivism. Intelligence may define the laws of science and history, but it is the human will that redefines them in terms of the moral goals of freedom. 'We do not believe in the fatality of history. There is no obstacle which cannot be broken down by wills sufficiently keyed up, if they deal with it in time.' For Bergson therefore, 'there is no inescapable historic law.'[3]

This is exactly the view to which Sorel came around to adopting. As early as 1895 we find him arguing against Durkheim's belief in strict social causality by maintaining that a Marxian position is concerned with general categories, not with real causation.[4] Several years later, under the pressure of distinguishing himself from orthodox

---

[1] Henri Bergson, *Matter and Memory*, p. 279; also p. 332.
[2] Letter of October 24, 1908, *La Critica*, XXVI (1928), p. 191.
[3] Henri Bergson, *The Two Sources of Morality and Religion*, p. 282.
[4] 'Les théories de M. Durkheim,' *Le Devenir Social* (April–May 1895), nos. 1–2.

Marxism, the same Bergsonian theme is used to show that contingency is the mark of the creative workshop specifically and historical events generally.[1] This move from a justification of indeterminism on Marxian grounds to an open schism with Marxism on Bergsonian grounds was of exceptional importance for Sorel. For in the three year period marking this shift, we find Sorel deeply engaged in an evaluation of the work of Fouillée, Guyot and Payot, the very men who anticipated the direction and content of Bergson's work.[2]

Evolution becomes capricious in Bergson's thought the way revolution becomes anarchical in Sorel's approach. The *élan vital* develops 'fan-wise, creating, by the mere fact of its growth, divergent directions, each of which will receive a certain portion of the impetus.'[3] This pluralism is in itself not an objectively determined process; not the pluralism of an optimistic and bouyant American instrumentalism. What Bergson confronts us with is the pluralism of backwardness; of a petit-bourgeoisie, content with the way things are. 'The origins of the process of mechanization are indeed more mystical than we might imagine. Machinery will find its true vocation again, it will render services in proportion to its power, only if mankind, which it has bowed still lower to the earth, can succeed, through it, in standing erect and looking heavenwards.'[4]

Sorel realized how well Bergsonism fitted the conditions of a petit-proletariat, no less than the petit-bourgeois. Looking towards heaven takes on the symbolization of a factory aesthetic. Sorel fuses the energy of the machine and the energy of man as a labour idyll.[5] The image of the small, intimate factory, where labourer and owner share a mutual pride in the material values created, and yet manage to spend their extra-curricular time glaring at each other with clenched fists, is at the basis of Sorel's identification of liberty of judgment and artistic activity.[6]

The clear lines of a backward, almost feudal sense of craft, embraced and encased Péguy, Pelloutier and Sorel in distinctive ways. *Fin de siècle* radicalism took comfort as well as glory in the medieval

---

[1] 'La necessità e il fatalismo del Marxismo,' *Riforma Sociale* (August 1898).
[2] Cf. the reviews of Fouillée, *Le mouvement positiviste et la conception sociologique du monde*; Guyot, *L'économie de l'effort*; Payot, *De la croyance*. All appeared in *Le Devenir Social* (February 1897).
[3] Henri Bergson, *The Two Sources of Morality and Religion*, pp. 282–3.
[4] Henri Bergson, *Ibid.*, p. 299.
[5] *De l'utilité du pragmatisme* (Paris, 1921), pp. 321–2.
[6] *Ibid.*, pp. 129–41, 320–1. See also *D'Aristote à Marx*, pp. 193–201.

synthesis. For Péguy there was the obvious glory of a virile and united Christian world. Pelloutier could fairly smell the honour and morality of the labour process. Sorel shared with Burke a vision of feudalism as an age of chivalry and glory for Europe, a time of sensitivity to principles, chastity of honour and loyalty to rank and sex. Bergson's growing response to the Church was prevented from fulfilling itself in baptism only by the desperate plight of the German Jews. To a greater or lesser degree, all saw in the machine an agent of dehumanization brought about by rational intelligence. The will was to become the ultimate barrier against a technical de-activization of the intelligence. It was therefore necessary for the will to assert its moral supremacy over reason.

Fear of the intellect's destructive potential was a significant element in anti-rationalism. Reason no longer held out the promise of progress as it did for eighteenth century men like Lessing and Diderot. The historical workings of reason were seen as productive of social and moral chaos. Both Bergson and Sorel saw the choice as one between rationalism and humanism, rather than a decision on behalf of the irrational. The irrational was but one of several agents, others being mysticism, indeterminism in physics, relativism in sociology, and the unconscious in psychology, which could re-establish the primacy of the individual in the face of an onrushing mechanical civilization. This was the primary form in which the honest French peasant spirit joined hands with a timid small middle class to counter the claims of technology and social reconstruction. This spirit was particularly effective in distinguishing the virtues of France from the vices of Paris. It played a considerable ideological role in the lower rate of industrial velocity and social mobility than was the case elsewhere in Europe.

What enables men to act remained the essential problem for both Sorel and Bergson. Rationalism is rejected not simply because of its mechanistic way of measuring progress, but no less because the mechanical civilization becomes a substitute for human action. Reason procrastinates, the Will moves man to act. 'The symbolic knowledge of pre-existing concepts, which advance from the fixed to the moving, is relative, but it is by no means the intuitive knowledge that projects itself into the moving and adopts the life of the things themselves. This intuition reaches the absolute.'[1] And though

---

[1] Henri Bergson, *Introduction à la métaphysique* (translated as *The Introduction to a New Philosophy*) (Boston, 1912), pp. 86–7.

Sorel denied the Bergsonian claim that this intuitionism achieves perfection and teleological certainty, he could not help but exclaim that this holistic view of intuitive knowledge 'leads precisely to the catastrophic conception of socialism.'[1]

For his part, Bergson did not particularly relish the use of his intuitionism for socialist ends—catastrophic or gradualist. Nonetheless, even he could not fail to see how, from a certain viewpoint, his theory of images could lend itself handsomely to a doctrine of myths. Even more than Péguy, Bergson's psychology provided a foundation to Sorel's myth of the general strike, since images, unlike the mystique, were a human creation and not something found in the spirit of society. Bergson's human being was manipulatable and plastic, 'an object destined to move other objects.' Man becomes 'a centre of action' rather than a centre of cognition.[2]

Bergson's provisional definition of images clearly indicates a prime source of the general theory of myths. Bergson defines matter as 'the aggregate of images, and perception of matter these same images referred to the eventual action of one particular image, my body.'[3] And the less provisional and more certain Bergson becomes of his definitions, the closer does he reach a theory of action common to intuitionist psychology. 'We start from action, that is to say from our faculty of affecting changes in things, a faculty attested to by consciousness and towards which all the powers of the organized body are seen to converge.'[4] Relating human consciousness to an action situation proved a basic form for Bergson to resolve the antinomy of matter and mind in the stream of time.

For Sorel it was still more. Intuitionist psychology was the way out of the dilemmas arising from getting men, despite their physical contentment and work efficiency, to struggle on behalf of socialism. Itself transferred from a realm of material necessity to one of spiritual urge, socialism too could be viewed as a convergence point for an aggregate of images. Social conflict must be pictured with the sharpest possible relief, without consideration for sociological nuances. Positive results are not a consequence of the application of science to social events. To gain socialist objectives, 'use must be made of a body of images which, by *intuition alone*, and before any considered ana-

---

[1] *Réflexions sur la violence*, p. 174 (140).
[2] Henri Bergson, *Matter and Memory*, p. 5.
[3] Henri Bergson, *Ibid.*, p. 8.
[4] Henri Bergson, *Ibid.*, p. 67.

lyses are made, is capable of evoking as an undivided whole the mass of sentiments which corresponds to the different manifestations of the war undertaken by socialism against modern society. The syndicalists solve this problem perfectly, by concentrating the whole of socialism in the drama of the general strike; there is thus no longer any place for the reconciliation of contraries in the equivocations of the professors; everything is clearly mapped out, so that only one interpretation of socialism is possible.'[1]

With knowledge no longer autonomous, no longer able to critically reflect upon events, ideas themselves become subject to the rule of action. Their worth is measured in terms of provocation rather than information. As Bergson summed up this Sorelian dictum later in life: Intelligence cannot predict where things will go, 'since action on the move creates its own route, creates to a very great extent the conditions under which it is to be fulfilled, and thus baffles all calculation.'[2] Given this position on the function of knowledge, it follows for both men that action is the supreme basis of morality as well as of critical judgment.

The sources of Sorel's pragmatic socialism are embedded in Bergson's image of the undivided whole as simply and 'in fact reduced to the image of that which interests you.'[3] Sorel's pragmatic vision is not a later development of his thought; it does not await the coming of James to French shores, but is already demarcated in the psychology of Bergson and his predecessors. The notion that the datum of sensation which perceives movement is not to be confused with the artificial constructions of the mind that wills, is clearly a cornerstone of *fin de siècle* ideology. Movement replaces structure in Bergsonian thought as a means toward the realization of human liberty. Sorel simply transposes this concept into social life. The movement toward socialism is itself the definition of its qualities. Bergson becomes the thinker who is best able to illumine the steady and spontaneous growth of technique and industry; a growth which for Sorel obviates the need for utopian prognosis of the socialist future.[4]

The point of essential disagreement between Bergson and Sorel came, strangely enough, just at the point of widest agreement. Bergson regarded the doctrine of creative evolution as entailing a commit-

[1] *Réflexions sur la violence*, p. 173 (140).
[2] *The Two Sources of Morality and Religion*, p. 285.
[3] Henri Bergson, *Matter and Memory*, p. 268.
[4] *De l'utilite du pragmatisme*, pp. 415–16.

ment to teleology; to a knowledge of the goals towards which things were evolving. Sorel believed that such teleological constructions properly belong to *nature artificielle* and not *nature naturelle*. Once Bergson is stripped of his teleological pretensions and cosmic designs, Sorel believes we are left with a theory of activity, pragmatism.[1]

The appreciation of Sorel for James was largely a consequence of the American philosopher's refusal to abandon a pluralist attitude at the critical moment of prediction. On the other hand, Bergson works out a doctrine of spiritual evolution as binding as the mechanical evolutionism of Spencer. The vital impulse was not just a feeling in men, but an intuitionist instrument for pure knowledge. The grandiose terms of freedom, necessity and causation were just as fervently believed in by Bergson as they were by the system-builders of earlier ages. This was not the case for either Sorel or James. Bergson made the fatal blunder of believing in the ultimate reality of his images. Sorel never confused profane reality with the sacred myths.

A further difficulty which Sorel found with the intuitionism of Bergson was its essentially tragic view of social life. The unfettered activity of the will yields chaos rather than freedom. It creates conditions of mind that lead further away from the grandeur it initially pledges. The pessimism of much *fin de siècle* psychological thought was truthfully captured by Bergson. The loss of social and philosophical roots created conditions for a desperate pragmatism, rather than for an optimistic, buoyant variety found in America. Bergson looked straight ahead at the tower, but manages to land quite decisively in an abyss where death alone is victor. 'Murder has all too often remained the *ratio ultima*, if not *prima*, of politics, an abomination no doubt, but imputable to nature as much as to man. For nature has at her disposal neither imprisonment nor exile; she knows only the sentence of death.'[2]

Bergson's assertion of the unlimited freedom engendered by the will is more a frantic cry against where organized intelligence had led mankind, than a promise of better results if the will were to take over. 'Mankind lies groaning, half crushed beneath the weight of its own progress.' The choice before civilization is stark. The task of men is 'determining first of all whether they want to go on living or not.'[3]

---

[1] *De l'utilite du pragmatisme*, p. 425.
[2] *The Two Sources of Morality and Religion*, p. 268.
[3] Henri Bergson, *Matter and Memory*, p. 306.

There is no hint however of the possibility of organized intelligence making constructive choices. Rather, these agonizing words follow hard on the heels of a discussion of the value of mental telepathy. Mysticism, which was to liberate men from the terrors of the mechanical universe, ends up by enslaving man in the hopelessness of living at all. Liberation from intelligence led Bergson to a helplessness in the face of challenges from nature and society alike.

Sorel too exhibited antagonism for the optimistic meliorism stated in the eighteenth century idea of progress. Like Bergson, he attempted to exhibit the moral philistinism of that doctrine by examining the psychological and political conditions out of which it grew and the bourgeois interests it served. Nor was Sorel oblivious to the weaknesses of the flesh that gripped large segments of society. But Sorel was no less troubled by the pessimism of *fin de siècle* ideology than he was by the bland optimism of the *philosophes*.

It was James who helped extricate Sorel from this dilemma. The American pragmatist saved Sorel's thought from falling victim to the deadening monism of European intellectualism.[1] American experience, which included concreteness in attacking problems, a regard for the unity of spiritual activities without involving itself in religious sectarianism, the imaginative confrontation of problems in which a combination of head and hands were required, all of these seemed to find their way into the Jamesian vision.[2] Even the roughness of American life, its attachment for the violent, direct act, rather than the fixed theories of European existence, greatly appealed to Sorel's imagination. James' psychology equipped the revolutionary for action better than Bergson's intuitionism.[3] If truth is nothing over and above the relation between things, the worker-hero could manufacture revolutions the way he could commodities. If science is really confined to the realm of *nature artificielle*, then what need is there of Bergson's pretensions at having probed the essence of *nature naturelle*? The tantalizing doctrine of truth as *relation* which James developed made the myth as 'real' in a functional sense as any so-called 'fact.' Reality became a thing to be operated on by men, and not just an epistemological nicety of the metaphysician.

This Jamesian vision was well suited to Sorel. The universe of chance guaranteed neither optimism nor pessimism; in fact, it made discussions of this kind meaningless. Furthermore, James' wide-open

---

[1] *De l'utilité du pragmatisme*, p. 70.
[2] *Ibid.*, pp. 71–2.   [3] *Ibid.*, pp. 74–5.

universe was easier to square with a theory of wide-open socialism, than a Bergsonian teleology converted into social theology. Through James, Sorel managed to escape the negativism of *fin de siècle* thought. It was not an intellectual escape to be sure. However, in not demanding of the will a metaphysical prop, Sorel was able to stand apart from the death-image through which the age saw itself.

In distinguishing between philosophy and sociology Sorel went far beyond the negativism of Bergson. He was able to avoid Bergson's fatal blunder of thinking that in showing the emptiness of consciousness he thereby provided an account of the consciousness of emptiness.[1] Sorel never abandoned a doctrine of proof as empirical. He maintained that although there could not be a scientific society in the utopian sense, this did not prevent the formation of a scientific sociology. This was possible since the irrational impulses conditioning social action were nonetheless materials for scientific investigation. The great difficulty which arises for Sorel is to show how a scientific sociology is both attached and detached from the myths and ideologies sustaining social life. In addressing himself to the dual relation of science to ideology, Sorel was forced to abandon Bergsonian metaphysics and labour in the vineyards of politics and sociology.

[1] The most succinct critique of Bergson to come out of the post-War period is Maurice Merleau-Ponty's *Éloge de la philosophie* (Paris, 1953). It is Merleau-Ponty who first drew attention to Bergson's peculiar logical inversion of consciousness and being; esp. p. 31.

III

STATE, SOCIETY AND SOCIALISM

'The parliamentary life sacrifices the man who thinks and who is active, to the man that speaks.'
André Tardieu, LA RÉVOLUTION À REFAIRE

IT is one of the classic features of political realism that the organism known as the State is conceived of as the central nervous system of modern politics. Because this is the case, and because Sorel was in an exact sense a realist, he sought to anchor his system of political theory to an analysis of the State and its subjects. In the present period it is no longer possible to suppress the significance of the State by maintaining that it serves as the corporeal medium for expressing divine law, or, as is now more fashionably the case, a spiritual medium for expressing natural law. Nor does the classic liberal posture, in which the State is represented as a philanthropic fusion guarding the most sacred rights of the citizens on one hand and the profane rights of property on the other, offer much comfort in a situation in which both political and economic power is concentrated rather than diversified.

1. The Magical Force of the State

It has become a test of political realism to recognize that in no modern, economically advanced social structure does the State perform its functions with Olympian impartiality. Efforts to restate or develop such a perspective are invariably viewed as apologetics—sacred or profane—no matter on what level of abstraction such statements are made. The pernicious idea that the State could have a double standard of being pacific and impartial in relation to its citizens and warlike in its foreign policy only; or *eo ipso*, repressive to its citizens and pacific in the conduct of foreign affairs, found no support in Sorel. From Proudhon, Sorel inherited the view of the warlike nature of the State, and the reflection of State coercion in all levels of life.[1] It was Sorel's belief that the external relations of the State, its foreign policy, employment of the art of diplomacy and deceit of the masses in support of 'national' causes, were reproduced on an internal level in dealing with issues arising out of the class conflict.[2]

The importance of Sorel for political theory is that he not only offered a unified theory of the State in space, how it functions locally, nationally and internationally, but also in time, how it functions in different economic systems in history. The State is repressive in the nature of things. To speak of this repression as a characteristic dispensable at a higher level of economic existence (like socialism) was for Sorel a contradiction in terms no less than in fact. It is thus illusory to believe that a socialist State would substantially improve or alter the classic relations between Leviathan and Citizen. Quite the contrary. As he said in a prophetic moment, socialist politicians, if victorious 'would very probably be less able than those of today; they would make more flowery speeches than the capitalists, but there is every evidence that they would be much harder and much more insolent than their predecessors.'[3] His evidence was the behaviour of socialist politicians within the government and unions. The foundations of a proletarian outlook must therefore begin with a theory of State power which is uniformly valid and universally recognizable as a testable proposition.

Since Sorel owes so much of his appeal in the popular imagination to his defence of violence, it might be wondered how it came to pass that he possessed such an unlimited disdain for the State *qua* State. The answer is to be found in his distinction between types of coercion. Since this is one of the few occasions on which Sorel takes the trouble

---

[1] Pierre Joseph Proudhon, *La guerre et la paix; recherches sur le principe et la constitution du droit des gens* (Paris, 1861), Vol. II, chap. xi.

[2] *Matériaux d'une théorie du prolétariat* (Paris, 1919), pp. 29–30.

[3] *Réflexions sur la violence*, p. 265 (199–200).

to offer linguistic distinctions of any kind, there is no question that he placed prime value on the dual form of violence existing in modern society. He first asserts the existence of two types of coercion—acts of authority and acts of revolt.[1] Now the State employs coercion for a very specific end: 'to impose a certain social order in which the minority governs.'[2] This form of coercion stands in clear contrast to the popular will, to the masses of people. It represents the arbitrary and capricious use of force.[3] In this capacity the State is 'in fact, the organizer of the war of conquest, the dispenser of its fruits, and the *raison d'être* of the dominating groups which profit by the enterprises —the cost of which is borne by the general body of society.'[4] Precisely this function of the State is disguised behind a veil of popular sovereignty and democracy. One could measure the strength of State power by the currency in official academic circles of theories of divine and natural law.

In many particulars, Sorel's view anticipates the position taken by Lenin, even to the extent of claiming that middle class democracy is the most perfect chimera behind which the ruling class can perform its distinctive oppressive role.[5] Without labouring the comparison, and without denying a wide divergence on basic issues, it shall be seen that more than surface resemblances are at stake, this despite Lenin's summary dismissal of Sorel as a muddlehead.[6] For it should be noted that Lenin's criticism of Sorel as a muddler was made with *specific* reference to Sorel's entrance into problems relating to epistemology and the philosophy of natural science.

The primary illusion of the ruling class, and one which, when taken up by the avant-garde of the proletariat, becomes an inverted illusion, a utopian phantasy, is that the goal of 'capitalist society would be a compromise between *conflicting appetites under the auspices of political lawyers* (avocats politiciens).[7] This illusion functions socially

---

[1] *Réflexions sur la violence*, pp. 256–7 (194).   [2] *Ibid.*, p. 257 (194).

[3] *Ibid.*, pp. 153–4 (127–8).   [4] *Ibid.*, p. 249 (189).

[5] Of particular interest in any comparison of the two men are the following writings of Lenin: *The State and Revolution* (Selected Works, Vol. 7) (New York, n.d.); *The State* (Selected Works, Vol. 11) (New York, 1943); *Collapse of the Second International* (Selected Works, Vol. 5) (New York, 1943).

[6] Lenin, *Materialism and Empiriocriticism* (Moscow, 1947), p. 301. While this statement is widely cited, the context of Lenin's remark has not been indicated. Thus, even George Lukacs, in *Die Zerstorung der Vernunft* (Berlin, 1954), p. 27, has drawn a general characterization of Sorel from Lenin's few words on Sorel's philosophy of physics.

[7] *Réflexions sur la violence*, p. 311 (229).

to corrode the effectiveness of revolutionary elements within society. Reformism becomes the dominant political motif of the proletariat, a reformism expressed in political practice through the fetish of free elections. 'The more readily the electors believe in the *magical forces of the State*, the more will they be disposed to vote for the candidate who promises marvels; in the electoral struggle each candidate tries to outbid the others; in order that the socialist candidates may put the Radicals to rout, the electors must be credulous enough to believe every promise of future bliss; our Socialist politicians take very good care, therefore, not to combat these comfortable Utopias in any very effective way.'[1] A vast literature has been written to justify the independence of commodity production from State control in the name of natural law and the freedom of market exchange. But in this process of separating functions, the State can more readily assume a posture secured in legal codes, and accepted by the utopians, of its essential impartiality in relation to the class conflict.[2] It is this bourgeois myth with which utopianism expects to make a pacific revolution.[3] The doctrine of the metaphysically secured and juridically applied automatic harmony of economic interests implies this conception of the impartial state.[4]

The reality which the illusion of the popular State beclouds is that control of the State leads to control of all social power. The State, for Sorel, is in its very conception an organ of class power, an instrument of one entrenched socio-economic grouping over all others. The right to rule is bitterly contested precisely for this reason. Every class out of power argues against the State as an institution only so long as it remains out of power. When the élite of a new class assumes control, a transvaluation of socio-economic values magically occurs. What becomes a focal point of contention is not the legitimacy of the State as such, but the legitimacy of the old rulers to continue in control of the State apparatus. 'When the force of the State was in the hands of their adversaries, they acknowledged, naturally enough, that it was being employed to violate justice, and they then proved that

---

[1] *Réflexions sur la violence*, p. 184 (146).

[2] *La décomposition du marxisme* (Paris 1908, 1910), pp. 13–14.

[3] *Matériaux d'une théorie du prolétariat*, p. 36.

[4] On several occasions Sorel recommended Vilfredo Pareto's *Les systèmes socialistes* as a significant critique of the doctrine of the harmony of economic interests in a class-divided society. The underlying political power thesis held by Pareto, its *realpolitik* extension of Marx's efforts, accounted in large measure for Sorel's endorsement of it.

one might with a good conscience "step out of the region of legality" in order to enter that of justice; when they could not overthrow the government, they tried at least to intimidate it. But when they attacked the people who for the time being controlled the force of the State, they did not at all desire to suppress that force, for they wished to utilize it some day for their own profit; all the revolutionary disturbances of the nineteenth century have ended in reinforcing the power of the State.'[1] The proletariat alone can alter this cycle of struggle for State power, for it alone represents social interests rather than selfish interests.

What distinguishes Sorel from Marx in this instance involves the different uses of the term interests. Marx held that the proletarian revolution is the historical completion of the class epoch because it links its particular class ambitions to the general social interest. Whereas, for Sorel, the proletarian revolution is the completion of the class epoch because it immediately destroys all specific class interests, leaving behind the altruism of those who make revolution as a general social component. It was this difference which led to a theoretical rupture of socialism and anarchism. What was at stake in this seemingly moral definition of interests was the major political question: what should the attitude of the revolutionary be toward the chief instrument of coercion and social domination—the State.

2. Socialism and the Future of State Authority

French political theory has been particularly sensitive on the question of the State. Nowhere else did the bourgeois revolution take such a pure form, both in its physical cleavage with the *ancien régime*, and, after the downfall of Mirabeau and Lafayette, in its total annihilation of divine right theories. Yet nowhere else did the revelation become so clear that bourgeois aims diverged radically from its universal claims of brotherhood and equality. *Encyclopédistes* enshrined the bourgeois ideal as the rational, historical ideal; while the revolution succeeded only in a universal redivision of property relations and in enshrining the middle class State as the rational State.[2]

While the lofty aims of overthrowing the sanctity of State authority

[1] *Réflexions sur la violence*, pp. 28-9 (46).
[2] For a penetrating account of this divergence between aims and achievements in the French Revolution, see Harold J. Laski, *The State in Theory and Practice* (New York, 1935), pp. 241-9; and his study, *The Rise of European Liberalism: An Essay in Interpretation* (London, 1936), pp. 227-36.

was not achieved by the French Revolution, Sorel nonetheless had hopes, tempered by the ever-present nagging fear of socialist politicians, that the producing classes would finally succeed where the propertied classes had failed. In this belief in the sanctity of the masses, in its capacity to rid society of that cancerous growth, the State, Sorel distinguishes himself from Renan. His primary teacher in historical studies, Renan's infatuation with Germany, led him to a view of an ideal France as a carefully structured hierarchical society, in which a political–military–intellectual aristocracy would control State power and mediate the claims of grasping bourgeois and gasping proletariat alike.[1] The State as such for Sorel, far more than any economic considerations, was the primary element of social decadence. This belief in the primacy of politics distinguishes Sorel just as sharply from his economic mentor, Marx, as it does from his mentor in history, Renan.

Sorel's total rejection of the State as a necessary evil, generated as it was by his pessimistic view of French history, led to a decisive break in theory and action between syndicalism and bolshevism. Whereas Lenin argues for the practical necessity of replacing the bourgeois State with a proletarian State, that is, for a dictatorship of the proletariat, Sorel argues vehemently against either the resurrection or revitalization of the State apparatus. For him, the central task of the producing citizens is not seizure of power, but emancipation from State power. 'Proletarian violence entirely changes the aspect of all the conflicts in which it intervenes, since it disowns the force organized by the middle class, and claims to suppress the State which serves as its central nucleus.'[2] To those who argue that the State, despite its coercive features, is necessary in a modern society because of its enormous role in regulating the economy of the nation, Sorel offers as his rejoinder that while this is the situation based on economies structured on a labour theory of value, it need not be enshrined as the only possible social instrument regulating the economy.[3]

The heart of Sorel's thrust at Marxian political theory is that, although in its theoretical moorings Marxism does not deny the oppressive nature of the State, it places its elimination from the historical scene into a relatively distant future. Marxism assumes

---

[1] For Renan's views, see 'Questions contemporaines' and 'La réforme intellectuelle et morale,' in *Oeuvres complètes d'Ernest Renan* (Paris, 1947), Vol. I, p. 23, 513–14.
[2] *Réflexions sur la violence*, p. 29 (46).   [3] *Ibid.*, pp. 170–1 (138).

an equivocating position in that it places the achievement of certain goals prior to any possibility of eliminating State power. The context of Marxian discussions on future society shifted from the structure of State power as such to the pre-conditions for an economy of material abundance and cultural achievement; and to the internal political power base that would be required to allow for the harmonious evolution of diverse sections of the economy. It was Sorel's contention that even if these were useful social goals, the need to anchor a theory of State liquidation to such goals, however noble, was for all practical purposes a devious form of support for the continuation and even extension of State power.

Ideologically, such a political sociology supports the State by terming the dictatorship of the proletariat a 'higher form' of democracy than the rule of capitalist democracy. Sorel's support for the Bolshevik revolution was on precisely the reverse grounds. The lesson of events in Russia indicated to him that there was 'a contradiction between democracy and the mission of the proletariat.'[1] He undoubtedly believed that the Soviets would constitute themselves as the Russian phalanx of syndicalism, and in so doing overcome both the bourgeois State and bourgeois democracy.[2]

It was Sorel's belief that orthodox European Marxism of his day, like *Encyclopédism*, placed itself on the side of universal democratic precepts by repeating the time-worn critique of abusive State power, while in fact promoting and promulgating its own version of the bureaucratic State. 'In the end the State must disappear—and they [the orthodox socialists—I.L.H.] are careful not to dispute what Engels has written on this subject—but this disappearance will take place only in a future so far distant that you must prepare yourself for it by using the State meanwhile as a means of providing politicians with tidbits; and the best means of bringing about the disappearance of the State consists in strengthening meanwhile the Governmental machine.' As a final peccadillo Sorel points out that 'this method of reasoning resembles that of Gribouille, who threw himself into the water in order to escape getting wet in the rain.'[3]

The criteria for reform socialism therefore is not simply, or even primarily, the attitude taken on evolutionary or revolutionary means of bringing about a co-operative society of producing classes, but

---

[1] *Matériaux d'une théorie du prolétariat*, p. 53.
[2] *Réflexions sur la violence*, pp. 437–54 (303–11).
[3] *Ibid.*, pp. 170–1 (138).

rather whether the preservation of the State is in practice desired or repudiated. Some of Sorel's harshest comments on reform socialism are directed at those who defend with subterfuge and verbal chicanery the need for a State machinery. Reform socialism fills bourgeois needs in that it channelizes the instinct of revolt possessed by the masses into a basis for promulgating the so-called popular State. This popular State is for Sorel the best means possessed by the bourgeoisie of maintaining its stranglehold on the organs of social power, while at the same time allowing it to do verbal shadow-boxing with the wide and varied demands of the producers.[1] Sorel harboured a profound mistrust for those who transform middle class vices into working class virtues. Social reformers like Eduard Bernstein, who at least have the courtesy and honesty to drop the mask of orthodoxy, take great trouble to 'explain to the middle class that they do not by any means dream of suppressing the great State machine, but wise socialists desire two things: (1) to take possession of this machine so that they may improve its works, and make it run to further their friends' interests as much as possible and (2) to assure the stability of the Government, which will be very advantageous for all business men.'[2]

Revolutionary socialism stands in direct opposition to this line of economic, reform socialism. Since the root and branch of proletarian political action is its organizational purity, that is, the elimination of professional time-servers and professional pundits, the workers will have no need to replenish the State machine or take refuge in false notions of 'L'État populaire.'[3] Their only need will be to destroy it.

Sorel was so taken with the intrinsic corruption of the State-Government apparatus of the French middle class that he tended to equate corruption with impotence and ineffectiveness. This was clearly evident even in his estimate of the Dreyfus affair. The exposure of the timidity of the government was alone held responsible for the benefits which accrued to labour in consequence of revealed administrative and military corruption in high places.[4] This strengthened Sorel's belief that the State could easily be defeated by the unified power of proletarian uprising. Before the onrushing general strike the middle class State would quake with fear and capitulate.

---

[1] *La décomposition du marxisme*, pp. 26–9.
[2] *Réflexions sur la violence*, pp. 238–9 (182).
[3] *La décomposition du marxisme*, pp. 26–7.
[4] *Matériaux d'une théorie du prolétariat*, pp. 283–4.

How to secure power and what to do with power once achieved, are passed off by Sorel as minor considerations, tactical matters that are resolvable only at the moment of crisis and revolt.

Like the German Spartacists, who in many ways shared Sorel's attitude to spontaneity and organization, he was so fearful of utopian projections, that he paid scant attention to the question of political organization. The unfettered action of the masses, the assumption that the myth of socialism would sustain them even in the details of revolutionary change, keynoted the anarchist attitude. The Spartacist uprising of 1919, which can serve as a case study of Sorelian methodology, revealed the disastrous consequences of operating within a pure theory of revolt. All contact with the bureaucratic State and with the bureaucratic socialists was considered alien to the purity of revolution from below. Freedom of action was held in such high repute by anarchism that at critical junctures in contemporary history, when organized direction was imperative for success, none was forthcoming. The myth of anarchism, in both France and Germany, was that it might, by the feather of freedom overcome the lash of authority.[1]

Several lines of criticism suggest themselves in evaluating Sorel's dire predictions for the future of State authority. In the first place, Sorel was quite incapable of stating just what forms of coercion might be necessary to maintain an advanced technological civilization under proletarian direction. Beyond the generalization that all labour would be evaluated for its social efficacy, he declines to venture an opinion on the contours of socialist society. If we assume, with Sorel, that only problems connected to the labour process would arise in a socialist directed economy, serious questions might be ventured: elementary issues of proper wage norms, hours of employment, gross national income distribution, the role of banking and commercial reserves and the measurement of value itself. Such questions seem to require some specially designated force in society which can both legislate and enforce legislation. The verbal and emotive distinctions between 'bourgeois State power' and 'proletarian syndicate power'

---

[1] The idea of paralleling syndical socialism with Spartacism was first offered to me by Aviva L. Futorian. For information on the extent to which Rosa Luxemburg's theory of spontaneity coincided with Sorel's doctrine of the political apocalypse, see her essay, *The Russian Revolution* (New York, 1940), pp. 46–7; also her programme on the demands of the Spartacus League, adopted by the German Communist Party on December 31, 1918, published in *Illustrierte Geschichte der Deutschen Revolution* (Berlin, 1929), pp. 259–63. A very useful estimate of the Spartacists' anarchist tendencies is in Carl E. Schorske, *German Social Democracy: 1905–1917* (Cambridge, 1955), pp. 318–21.

merely disguises the problem of coercion, freedom and the role of the élites. It is on just this point that Michels, Pareto, Mosca and a whole generation of Italian neo-realists took profound issue with Sorel's bland conviction that the future will take care of itself.

The purely regulative, administrative needs of a highly developed industrial civilization suggest that some form of State power is necessary for at least as long as human-kind endures. Even presuming a society of extraordinary abundance, decisions as to how to distribute wealth and assure the continuation of abundance remain. In a more immediate sense, problems of differing cultural and ethnic values, differences in psychological temperament, religion, climate and geography, all have to be dealt with. The disappearance of class antagonisms might indeed make it easier for an administrative force to regulate these problems harmoniously, but that they remain problems to be dealt with is a fact which the history of socialism and social reform since Sorel's time verifies. To put the matter directly, there exists an enormous gap between the elimination of the State whose primary feature is class coercion and the elimination of the State as a law-making and law-enforcing agency. To call only the former, only that condition in which the will of some ruling class is involved, a State, in no way dissolves the State in existential terms. In this identification of the State with class power rather than public authority, Sorel forms a common ground with Lenin in quite total disregard of both their mentors, Marx and Engels. The consequence of the Lenin–Sorel thesis results not in the liquidation of the State, but in a liquidation of the traditional linguistic forms of examining the State in theory and practice.

Because Sorel decries as utopian phrase-mongering all attempts at anticipating problems which might arise in a socialist society, nothing in his work enables one to understand how changes in the rules of conduct can be brought about in a cohesive and coherent form, much less be enforced. In failing to provide a distinction between oppressive class-State functions and civil functions fulfilled by State power from pre-class society to the present, the impact of his critique of the State is severely circumscribed in both time and space to the France of the early twentieth century.

Let us assume that Sorel is correct in saying that history marks the passage from obligations to rights, in itself a difficult assumption since these terms might imply rather than exclude each other. Does this alter the need for some public authority to regulate the harmonious distribution of these rights, or at least ensure that no infractions of these rights occur? What Sorel ignores is that discussion of rights immediately involves questions of obligation, just as in a more general way, discussion of liberty involves discussion of the admissible range of coercion.

Then of course there are empirical problems related to the functioning State in specific contexts at given historical moments. For example, granting that the bourgeois State generates socio-economic strife by fostering the economic interests of one class over another, does it not have at least the auxiliary function of regulating the civil relations between people and people and people and things? It was one of the greatest contributions of classic political philosophy, of Hobbes in particular (of whom Sorel knew little, if anything), that this dual functional role of State sovereignty was recognized. Undemocratic and oblivious to the fundamental interests of producing classes a State may be, it still remains that regulative lever by virtue of which man in an industrial society is guaranteed a certain amount of stability and harmony. Hobbes felt so keenly this relationship of the State to the Citizen, that he maintained that revolution was acceptable only at that point where State power failed to provide the people with the security for which it was organized in the first place.

Sorel further failed to indicate that the relationship between the State and the dominant economic forces is not a static relation. Power is never stationary. Power is the measure of disequilibrium. In times of general socio-economic strife the State may necessarily waver in its allegiances. The shortcomings of the dominant class, any procrastination on basic labour, health and welfare measures, any inability to provide for maximum full employment over a long period of time, any reduction of the economic capacities of the ruling classes, inevitably leads to a situation in which the State may function as an instrument of mass interests over against narrower class interests. Frederick Engels admitted as much when he said: 'By way of exception, however, periods occur in which the warring classes balance each other so nearly that the state power, as ostensible mediator, acquires, for the moment, a certain degree of independence of both.'[1]

[1] Frederick Engels, *The Origin of the Family, Private Property and the State*, in *Marx/Engels Selected Works* (London, 1950), Vol. II, p. 290. The exact wording in this version differs in emphasis from the earlier Kerr edition of the same work (p. 209). Nonetheless, the impact of Engels' statement is to introduce the fact of the existence of the State in pre-class history, a State which is not primarily a tool of a class. His statement further enables us to distinguish the point in human

It is in this direction that certain monarchical regimes of seventeenth century England, eighteenth century France and nineteenth century Germany functioned, and it is no less a tendency in the way the State functioned in a Labour-governed England, a New Deal America and a government of the 'popular front' in France. Such distinctions are not reducible to logic chopping, for they cut through the essentially one-sided Machiavellian view of the State held by Sorel.

How in point of fact a State apparatus functions at a particular moment is far less a matter of general theoretical or historical principles, than a concern for sociological investigation. There is a significant distinction between the *primary purposes* of the State and the *total functioning* of the State. In like manner there is a clear logical disjunction between how the State conducts itself *sometimes* and how it conducts itself *always*. These types of distinctions which would either validate or invalidate Sorelian theory were brushed aside by Sorel himself. In consequence, capricious interpretations were put upon his view with impunity. Even the most perfect examples of State power operating to protect the interests of industrialists and militarists (Nazi Germany and Fascist Italy) sought and received sanctuary in Sorel's political philosophy.

A third and ancillary criticism of the Sorelian theory of Statecraft is his naïve faith in the conviction that the State is *always* intimidated by proletarian violence. If we assume with Sorel that the State is an arm of the dominant economic forces of society, then the question of how difficult or complex it is to replace one State power with another can be seen for what it is—a problem of concrete history. When State power is viewed through the perspective of the myth of the general strike, which, it might be added, involves a myth Sorel does not discuss—the total disunity of the ruling classes and the total unity of the ruled classes—analysis of the State vanishes into personal wish-fulfilment. To assume, as Sorel does, that a vigorous and prospering middle class State would succumb to a vigorous and prospering proletariat, or that this economic condition is best for revolutionary activity, is naïve. Classes most often succumb when they have decayed, not when they are healthy.

A State apparatus tends to remain intact long after the class which

---

history when the State is transformed from an instrument of public authority into one of class authority. For a concise exposition of this point see Stanley W. Moore, *The Critique of Capitalist Democracy: An Introduction to the Theory of the State in Marx, Engels, and Lenin* (New York, 1957), pp. 17–57.

gave it its original nourishment ceases to perform decisive economic functions. The final break-up of feudalism in France occurred no later than 1715; yet the actual transference of political power, i.e., of State power, did not take place until 1789—this in a social situation in which the *ancien régime* was neither particularly vigorous nor numerically powerful. This historical example is merely indicative of the many elements which must be present before a State machinery can be replaced. It is historically more accurate to say that the unification of social aims which grips large masses at points of revolution is in itself a reflection of weakness and disorganization on the part of the dominant ruling classes. It is not, as Sorel maintained, something which automatically comes about through the establishment of the myth of the general strike.

In sum, Sorel suffered from an inability to distinguish between government and State, between the machinery of administration and the machinery of exploitation. It is widely realized, for example, that the frequent South American revolutions, however fratricidal, do not touch the economic foundations of State sovereignty. The same can be said for counter-revolutionary movements in Italy and Germany during this century. What is at stake in this distinction is of major consequence. When the structure of government is considered to be an administrative apparatus, there is no need, either on radical or conservative grounds, to assume the 'withering away' of government with the destruction of the coercive features of State power. The failure to bear this distinction in mind subjected Sorel to a position in which the only legitimate alternative to State power is a power vacuum. Government being conceived of as merely a subsidiary appendage to the State apparatus, no possibility of developing a rational approach to the politics of socialism was possible in Sorel's standpoint. This lack of elementary distinctions, which is characteristic of Sorel's writings, led him to hasten his abandonment of objective political analysis in favour of the greener pastures of a voluntaristic philosophy of history and an atavistic psychology.

Sorel's theory of the State, while on the surface a vigorous defence of revolutionary possibilities in mass action, is at its core more closely related to fantasy than to science. It offers no guarantee that the syndicate, the fundamental unit of proletarian organization which is to become the centre of polity under socialism, will not reproduce every miscarriage of human rights committed by the State in class society. As Michels brilliantly noted: 'The more syndicalism endeavours to displace the axis of working class policy towards syndicalist action, the greater is the danger it runs of itself degenerating into an oligarchy. Even in the revolutionary syndicalist groups the leaders have frequent opportunities of deceiving the rank and file. The treasurer of a strike, the secretary of a trade union, even the participator in a conspiracy or the leader upon a barricade, can betray those from whom they have received their instructions far more easily and with much more serious consequences than can a socialist member of parliament or a municipal councillor. French syndicalists,' continues Michels, 'arbitrarily restrict their one-sided theory to the political party alone, as if it were not inevitable that like causes should produce like effects when their action is displayed upon the field of the syndicalist movement. They reason as if they were immunized against the action of sociological laws of universal validity.'[1]

Its exemption from social laws is the personal embodiment of utopian reasoning in Sorel's syndicalism. The mythological basis of his doctrine of the State, far from being an asset to a revolutionary theory of society, proved to be Sorel's greatest liability, for he reproduces a portion of the pragmatic acquiescence: an acceptance of the spontaneous and apocalyptic view of social change. The very view of history and change which Sorel ridicules in Enlightenment philosophy, becomes his supreme ideological burden. And since he eschewed the possibility of a scientific sociology, he was left with a dogmatic emotivism emulating in ferocity anything produced by internecine tendencies of medieval society.

3. Democracy and the Role of Coercion in Human Affairs

The question of the relationship between democracy and coercion has come to play an increasingly important part in contemporary studies of political thought and behaviour. As recent major discussions have made rather clear, whatever the philosophic pose, the problem of democracy cannot be resolved outside analysis of the coercive features that the State steadily employs.[2] The distinctions between democratic and authoritarian modes of rule are not so much

[1] Roberto Michels, *Political Parties: A Sociological Study of the Oligarchical Tendencies of Modern Democracy*, p. 347.

[2] *Democracy in a World of Tensions*, edited by Richard McKeon (Chicago, 1951). See also on this Arne Naess, *Democracy, Ideology and Objectivity: Studies in the Semantics and Cognitive Analysis of Ideological Controversy* (Oslo and Oxford, 1956).

questions of the economic supports of government, as they are quantitative differences between the use of coercion and consensus.

Democracy is more easily identifiable with the ends to which coercion is put and the limits with which coercion may be employed to secure these ends, than by purely formal or semantic appraisals of universal qualities of democracy. On the sociological side, it is likewise more important to identify the level of democracy with types of class structure than with a simple numerical majority or plurality covering many classes. It was the virtue of Aristotle's view of democracy that he identifies it in just such economic and class terms. It is likewise a decided asset in Sorel that he saw the problem of democracy in this two-fold way: as related institutionally to the problem of coercion, and as related sociologically to the problem of economic classes. This is a starting point of any mature political sociology.

The first stage in Sorel's argument was to distinguish between violence and force. Basically an act of force is said to represent an act of officialdom—of established authority. Force is that which is employed by the State to defeat its only potent adversary—those able to employ counter force.[1] Now counter force, the force not of established authority but of producers in capitalist society (and by inference, the middle class in feudal society, the industrialists in mercantile society, etc.), is given the designation—violence. 'A terminology which would give rise to no ambiguity' would be one in which 'the term violence should be employed only for acts of revolt,' while 'the object of force is to impose a certain social order in which the minority governs.'[2]

Sorel did not think himself arbitrary in advocating the use of violence to counter the force of the State. To be sure it was his primary theme that 'whether we approve or condemn what is called the *revolutionary* and *direct method*, it is evident that it is not on the point of disappearing.'[3] The establishment of a correlation between subjective ambitions and the objective use of force led Sorel to an empirical and not merely a normative guide for the advocacy of violence. *It is not that force simply ought to be employed, but that it is employed.* Advocacy is not to be confused with description.

The problems involved in jumping from description to prescription in political theory are clearly evident in Sorel. For the fact that vio-

[1] *Saggi di critica del Marxismo* (Palermo, 1903), pp. 38–40.
[2] *Réflexions sur la violence*, pp. 256–7 (194).
[3] *Ibid.*, p. 95 (90).

71

lence is used to counter force is not logically an argument for its continued use—only a statement of fact. That Sorel makes this jump hurriedly is indicative of the loose empirical evidence supporting his contentions. It was after all in 'warlike France' that Sorel saw the most insidious inroads of the 'pacific spirit' in both domestic and foreign affairs, and in both the proletariat and the middle class. The statement that violence is the main fact of the growth of civilization has far-reaching consequences for Sorel's *Weltanschauung*, since another anchor point of his theory of force and violence is that civilization, through its continued stress on utilitarian modes of behaviour, does indeed negate the warlike spirit. The gravity of Sorel's paradoxical position might be summed up by pointing out that if violence is an objective fact of socio-economic existence, why the need to urge producers to adopt violent tactics as the only road to emancipation? On the other hand if violence is progressively being replaced by other methods of reconciling social antagonisms, where is the objective basis for the prolongation of the method of violence? On this theoretical polarity Sorel floundered badly. The political *volte-face* that he periodically underwent is indicative of an essential confusion between arguments based on moral sentiments and arguments based on empirical measurements.

Sorel's view of coercion is fundamentally conditioned by an acceptance of the Marxian view of the supremacy of the class struggle over all other forms of human association and rivalry: 'The class struggle is the alpha and omega of socialism.'[1] The struggle between plebeians and patricians, poor and rich, has roots as far back as Hellenic civilization. The unequivocal and categorical presentation of this struggle is the underlying source of socialism's strength.[2] As long as economic roots are clearly divided between owner and owned, employer and employed, there is no question in Sorel's mind that power remains the sole basis for resolving differences. What he resents most in modern society are those social forces which tend to obfuscate primal economic relations, i.e., the lower middle classes and the aristocratic echelons in the labour movement. This vast middle economic sector operates to vitiate and neutralize class warfare, and beyond that, to assume power by mediating the claims of wealth and privilege against those of labour and poverty.

[1] *Matériaux d'une théorie du prolétariat*, p. 67.
[2] *La décomposition du marxisme*, pp. 22–4.

The political reflection of this middle portion of the economy is liberalism and democracy. This sector corrupts the purity of both the *haute bourgeoisie* and the proletariat by proclaiming a series of reformist platitudes that dulls the edge of violence. 'The whole future of democracy might easily depend on this *lower middle class (basse bourgeoisie)*, which hopes to make use of the strength of the really proletarian organizations for its own great personal advantage. The politicians believe that this class will always have peaceful tendencies, that it may be organized and disciplined, and that since the leaders of such sane syndicates understand equally with the politicians the action of the State, this class will form an excellent body of followers.[1] Democracy is therefore not a form of political rule sanctioned by the ruling classes, but an economic tactic of the weak. It is offered up to the masses by those *basse bourgeois* alienated from the cleansing force of production. Its major function is to secure State control with the minimum political strife.[2]

The divergence of Sorel's view from traditional Marxian political theory, which asserts that democracy is the most efficient political shell for the *development* of capitalism, is important from a theoretical point of view. In this divergence is revealed the gulf between Sorelian syndicalism and Marxian socialism. Spontaneity and mass action became the highest ideals, replacing political organization and parliamentary action. Socialism is emptied of all democratic content. The liberating violence of the revolutionary situation becomes an end in itself. Whatever justification for revolution inhered in Marx's socialism, the effort to establish a broader and more pervasive form of democracy, is dissipated by the anarchist repudiation of any specific programme for social change. This Sorel did through a rejection of the worth of social consensus and also through an assertion of the negative character of democracy.[3] Of equal interest is the agreement *in principle* between fascism and syndicalism on the decadence of the middle classes. The facts are something else again. Fascism relied heavily for its support on the lower middle classes. It was when this stratum of the population became discontented with its share of the national produce, disenchanted with the goals of proletarian socialism and disaffiliated from bourgeois democracy, that fascism and nazism were in a position to come to power. As one authority points

---

[1] *Refléxions sur la violence*, p. 265 (199).
[2] *La décomposition du marxisme*, p. 25.
[3] *Matériaux d'une théorie du prolétariat*, pp. 384-9.

out: 'The Nazis recruited their millions from the middle class parties as well as from the non-voters.'[1]

Just as the producers are the bulwark of modern social revolutionary movements, so, too, the lower middle strata of the economy have come to perform a similar function in social counter-revolution. Far from playing the role Sorel attributed to them, the lower middle class, 'the protagonists of repressed nature, the victims of instrumentalized reason,' has in modern history not infrequently exhibited profoundly warlike and anti-democratic attitudes.[2] In contrast to this is the propensity of labour in developed capitalist societies exhibiting rapid social mobility to eschew the method of violence where possible. Labour unions tend to hold their power of organization as an ultimate weapon—to be used only where all other means of gaining their ends fail. The method of violence tends to be employed by the proletariat when other methods are not available. This is a point worth making in view of Sorel's belief in the instinctual proclivity to violence on the part of the producing classes.

It was Sorel's contention that 'no historical experience justifies the hope that a democracy can be made to work in a capitalist country, without the criminal abuses experienced everywhere nowadays.' Instead of granting the possibility that socialism may develop a form of democracy which cancels out political–criminal associations, he enshrines this relation between democracy and criminality into an instinctual, permanent verity: 'we ought to learn from experience that there is no way of bringing about their disappearance.'[3] This is clearly reduced to the view that democracy is at best a disguise for coercive activities. Since this is the case, democracy cannot be utilized by the producers as a method of greater worth than that of force, since the two terms describe antagonistic social interests. Thus, the social changes required are capable of being brought about by violence which the proletariat brings to bear on the force of middle class democracy.

Democracy in itself cannot be an instrument of progress, or even an indication that greater progress has occurred. It can only be an instrument cleverly disguising the defence of the *status quo*. Sorel further makes the interesting observation that the social cohesion which democratic rule tends to promote is not in fact a consequence of the

[1] Cf. Peter Gay, *The Dilemma of Democratic Socialism: Eduard Bernstein's Challenge To Marx* (New York, 1952), pp. 207–12.

[2] Max Horkheimer, *Eclipse of Reason* (New York, 1947), pp. 121–2.

[3] *Réflexions sur la violence*, p. 298 (220–1).

ability of education, persuasion and knowledge to render the method of violence obsolete in settling conflicts, but is in reality a social product of force itself. 'Social unity presses upon us from all sides, so to speak, in the ordinary course of life; because we feel, almost always, the operation of the effects of hierarchical authority which imposes uniform rules on citizens of the same country.'[1] It is coercion, legal and extra-legal, which underlies the unity of the nation far more effectively than supposed common economic and social interests. This being the case, the maintenance of social unity was for Sorel no more an argument for the promotion of pacific means as against violent means, than social divisions can be an argument for the promotion of a democratic polity.

Cutting across Sorel's argument and cushioning it from criticism, is the idea that parliamentary activities and all political products of the modern democratic State are fig leaves in the great struggle *between* force and violence, between owner and producer.[2] Sorel has a disquieting reproach for reform socialists who are under the impression that social revolution is a consequence of fine rhetoric made in the counsels of the politically powerful. 'From the moment one has anything to do with elections, it is necessary to submit to certain general conditions which impose themselves unavoidably on all parties in every country and at all times. If one is convinced that the future of the world depends on the electoral programme, on compromises between influential men and on the sale of privileges, it is not possible to pay much attention to the moral constraints which prevent a man going in the direction of his most obvious interests. Experience shows that in all countries where democracy can develop its nature freely, the most scandalous corruption is displayed without anyone thinking it even necessary to conceal his rascality.'[3]

He goes on to compare the activities of parliamentarians to financiers who place worthless stock on the commercial exchange. Both offer commodities that are intrinsically worthless.[4] For in this transformation of democracy into parliamentary demagogy, the actual socio-economic needs of the masses are continually violated. Instead of being the sensitive instrument through which such needs are registered, democracy becomes the enemy of the producers, functioning as

[1] *Réflexions sur la violence*, p. 392 (279).

[2] For a brief, pointed examination of anti-parliamentarianism in Sorel, Pareto and Lenin, and psychological co-efficients of authoritarianism see Jules Monnerot, *Sociology and Psychology of Communism* (Boston, 1953), pp. 31–3, 146–7.

[3] *Réflexions sur la violence*, p. 341 (247). [4] *Ibid.*, p. 342 (248).

the shell through which politician and professor, socialist and capitalist alike, thwart the ambitions of labouring classes.[1] Democracy *promises* the good life for these masses; it *secures* this good life only for the economically prosperous.[2] In addition, democracy is, by definition, a form of political rule, not a method of direct popular rule. This dichotomy becomes particularly clear when a parliamentary system is developed to act as the legislative arm of State power. Through the machinery of these State-dominated parliaments, and the educational system it brings into existence, democracy carries on the task of coercing the masses with an effectiveness and mendacity unknown to the ancients.[3]

The appeal of Sorel's position is evident to all who have been disconcerted by the division between liberal democratic pledges and practices. He made it clear that power is at the basis of political change. The force of democracy can be essentially conservative particularly when it obstructs the desire for change behind a veil of electoral procedures.

What is lacking in Sorel's appraisal, however, is an appreciation of the possibility that power can be consciously represented by democratic procedures. If one source of power confronts another source of power directly, in the field of combat, this does not mean necessarily that in every instance this is the logically superior method of resolving political or economic differences. The fact that force is the purest way of resolution does not constitute logical proof that it is the only or the most desirable way. For as one critic of Sorel indicates: 'It may be, on occasion, necessary to fight, and cowardice not to; but fighting is always at best a necessary evil, and there is nothing ennobling about it. Quite the contrary. It is perfectly possible to admire initiative, *élan* and determination without falling into the evil position of admiring combativeness in its own right.'[4] This prescriptive attitude towards violence, rather than its necessity, separates Sorel from liberal socialism, more profoundly than any specifically doctrinal differences.

Surely the growth of civilization and the worth of democracy itself rests not so much on how it obfuscates conflict, but on how it points to a resolution of conflict within commonly accepted rules. Too often,

---

[1] *Insegnamenti sociali della economia contemporanea*, pp. 397–8.
[2] *Les illusions du progrès* (4th edition), pp. 276–7.
[3] *Matériaux d'une théorie du prolétariat*, pp. 72–3.
[4] G. D. H. Cole, *A History of Socialist Thought*, Vol. III, Part I, p. 386.

critics of democracy call any non-violent resolution of differences obfuscation; this because they start with a definition of society as lawless. But democracy, in providing rules of procedure offers a method of channelizing and directing behaviour, despite the contentions of critics. Democracy can clarify the relative strength of contending forces in a conscious way. Democracy therefore is perhaps the most reasonable expression through which the issues dividing men can be resolved. The fact that power remains basic political capital in all existing societies is no serious critique against the employment of democratic procedures. Quite the contrary. The abuse of democracy is perhaps the soundest argument for broadening the scope of human involvement in political processes. This involvement would perhaps better reflect the actual balance of power sources than is the case at present. It thus may be argued that what is needed at this juncture in history is not the overthrow of democratic procedures, nor the substitution of Sorel's method of direct violence, but a stipulation of the contents of democracy in functional rather than normative terms: that is, into terms which have utility and relevance for the masses of men in a scientific and technological civilization; namely, a general theory of social organization.

Still another potential shortcoming in Sorel's theory of proletarian violence is the fact that raw power may often resolve antagonisms to the detriment of the great mass of people. If the numerically few possess overwhelming power, in the form of the State for example, then the popular will might be thwarted time and again. It is the ideal of democracy, and a genuinely functioning ideal in many of the lower layers of human intercourse, that it registers the wants, complaints and ambitions of the group or class out of power. A democracy is a real entity only in so far as its employment of coercion is so circumscribed as to allow those out of power, and perhaps without hope of achieving power, to share in the general material and cultural advances of society. It might be argued that the potentials of democracy are never fulfilled in a society rendered antagonistic by diverse economic interests. But such an argument is an empirical one, and does not necessitate an either/or posture with regard to the value of democratic process itself. Democracy has, in the context of class society, a double function, corresponding to a negative and positive role of social authority. In the first instance it is a technique for reducing violence and in the second place a technique for reaching rational consensus. What Sorel lost sight of was that the concept of rendering decisions in a non-violent way did not necessarily carry with it an assumption of philistinism. The radical critique of society does not imply therefore a radical *technique*, i.e., the method of absolute violence, but only the application of the historically evolved tools for the best possible social decisions. Sorel substituted a formal radicalism of content, a formal denunciation of the State, for the elimination of the problems connected with its genesis and evolution.

Judicial review, constitutional amendment, parliamentary statute, executive veto and the like, are elements (even in capitalist democracy) which mitigate and abate, no less than disguise the basis of political domination. That these activities of democracy are taken as a consequence of the potential power of various revolutionary currents in society is, it would seem, just as strong an argument for increasing the sensitivity of democracy to revolutionary approaches as it is for attempting a return to primordial modes of settling social and economic antagonisms. Contrary to Sorel's insistence, a reasonable defence of democracy would not rest upon subterfuge and reformism, but would show the essential sufficiency of political democracy for even the most radical far-reaching transformations in the economic institutions of human society. The degree of democratic safeguards possible in a given revolutionary context is an empirical question, which in no way cancels the values of democracy in modern society as such. In present society the methodological base of democracy is criticism. It is the social force of popular power—potential and actual.

4. Bureaucracy and Mass Politics

Democracy functions for Sorel as a protective mask for carrying on the coercive acts of the State with impunity and without criticism. It will occasion little surprise therefore that, for Sorel, democracy plays a like role in the relationship between the bureaucracy and the masses. That is, democracy instead of being an instrument of popular control is essentially a protective covering for the machinations of the bureaucracy. In Sorel's opinion, 'the greatest danger which threatens syndicalism would be an attempt to imitate democracy.' Since democracy is seen exclusively in terms of its being 'a political form of the middle class,' the aims of labourers cannot be resolved within the framework of democratic procedure.[1]

[1] *Réflexions sur la violence*, p. 268 (201).

This appeared as the decisive feature of Sorel's political thought when appropriated by fascist ideology. It too condemned democracy as an exclusively middle class phenomenon that corrupts and distorts the heroic instincts and appetites of *il popolo*.[1] The demogogic potential of Sorel's view of democracy is socially realized in a context in which the standpoint of an 'out-group' (not necessarily from a lower economic strata) sees itself frustrated by the effete virtues of the going institutional concern. The heroic passions revealed in direct action can only be suppressed in the immorality of democracy. In this way anti-democracy becomes a moral credo.

It should be noted, however, that Sorel differs from Vilfredo Pareto's argument that bureaucracy is built into all contemporary social structures, since they rationalize power relations in advanced societies. Sorel condemns the bureaucratic tendencies in modern civilization for talking on behalf of the producing classes while acting to frustrate their most elementary ambitions. The bureaucracy is for Sorel a powerful sub-class, with a will to survival that cannot easily be stifled, even by the conquest of socialism. Its tendency, to the contrary, is to become a special class, with a firm managerial mandate. The bureaucracy is recruited in the main from professional elements, engineers, lawyers, clerks and economists. Their 'natural tendency is to become a little aristocracy; for these people, State socialism would be advantageous, because they would go up one in the social hierarchy.'[2] The producing classes, even if successful in the social revolution, even if they seized control of the economic foundations, would be faced with the immense and drawn-out task of uprooting the bureaucratic aristocracy. Sorel's solution to this problem, the formation of an independent and strictly proletarian seat of power, tends to obscure the differences between the legitimate demands made by highly advanced technological societies for trained personnel at managerial and administrative levels, and the excessive waste created by an indolent group of bureaucratic time-servers.

Sorel assumed that every social need would be fulfilled within the framework of purely proletarian economic activity. These social needs would in short order create, from the working class itself if necessary, managerial and administrative elements which would

---

[1] Cf. Curzio Suckert Malaparte, 'Fascism as a Counter-Reformation and Anti-Risorgimento,' in Herbert W. Schneider, *Making The Fascist State* (New York, 1928), Appendix 30, pp. 352–6.

[2] *Réflexions sur la violence*, pp. 190–1 (150–1).

separate themselves out from actual productive processes. Lawyers, engineers and clerks would no more perish in a society of producers than they would in any other advanced industrial structure. Sorel's failure to discuss such eventualities, on the basis of their being essentially non-demonstrable and utopian, confirms the suspicion that he frequently confused political ideals and sociological realities.

In political life generally, Sorel sees the outlook of European social democracy as an essentially compromising force. Just as social democracy mediates the claims of workers and employers in economics, these oppositional claims in political life are mediated by the bureaucracy. There is a functional kinship between social democracy and bureaucracy. It is this entire economic stratum between the polarity of producer and owner that Sorel views with the greatest suspicion and mistrust. The pious rascality of the legal profession in medieval life, for example, has in no form been curbed in capitalism. It has merely been transplanted to a new and fertile ground. Whether industrial barons or church fathers are the great beneficiaries of the machinations of the lawyers is secondary. They form the higher echelon of the bureaucracy precisely because of their ability to deprive the producers of their fruits within the framework of the law.[1] Dominant classes utilize other segments of the bureaucracy in much the same way. The capabilities of the bureaucracy are turned to specific class needs. Its services are always offered to those in political control. Older revolutions did not disturb the bureaucracy, because its essential task of confounding proletarian needs remained built into new systems of oppression.

The State represents the interests of the owners as against the led. Sorel insists that the needs of the masses can only be fulfilled in direct conflict with the politicians from outside the structure of politics. This high caste of State organization is described by Sorel as being 'people whose wits are singularly sharpened by their voracious appetites, and in whom the hunt for fat jobs develops the cunning of Apaches (*ruses d'apaches*).'[2] Proletarian strength is tested not only, or even primarily, against the bourgeoisie as such; but more especially against the bureaucracy developed by the bourgeoisie in the course of its evolution. The distinction is important for it points up that the type of class warfare Sorel had in mind centred primarily in the political sphere, in the sphere of State power. To beseech the

---

[1] *Réflexions sur la violence*, pp. 313–14 (230–1).
[2] *Ibid.*, p. 221 (171).

wealthy for economic advantages, as socialist politicians and labour aristocrats do, is reformism. To abolish the *political* rule of capital, the governmental machinery it has erected, is the central goal of revolutionary socialism.

Sorel took seriously the question of the overthrow of the old capitalist political order. We know that he remained interested in the *Maffia* and *Cammorra*, secret and extra-legal terrorist organizations in Italy, during his entire life. They served as examples to him of how it is possible to maintain a semi-militarist organization operating outside the official State machinery, a force which shared the tenacious fanaticism of the manipulators of the State and yet escapes corruption by class society.[1]

From this regard for the direct method came Sorel's steadfast opposition to social legislation and social reconstruction through educational advances. He worked within an association of terms: the direct method of violence is the revolutionary approach, the indirect method of legislation and education is the reformist approach.[2] By adopting this equation Sorel felt himself to be a thoroughly consistent socialist, since any amelioration of the economic antagonisms of class society only provides the ruling, exploiting class with a longer, stronger lease on life. For if 'all social legislation is nothing but an element of proletarian decadence,' it becomes obvious that the path to change is not gradual but apocalyptic, involving a confrontation of the chief rivals for power in any given age.[3]

Sorel cast his spontaneous socialism in the form of the psychology of slave and master. True to his belief in the primacy of the political, he generally preferred to picture the class conflict in vivid images, rather than in economic terms. 'The masses who are led have a very vague and extremely simple idea of the means by which their lot can be improved; demagogues easily get them to believe that the best way is to utilize the power of the State to pester the rich. We pass thus from jealousy to vengeance, and it is well known that vengeance is a sentiment of extraordinary power, especially with the weak.'[4] The mass of producers are thereby induced to subdue their discontent in quietistic and pietistic ways, never really achieving the power they possess as producers. The only escape Sorel allows is revolutionary

[1] Michael Freund, *Georges Sorel: Der revolutionäre Konservativismus* (Frankfurt am/Main, 1932), pp. 63–4.
[2] *Matériaux d'une théorie du prolétariat*, pp. 73–4.
[3] *Insegnamenti sociali della economia contemporanea* (Palermo, 1906), p. 278.
[4] *Réflexions sur la violence*, p. 244 (186).

practice, the method of direct violence. Unlike the bulk of socialist intellects and politicians, he disallows the co-existence of immediate reform policies coupled with long-range revolutionary policies.

In adopting this socialism without tactics, Sorel reveals how thoroughly his commitment to and feeling for the problem of achieving socialism rested on psychological rather than economic grounds. 'The only means by which this pernicious influence of the demagogues may be wiped out are those employed by Socialism in propagating the notion of the proletarian general strike; it awakens in the depths of the soul a sentiment of the sublime proportionate to the conditions of a gigantic struggle; it brings to the fore the pride of free men; it forces the desire to satisfy jealousy by malice into the background; and thus protects the worker from the quackery of ambitious leaders, hungering for the fleshpots.'[1] Clearly, the core of politics for Sorel is not the outcome of the class war, but the mode in which the battle is waged. Cole put the matter rightly: 'What attracted him was the struggle, not the prospect of victory, except when he was thinking of the latter, not as victory, but as the defeat of the other side.'[2]

The enormous bureaucracy, subsidized and underwritten as it is by the bourgeoisie, expands to where it can lead a flourishing existence in quite different and varied economic soil. Bureaucracy becomes an independent political variable even in socialist politics. In this way Sorel perceived a relative independence of political life from its economic sources. He also perceived the potential of bureaucratic management to one day congeal as an economic entity rivalling older productive classes. The class allegiance of bureaucratic-minded politicians are continually being purchased. 'The reinforcement (of power)[3] of the State is at the basis of all their conceptions.' Indeed, the more perceptive politicians are 'already preparing the framework of a strong, centralized and disciplined authority, which will not be hampered by the criticism of an opposition, which will be able to enforce silence, and which will give currency to its lies.'[4]

To Sorel the huge and vital growth of productive techniques in the twentieth century makes possible an ultimate and final break with the bureaucratic State. 'Modern production requires mutual action of the

---

[1] *Réflexions sur la violence*, p. 246 (187).

[2] G. D. H. Cole, *A History of Socialist Thought*, Vol. III, Part 1, p. 383.

[3] Sorel's original statement does not contain the translator's phrase, 'of power.' It simply reads: 'Le renforcement de l'État est à la base de toutes leurs conceptions.'

[4] *Réflexions sur la violence*, p. 250 (190).

workers, a voluntary co-ordination of the systematic productive relations, that transforms an accidental agglomeration into an army
shown to possess a common enterprise.'[1] Thus the answer to State
power is economic power. The answer to the bourgeois State founded
on terror is the proletarian syndicate based on voluntary association.
The unusual aspect of this alternative to the State, is that Sorel derived it in large measure from reform socialism. Like Eduard Bernstein and German revisionism generally, he was mistrustful of the
implications that the concept of the dictatorship of the proletariat
held in store for the producing classes. For as Bernstein noted, the
consequence of the strengthening of State power would be a further
separation of the proletariat from the actual implements of political
rule and control.[2] This tendency of politics to separate itself from
economics represented for Sorel a corresponding extension of the
division of society into masters and slaves.[3] This is not for Sorel
allegorical theorizing. What is involved is a further development of
the conflict between the masses and the bureaucratic machinery.
This political conflict has an historical evolution of its own that
is not resolved automatically in the course of economic transformations.

The bureaucracy quite clearly cannot maintain itself without mask-
ing its relations to the proletariat. The disguise takes the form of concessions to the labourers in the form of the *political* strike. This phenomenon is properly speaking not a strike at all, but only a series of
party manoeuvres. It was, for Sorel, the logical labour tactic of reform socialism, particularly in Germany.[4] 'Enfeebled classes habitu-
ally put their trust in people who promise them the protection of the
State, without ever trying to understand how this protection could
possibly harmonize their discordant interests; they readily enter into
every coalition formed for the purpose of forcing concessions from
the Government.'[5]

The political strike is the precise opposite of the proletarian strike
in that it at least implicitly accepts the notion that several classes can

---

[1] *Matériaux d'une théorie du prolétariat*, p. 162.

[2] Eduard Bernstein, *Socialism théorique et social-democratique pratique* (Paris, 1900), pp. 226–8.

[3] *Réflexions sur la violence*, p. 253 (191).

[4] Eduard Bernstein, 'Der Streik als politisches Kampfmittel,' in *Neue Zeit*, XII, No. 1, 1894, pp. 689–95. This article contains a defence of the political strike, and of revisionist labour tactics in general, as opposed to the purely proletarian strike. See also *Der Streik, sein wesen und sein wirken* (Frankfurt a/M, 1906), pp. 109–17

[5] *Réflexions sur la violence*, p. 236 (180–1).

co-operate towards the same specific economic goal. Broadly speaking, the political strike was an effort made by German socialism and its leaders, Bernstein and Kautsky, to satisfy the ultimate demands of the working class for emancipation by gradually resolving the problem of its vast political disenfranchisement. The banner of reformism might well have read: from political power to economic supremacy. This for Sorel was anathema, since it involves an ultimate commitment both to co-operating with the class enemy, and what is worse, absorbing in producer organizations the worst features of the bureaucratic State.[1] 'The political general strike presupposes that very diverse social groups shall possess the same faith in the magical force of the State; this faith is never lacking in social groups which are on the downgrade.'[2] This quest for alternatives to revolution, in Sorel's view, separated Marx from the bulk of the Marxists.

The issue of reform or revolution pressed as hard in France at the turn of the century as it did in Germany. The general failure of the condition of the producers to deteriorate in either an absolute or relative sense, the fantastic growth of industrial output in western Europe at the time, and the development of the trade union movement on a mass, industrial scale, contributed to the growing feeling that socialism might be realized by strictly legal, evolutionary methods. Sorel improperly saw in Jean Jaurès the French counterpart to German revisionism. He drew this false image from a single fact: Jaurès' position on the function of the strike ran counter to Sorel's in every major detail. First, Jaurès held that the proletariat must be deeply convinced of the goals sought through the general strike, and not just be exclusively concerned with the mechanics of the strike. Second, a large section of public opinion and not merely a proletarian élite must be willing to support the legitimacy of the general strike. The third point is best stated in Jaurès' words: 'The general strike must not seem like a disguise for violence, but simply the exercise of the legal right to strike. More systematic in method and vaster in scope than usual, it is true, and with a more clearly marked class character.'[3]

The ideological conflict between reform and revolution, of which the debates concerning political strikes versus the general strike is but

[1] *La décomposition du marxisme*, pp. 10–11.
[2] *Réflexions sur la violence*, pp. 236–7 (181).
[3] Jean Jaurès, *Studies in Socialism*, 'The General Strike and Revolution,' (London, 1906), pp. 106–29.

a fragment, forms a continuing pattern in French political thought.[1] Indeed, among the advanced European countries, only in France can one speak of a steady questioning of reformism, rather than its unconscious acceptance as the only road for man to adequately adjust to his social milieu. Radicalism in France has therefore tended to consider reform policies not so much as a way of life, as a challenge to the life of change.[2]

Ultimately, reformism is a futile road for the producing masses because, in Sorel's view, an instinctual, psychological propensity for violence possesses the proletariat. In witness of this, we should note that Sorel at no point in his writings found it necessary to criticize the character of productive relations in capitalist society. Andreu has indicated that not a single line against capitalism as a regime of produc-

---

[1] It is important to distinguish the three types of strikes which Sorel deals with. First, there is the *proletarian* general strike, which is a protracted workers' strike at the bastions of government as such. It has as its chief aim the overthrow of capitalist society. Sorel restricted the content of socialism to this type of general strike. The *political* general strike is connected to the proximate goals of socialists in parliament and government generally. The political strike is a symbolic strike, revealing the extent of mass support for socialist political claims. The third type of strike is the more familiar *economic* strike; having as its aim the improvement in the status of the labourers. Political ends either do not enter, or enter only elliptically. Sorel was relatively indifferent to the economic strike. Like most social revolutionaries, although he supported the right of workers to improve their conditions of life, he was fearful of the reform ideology that ordinarily accompanies the purely economic strike.

[2] Political and philosophical thought in France after the conclusion of the Second World War bears witness to the extent to which it was still caught up in the historic debates of reform versus revolution. Raymond Aron has inherited the constitutional reform tradition from men like Millerand. In his justly famous essay, *The Opium of the Intellectuals* (London, 1957), he attempted to puncture the 'myth of the proletariat' and the idea of the inevitability of revolution in general. Albert Camus has offered a different phase of this debate in his *L'homme révolte* (Paris, 1951). Here, State terror is counterposed to rational terrorism, with a firm plea being made for the rebel over and against the revolutionist. The two contemporary views which show the most in common with Sorel are those of Emmanuel Mounier and, to an even larger extent, Maurice Merleau-Ponty. Mounier, the direct inheritor of the mantle of Péguy, offered, up to his recent death, the most consistent defence of revolutionary socialism from the viewpoint of the Catholic apocalypse. In particular, see his collection of essays in two volumes, *Feu la chrétienté* (Paris, 1950), and *L'espoir des désespérés* (Paris, 1953). Like Sorel, Merleau-Ponty is insistent on the special role of the proletariat in shaping the future of history. The proletariat is said to have a unique revolutionary destiny because it is the only class which embodies real universality and consciousness of historical direction. See in particular his *Humanisme et Terreur* (Paris, 1947) and *Les aventures de la dialectique* (Paris, 1955). Here we see just how much of the Sorelian legacy has been retained by present existential *philosphes* and *literati*.

tion will be found in Sorel's writings.[1] An astonishing fact in view of the extent to which socialist literature in the nineteenth century made use of Marx's argument against the efficiency and effects on labour of capitalist production. This being the case, why the producers should be desirous of taking up arms against the bourgeoisie in deadly combat is held to be less a matter of economic tensions than the psychological compulsion to assert its class muscularity and purity. The political union of diverse economic elements is criticized with such a viewpoint in mind. 'The political general strike does not presuppose a class war concentrated on a field of battle in which the proletariat attacks the middle class; the division of society into two antagonistic armies disappears, for this class of revolt is possible with any kind of social structure.'[2]

Lurking beneath the psychological dimension of proletarian purity was a view common to many revolutionary thinkers in Europe after the death of Marx: that substantial alteration would be required in theory to account for disturbing peculiarities in proletarian practice. As long as the social consciousness of the working class found appropriate expression in trade union activity, an implicit threat to a revolutionary standpoint was ever present. This is so since trade unionism, when left at the level of economic wants, involved an acceptance of the existing economic order and its ways of promoting men up the social ladder. Thus, Sorel was led to the conclusion that 'the proletarian general strike and the political general strike are diametrically opposed to one another.'[3] The latter receives its sustenance from parliamentary democracy and the State bureaucracy, the former from consistent opposition to these pernicious blandishments of capitalist existence which frequently manifest themselves in the economic ambitions of the proletariat. The true face of bureaucracy can only be uncovered through the steady opposition to encroachments on proletarian heroism and purity. As long as the State and its bureaucratic apparatus is seen as a neutral element of capitalist society, or even as a force sometimes receptive to working class interests, the possibility of developing a revolutionary situation tends to be undermined. For as Sorel would have it, the bureaucracy will then be in a position both to manipulate and to corrupt producers of the wealth of society.

[1] Pierre Andreu, *Fédération* (Paris, 1947), cited in James H. Meisel, 'Sorel Revisited,' *University of Toronto Quarterly*, Vol. XIX (1949), p. 54. For Sorel's *praise* of capitalist production, see *De l'utilité du pragmatisme*, pp. 350–1.

[2] *Réflexions sur la violence*, p. 233 (179).

[3] *Ibid.*, p. 228 (175).

The idea of ideological purity as necessitating a total separation of labour from the bureaucracy, extended even to the need of keeping apart proletarians and professors, the intellectual bureaucracy. Just as the syndicate is to grow outside and independent of the juridical and legislative devices of the State, so, too, it is to maintain careful watch over the intelligentsia, even that portion of it which professes sympathy for proletarian aims. Because practice resides in the proletariat, it alone can be the instrument of real change. The intelligentsia can at best perform auxiliary functions in the social revolution. Sorel was convinced that any relation other than dependence upon the producers would be equivalent to injecting impure ideological modes of thought that could only lead to an equivocating and procrastinating working class. Indeed, sociological methods that would take cognisance of alternative modes of action in a specific context would serve to undermine the mythological basis of mass action. In this way the intelligentsia, like the bureaucracy, comes to preach the gospel of reformism.[1]

Sorel is aware that his position on bureaucracy is extreme, and raises more questions than it answers. He therefore sought to distinguish the political bureaucracy from the future proletarian élite. This he was able to do by relating the former to advocacy of the political strike and the latter to the proletarian, revolutionary strike. There will be no bureaucracy, in the historic meaning of the term, under socialism. Administration is to replace bureaucracy.[2] But as is often the case with Sorel, after indicating the general features of future society, he does not indicate the precise mechanism by which proletarian administrators will be able to avoid differentiating itself from the labourers to form, once again, a distinctive social and political élite. What we are thus ultimately left with is Sorel's insight into the multi-levelled sources of political friction, without a corresponding ability to show the possibilities for non-antagonistic forms of social organization. Sorel pushed the central problems of socialist political theory into the utopian future. In so doing he abandoned the whole range of problems with which political sociology must grapple.

It is easy enough to summarize the crudities in Sorel's view of the relation of the masses to the bureaucracy: his one-sided concentration on the political forms of rule, the consequent absence of serious

---

[1] *Matériaux d'une théorie du prolétariat*, pp. 73–4, 132–3.
[2] *Introduction a l'économie moderne* (Paris, 1922), p. 247.

analysis of the economic sources of bureaucratic strength, his imprecision as to the actual mode of operation of bureaucratic apparatus and types of people involved in this apparatus, his linguistic vagueness on questions of control and levels of control of the State, his failure to clearly distinguish between the legitimate managerial functions of a highly developed industrial society and illegitimate power function exercised by an exploiting class. These are serious deficits indeed. They stem in part from Sorel's blind adherence to a partisan notion of truth, and in part from the pragmatic values implicit in his approach to revolutionary action.

The ray of light penetrating shady vagueness and inaccuracies is Sorel's perceptiveness, particularly his insistence on seeing the State and its bureaucratic apparatus as a self-perpetuating phenomenon. It is an apparatus that might change hands with succeeding revolutions, but an organism which nonetheless has remarkable qualities of endurance, much like institutional religions. That the bureaucracy may concentrate further and evolve to a point where, independent of older established classes, it might constitute itself as a political and economic force is a possibility Sorel raises that cannot be dismissed lightly. The bureaucracy, which can come to power only with the support of one or another contending economic classes, has shown signs of constituting itself as an entity over and apart from these classes, and in effect forms a distinctive social entity. Whether the bureaucracy can ever be a class in the classic sense of economic ownership of productive processes is still a future contingency. What can no longer be doubted is the bureaucracy's capacity for economic management and also social demands of a kind not normally associated with either the bourgeoisie or the proletariat.[1]

To justify élitist distinctions and to defend them in the name of State authority, is to Sorel tantamount to surrendering freedom to the false God of security. Those who make the guarantees, the mass bureaucratic network, attempt to make good by controlling economic and political upheavals through manipulation of the legal

[1] The following recent works have emphasized that common to different economic systems is a unique inversion of the political State and the national economy; an inversion accompanied by a much larger role for the State bureaucracy. See Franz Neumann, *Behemoth: The Structure and Practice of National Socialism* (New York, 1944); C. Wright Mills, *The Power Elite* (New York, 1956); Milovan Djilas, *The New Class: An Analysis of the Communist System* (New York, 1957); Joseph A. Schumpeter, *Capitalism, Socialism, and Democracy* (New York, 1947).

machinery of government. In so doing, the bureaucracy insidiously constitutes itself as a class independent of either industrialists or producers. This Sorel sees as the binding element between State capitalism and State socialism. The reconciliation of social needs and economic ambitions is not solved, in Sorel's system, by viewing material abundance as the automatic regulator of human strivings and passions. Such a hierarchical approach is too often a disguise for putting off into the future serious consideration of root problems of political sociology: the precise relation of authority to freedom, social control to individual fulfilment.[1]

It was Sorel's prime merit as a political theorist that his hopes for the future were not allowed to conceal concrete issues of the present. His focus by now has become common sociological currency as it shed light on the general features of the State. The bureaucratic components of the State, the effects of violence on the masses, the adopted stance of bureaucracy within various economic systems: on such vital issues as these, his work and insight assure him a significant place among efforts to construct a synthetic theory of politics.

[1] It should be mentioned that Sorel arrived at his position on the pivotal role of bureaucracy in modern society independent of and prior to Max Weber. The fact of their remarkable perspectival similarities has thus far not received the attention it merits from comparative sociologists. Talcott Parsons' justly famous *the Structure of Social Action* (New York and London, 1937), which deals extensively with the work of both Weber and Pareto ignors Sorel's germinal efforts completely. Reinhard Bendix's *Max Weber: An Intellectual Portrait* (New York, 1960) likewise makes no mention of Sorel. The excellent essay by J. P. Mayer, *Max Weber and German Politics: A Study in Political Sociology* (London, 1944), while noting Weber's 'European Outlook' does not indicate that Sorel shared with Weber the founding of the sociology of bureaucracy. What makes this so amazing is that Roberto Michels and Vilfredo Pareto had many years earlier already documented Sorel's role. While the literature of Weber in English is extensive, the best single source for his views on bureaucracy are contained in *From Max Weber: Essays in Sociology*, translated and edited by H. H. Gerth and C. Wright Mills (New York, 1946), esp. pp. 196–244.

IV

SACRED AND SECULAR
HISTORY

'We have begun to pose to ourselves the terrible question:
can it be possible that our civilization is not the civilization?'

Jacques Soustelle, LIBERTÉ DE L'ESPRIT

THE philosophy of history becomes a social force at that moment
when men realize that society not only possesses a structure but
also a process. Sorel was cognisant of the fact that notions of historical evolution become transformed into doctrines of revolution
when historical laws posit an end to the old order of institutions and
relations. The vigour of Enlightenment rationalism, no less than that
of Augustinian mysticism, stemmed from a discontent with existing
circumstances that pressed for an answer to the question: are these
the only circumstances possible? The need for a City of Man, and
prior to that, a City of God, were said to rest on historical sanction at
least as much as moral sanction. However fantastic these historical
claims might have been in fact, however tinged with 'charlatanism
and puerility,' they provided a rallying ground for the whole of discontented society on which to struggle to bring into existence a better
and different future.[1] The philosophy of history is that gigantic social
myth that makes revolutions possible, and even necessary.

[1] *Les illusions du progrès* (Paris, 1927, 4th ed.), pp. 6–8. Unless otherwise noted
all references to this work will be to this edition.

90

1. From Factual History to the Philosophy of History

The social myth is the instrument which triggers revolution. But when philosophies of history become enshrined as State religions, both they and the social forces fortifying them are no longer valuable as radical critiques. The total identification of Christian revelation with medieval Europe made messianism and the social interpretation of the gospels suspect and heretical. Mysticism, what for Sorel is the bearer of the apocalyptic vision, was replaced by a conservative scholasticism that argued the language and logic of problems. Even the question of social structure was examined only in terms which precluded an examination of social processes. Similarly, the complete identification of reason and progress with European capitalism led to a corruption of doctrine as soon as capitalism became entrenched. Capitalism became identified as the rational economy, and progress was reduced to a measurement of gains within the system. The revolutionary impetus which initially gave rise to a general theory of progress, was replaced by idealist bombast and vague references to the conquests of science.[1]

The trouble with past philosophies of history was that their formulators insisted on converting history into either religion or science. For Sorel, the philosophy of history when so converted is a corruption of the powerful and great social myths which inspired past ages to action. This was particularly evident in the dissemination of Enlightenment thought, about which Sorel felt most strongly. He felt it a central task of 'contemporary socialism to demolish the entire structure of conventional falsehoods and to ruin the esteem which those who popularize the popularizations of the eighteenth century are still held.'[2] What this requires for Sorel is a view of civilization as indeterminate rather than pre-determined. Each business depression, for example, is different owing to the real history, or 'durational factor' which contributes to it. Therefore the calculations of reasoned foresight are not valid in social movements.

Instead of pontifications about law-like statements, the worthy philosophy of history admits its essentially ideological and mythological character, serving as a passionate stimulant for rallying men to increased social activity. Ernest Hocking has caught this point very well when he notes that Sorel's 'portrait does not claim scientific

---

[1] *Les illusions du progrès* , p. 265.
[2] *Ibid.*, pp. 275–6.

exactitude; scientific exactitude is not what is wanted. The thing is to set the mind of men in the right direction; and the right direction is to conceive the existing order as hopelessly bad in order that the will to overthrow it may not flag. Rationalists may see in this reasoning a vicious circle, as if one had decided in advance to have a revolution at all costs. But no. This pessimistic judgment has a broader base; it is founded on a philosophy of history.'[1]

But Sorel would reject Hocking's support on the grounds that there can be no scientific philosophy of history. What exists and can be fought for is a theory of historical development which is nothing over and above the pragmatic use of theory in the struggle for human emancipation. The meaning summed up in the historical situation concerns the battles fought rather than the battles to be fought. History offers a sense of tradition rather than an ability to make accurate prediction.[2] The philosophy of history is therefore not so much an analysis of events as a super-imposed moral judgment. It fulfils psychological and social needs rather than scientific demands. The failure of the *philosophes* to distinguish between historical reality and their projections of that reality led to a corruption of their beliefs; to a spread of the gospel of progress rather than to a further study of history.[3]

Underlying Sorel's structural analysis of the politics of modern society is a view of history which was worked out over a period of thirty years. His initial entry into French intellectual life, following his career as an engineer, was through the empirical studies of past societies. He continually drew illustrative material for his general theory of politics from this formative acquaintance with the stages of history he knew best: Hellenic civilization, the origins and evolution of Christianity in the West, and the rise and transformations of the Roman Empire.[4] The analysis of action, heroism and virility, which were to form such a major part of his social psychology, was made possible by these early *fin de siècle* studies.

From the brilliant Italian precursor of a systematic philosophy of history, Giambattista Vico, Sorel derived his cardinal premise that the constructions of metaphysics could not explain social history;

---

[1] William Ernest Hocking, *Man and the State* (New Haven, 1926), p. 449.

[2] *De l'utilité du pragmatisme*, p. 185.   [3] *Les illusions du progrès*, p. 133.

[4] Sorel's major historical writings were all done prior to the turn of the century, but they already exhibit his characteristic partisanship. See *Le procès de Socrate* (Paris, 1889); *Contribution à l'étude profane de la Bible* (Paris, 1889); and *La ruine du monde antique: conception matérialiste de l'histoire.* (Paris, 1902).

whereas the study of social history could do much to explain the origins of metaphysics. Sorel's regard for Marx is in no small part a consequence of this adherence to Vico's historical sociology. They shared the belief that men must 'look for the origin of our metaphysical constructions in the more or less empirical constructions of social existence, just as we find the origin of our scientific theses in the observations of technicians in the arts.'[1]

Sorel's kinship to Italian social theory, and no less his antagonism for German sociology, stem in part from his immersion in the writings of Vico rather than Hegel. The certainty of the historical future, its culmination in the pure rational order, which was to be found underlying the Hegelian philosophy of history, irritated Sorel. It tended to fix responsibility for historical evolution on a teleological level rather than in the specific and concrete relations between nations, classes and individuals. In so doing, Hegelianism in relation to individual activities was nihilistic in just that degree to which human beings were relieved of responsibility for action. The psychologically-rooted outlook of Vico offered Sorel wider possibilities for understanding human history precisely because its focus upon individual actions made social determinism easier to challenge. Personality had more significance for Vico than for Hegel.[2]

This psychological approach to historical understanding, as well as a functional appraisal of religions in history, attracted Sorel to the author of *Scienza Nuova*. The idea that governments must conform to the nature of the governed, the capacity of the masses to change the political regime in any way they see fit, the conception of civilization as essentially the progressive clarification of conscience and social behaviour, were all central concepts in Sorel's thinking. He was impressed by Vico's insistence on a firm separation between history and metaphysics: the social world is the world of man, the divine world the work of providence. What man makes, unlike what God creates, is subject to constant change and decay. It is this creative, yet 'open' element in Vico's theory that captivated Sorel's imagination.[3] Vico's 'ideal eternal history' which every nation undergoes, and which in microcosmic reflection every individual passes through, 'rise,

---

[1] 'Étude sur Vico,' in *Le Devenir Social* (Oct.–Dec. 1896), p. 801.
[2] *Matériaux d'une théorie du prolétariat*, pp. 39–41.
[3] Vico's *Scienza Nuova* (translated as *The New Science of Giambattista Vico*, by Max H. Fisch) (New York, 1948).

development, maturity, decadence and dissolution' offered richer possibilities for historical research than the study of human affairs.[1] It was Vico who convinced Sorel that Hegelian predeterminism, when taken seriously, is a ground for inaction, a form of fatalism. The idea that Reason is infallible and supreme had no place in Sorel's psychology of action. Vico's notion of the 'barbarism of reflection,' reinforced as it was by Renan's critique of the distorting influence of abstract metaphysical notions in historical struggles, fitted in neatly with Sorel's own world picture.[2]

In his later writings, Sorel worked out the implications of his early historical studies. The philosophy of history that he developed not only supports the structural analysis of the relation of the State to the Citizen but is offered as empirical evidence for the motivational psychology for which Sorel is best known. Sorel's philosophy of history elevates his writings on other themes from existential speculation to considered contextual analysis. This phase of his work most clearly separates him from his close followers. They were able only to use the vocabulary of realism. He was alone in probing the contents of social struggle. The rationalization of politics and psychology was his primary concern. Precisely because of this, Sorelian theory is more easily accessible here than at any other point.

History is divided by Sorel into two basic parts. On one side there is factual or empirical history; on the other, mythological history. This construction immediately raises problems which Sorel never resolved. For while he insisted that socialism can be discussed meaningfully only if 'we pass to the domain of real history, to the interpretation of facts,'[3] he believed that the evaluation and interpretation of history is entirely subjective.[4] This bifurcation was a continuous plague: while Sorel the empirical historian flayed utopianism for its insatiable desire to 'fix dates for the arrival of the millennium,'[5] Sorel the advocate of the myth urged a revolutionary course of action on

[1] An excellent appraisal of Vico's open historicism is contained in Max Fisch's review of Robert Caponigri's *The Theory of History in Giambattista Vico.* Cf. *The Journal of Philosophy*, Vol. LIV, No. 21, 1957, pp. 648–52.

[2] Cf. Michael Freund, *Georges Sorel: Der revolutionäre Konservativismus*, pp. 78–80. See also Ernest Renan, *L'Avenir de la science*, in *Oeuvres complètes*, Vol. III, pp. 773–4.

[3] *Réflexions sur la violence*, p. 389 (278).

[4] 'Étude sur Vico,' in *op. cit.*, pp. 796–7; also *l'utilité du pragmatisme*, p. 336.

[5] 'L'éthique du socialisme,' in *La Revue de Métaphysique et de Morale* (May 1899), p. 297.

the producers—even though historians eventually discover that such action was based on illusions.[1]

The Hegelian dialectic is considered 'unsatisfactory past the time that Marx termed pre-history.'[2] Not only are social facts decisive to historical investigations, but also such phenomena as the ideological standpoint of the subject and the sensitive differences in each person's group context. Since the ground of history is the individual, Sorel saw relativism no less than subjectivism as the basis of adequate description and prescription. In his opinion the proletariat must not heed the inherited delusions as to how it can take power by standardized recipes. Revolution and counter-revolution is made first by the sword and then by the pen. This is the first stage in a realistic philosophy of history.[3] What really distinguishes Sorel from Hegel and Marx is not so much the use of historical sanction as just cause for supporting revolution, but the type of historical doctrine best suited to bring revolutions about. Hegel derived revolutions from history, while Sorel derived history from revolutions.

The transition from empirical to mythological history involves several crucial layers of development. Scholarly interest in Sorel's efforts to stave off a dualism between empirical and subjective history has thus far been concerned with his placing of practice in the central role as mediator of the two types of historical explanation. It is my contention that Sorel operated with false alternatives. A cosmic determinist view of history when countered by an indeterminist theory of human nature, does not lead to concrete historical discoveries, but simply to a new variety of social metaphysics. Unconsciously, but not unwillingly, Sorel passed from an historical *is*, 'the function of violence in the working classes,' into a metaphysical *ought*, 'a perpetrator of violence.'[4]

The understanding of real history requires, in a strict sense, active participation in history. From Renan, Sorel derived the idea that an 'intellectualist philosophy is entirely unable to explain the great movements of history.'[5] The passive man in Renan's outlook observes human change in an alienated way because he is estranged

---

[1] *Réflexions sur la violence*, p. 219 (169).
[2] *Matériaux d'une théorie du prolétariat*, p. 41.
[3] *Ibid.*, pp. 55–6.
[4] *Réflexions sur la violence*, pp. 63–4 (70).
[5] *Ibid.*, p. 38 (52).

from the historical flow itself.[1] History as analogical, as being the social representation of physical events, is but a sterile scientism lacking a perspective on the distinctly bio-social character of historical truths.[2] The initial phase in a comprehension of history involves an acceptance of the primacy of activity, the participation of man in shaping his destinies. Just as for James and Bergson a functional theory of knowledge requires the involvement of men in the specific forms of doing and changing, so for Sorel history demanded a like commitment to action. Activity is incompatible with determinism. Consequently, history offers the same likelihood of reward and success as the intelligence and activities of the men who take part in events. Socialism becomes a risky venture, the worth of which can only be guessed at, not predicted.

As prospects for international social revolution grew dimmer, Sorel shared in a general anxiety over the growth in political passivity which seemed to accompany the expansion of the European economy. Even the orthodox Marxians were anxious to establish the need for spontaneous political action to cope with the amazingly virile class foes. Only human activity, and not any abstract historical inevitability, could hasten the revolutionary process. This was clearly the message of the precursors of organizational Marxism, Antonio Labriola and George Plekhanov.[3] It was not listened to by the social democratic politicians of Western Europe.

What distinguished socialist thinking in the first decade of the twentieth century was a search for organization, a political form through which the proletarian socialist could establish his supremacy. An underlying premise of this organizational emphasis was a downgrading of the role of Hegelian dialectic in the ideology of political man. The left-Hegelians countered by insisting that the activism of men like Sorel reduced itself to a tautology that one should stress action simply for its own sake. Revolutionary activism reduced itself to revolutionary phrases. Lenin went so far as to con-

---

[1] Ernest Renan, *Histoire du peuple d'Israël*, Vol. III, p. 497; *Nouvelles études d'histoire religieuse*, p. 7; and *L'église chrétienne*, p. 317. Sorel steadily cites these works in support of an activist theory of history. The points of similarity with Vico's *ricorso* are clear. Sorel viewed Renan as the empirical proof of Vico's historicism. Cf. 'Was man von Vico lernt', *Sozialistische Monatshefte* (June 1898), pp. 270–72.

[2] *Matériaux d'une théorie du prolétariat*, pp. 14–5.

[3] For examples of the new note of realism that swept Marxism, see Antonio Labriola, *Essays on the Materialistic Conception of History* (Chicago, 1903); and George Plekhanov, *The Role of the Individual in History* (New York, 1940), and *The Materialist Conception of History* (New York, 1940).

tend that the revolt against the dialectic had as an ultimate purpose the substitution of prejudices for principles, and made of revolution a matter of caprice rather than necessity. Lenin once even urged a Russian journal to function as a sort of 'Society of Materialist Friends of Hegelian Dialectic.'[1]

To speak of an upward sweep of history is an abstraction fostered by the Enlightenment notion of eternal progress. Sorel does not deny that history reveals patterns of organized change and growth, but not as a consequence of a hidden *deus ex machina*. Upward movement in history takes place only as long as men are active. When they try to escape through false linguistic idols, by which Vico called the 'barbarism of reflection,' then this upward movement is reversed. We are thrown back to adopting the worst features of barbarism; and what is worse, a barbarism having the additional curse of appearing in the guise of civilization.[2]

The doctrine of development through harmony is, for Sorel, no less chimerical than the dialectic. It results in a theory of history which replaces human activity with universal design, even when such historicism takes an avowedly naturalist form. It was Vico's merit to indicate that empirical history shows progressions only when a cycle of human consciousness is present: violence to equity to violence, sensations to reason and back again to sensations. 'The ruling class of nobles meant to abuse their lordly freedom over the plebeians, and they had to submit to the laws which established popular freedom. The free peoples meant to shake off the yoke of their laws, and they became subject to monarchs. The monarchs meant to strengthen their own positions by debasing their subjects with all the vices of dissoluteness, and they disposed them to endure slavery at the hands of stronger nations. The nations meant to dissolve themselves, and their remnants fled for safety to the wilderness, whence, like the phoenix, they rose again. That which did all this was man, because men did it with intelligence; it was not fate because they did it by

---

[1] Vladimir Lenin, *Marx-Engels-Marxism* (New York, n.d.), pp. 56–9, 71–9, 208–11.

[2] 'Étude sur Vico,' *loc. cit.*, p. 799. Although Sorel counted the dialectic among the false linguistic idols, he would have agreed with Lenin as against the Mensheviks and the German social democrats on the nature and primacy of human action. Discussions on this topic, while never completely absent in socialist circles, took on particular sharp political tones during the 1895–1905 period in both western and eastern Europe. See E. H. Carr, *The Bolshevik Revolution, 1917–1923*, Vol. I of his *A History of Soviet Russia* (London, 1950), esp. pp. 26–44.

choice, not chance . . .'[1] This beautifully written passage indicates that Vico was convinced that the process of conscious activity gives a distinctly voluntaristic note to the course of historical development. History may not be a smooth process, but it nonetheless is a distinctly human process.

Sorel's appraisal, which follows closely the Vico *ricorso*, makes the very same errors as his Italian mentor. Both assumed that gradual change implies the absence of conflict. It seems clear that a doctrine of consensus has no more priority than a theory of violence when related to measuring the growth and expansion of a given society. It is furthermore not clear why a principle of development outside of history itself must govern the movement of things: in Vico this principle is Divine Providence and in Sorel it is the myth. Both men reproduced the search for a *deus ex machina* to govern the working of human society.

It is not that Sorel thoroughly rejected the idea of a progressive evolution of society. His difference with the *philosophes* is essentially over the character of progress. The dynamics of Sorel's position rests on an insistence that progress involves the preservation of past traditions and productive achievements, no less than the political fetters which bind men to the archaic.[2] This has led to a view of Sorel as essentially conservative in temperament and orientation.[3]

The difficulty of such a critique is that it vitiates any distinction between conservatism and radicalism. Few philosophers of change would consider that the growth of a new political or economic system could be achieved without preserving past accomplishments. It was often Sorel's maturity, rather than a raw traditionalism, that led him to perceive the need for retaining the old material and cultural gains in efforts to develop new societal forms. He saw himself as the defender of heritage and tradition. He opposed utopian radicals who for centuries had preached that the implementation of great reform projects, under the guidance of the established rulers of society, is sanctioned by laws of history, and makes obsolete all past achievements.[4]

The confusion over Sorel's conservatism stems in part from his piquant flirtation with royalist-restoration French politics. However,

[1] Giambattista Vico, *Scienza Nuova*, Article 1108, p. 382.
[2] *Le Système historique de Renan* (Paris, 1906), pp. 171–2.
[3] Michael Freund, *Georges Sorel: der revolutionäre Konservitivismus*, see especially Chapter Two.
[4] *Matériaux d'une théorie du prolétariat*, pp. 16–17.

on the theoretical side, it seems to be caused by Sorel's woeful mis-understanding of the nature of democracy. His conception of demo-cracy was restricted to the view that it implies a levelling process, leading to social uniformity. Negatively, this view of democracy in-volved the belief that a democratic *polis* would annihilate all tradi-tion. And since for Sorel tradition is a necessary aspect of revolu-tionary processes, he took the next fatal step, which was to deny that democracy had anything to do with revolution.[1] Nonetheless, the evidence indicates that it was the incompleteness of middle class de-mocracy, its duplicity and negligence in terms of the needs of labourers and peasants, rather than a conservative spirit, that moti-vated Sorel's anti-democratic posture. This is not to deny the essen-tially quixotic character of such a separation of political democracy from the question of revolutionary action. It is to reject the opinion that such a separation is *eo ipso* a characteristic of political or theoretical conservatism.

Tradition functions unconsciously for Sorel. He followed the Marxian analysis of unconscious motor-forces as directing history indicating that capitalism by its own inner mechanism prepares the ground for the future.[2] Elsewhere he writes that: 'Capitalism plays a part analogous to that attributed by Hartmann to the Unconscious in nature, since it prepares the coming of social reforms which it did not intend to produce. Without any co-ordinated plan, without any directive ideas, without any ideal of a future world, it is the cause of an inevitable evolution; it draws from the present all that the present can give towards historical development; it performs in an almost mechanical manner all that is necessary, in order that a new era may appear, and that this new era may break every link with the idealism of the present times, while preserving the acquisitions of the capitalis-tic economic system.'[3] Sorel makes perfectly clear that this dialectic of tradition in no way cancels out the need for a scientific reconstruc-tion of society. 'How absurd the idea is then of borrowing from some dead and gone social structure, a suitable means of controlling a sys-tem of production, whose principal characteristic is that every day it must become more and more opposed to all preceding economic systems.'[4]

The fusion then of conscious and unconscious elements (of science

---

[1] *Introduction à l'économie moderne*, p. 246.
[2] *Insegnamenti sociali della economia contemporanea*, pp. 180–5.
[3] *Réflexions sur la violence*, p. 113 (102).   [4] *Ibid.*, p. 387 (277).

and myth) produces real progress. This reciprocity discredits the Enlightenment conception of rational history and its romantic nineteenth century utopian extensions. The appeal to rational consciousness as the mainspring of history from Holbach to Hegel ignores the decisive role of unconsciousness. It is precisely the knowledge of this unconscious that 'permits us to explain historical phenomena of the most complex kind without the least difficulty.'[1]

Real evolution has nothing in common with Fabian appeals to the law-makers for amelioration. Such appeals move counter to the actual unconscious centre of human existence that prepares on the ground of existing clashes, the future proletarian revolution.[2] It was in a similar spirit that Plekhanov castigated the *philosophes* 'joyless chase of some happy historical accident.'[3] What distinguishes Sorel from Plekhanov is the unwillingness of *notre maitre* to grant the Enlightenment concept of progress its advanced function of restoring to human control the historical events which scholasticism attributed to providential edict.

Sorel remained convinced from the outset that Western European socialism retained the Enlightenment position on historical change because it was more concerned with reform than with revolution: with the preservation of special political and economic privileges for the organized craft workers rather than with the emancipation of the labourers as a whole. This was the essence of the 'corruption of Marxism.' This is how Sorel characterized what later became a furious debate within socialist ranks. Advocates of the dictatorship of the proletarian class maintained that it was rank fantasy to think that socialism could come about without the organized seizure of political power. Critics of this notion held that the dictatorship of the proletariat inevitably and invariably invites its transformation into a new stage of élitism, into a dictatorship of the party. It is interesting that opponents of 'Jacobin' dictatorship *within* orthodox Marxism, such as Rosa Luxemburg in Germany and Leon Trotsky in Russia, based their conclusions precisely on that tradition which Sorel saw as the leading culprit, the Enlightenment.[4]

[1] *Matériaux d'une théorie du prolétariat*, p. 190.
[2] *Les Illusions du progrès*, pp. 58–9, 133 (1st ed.).
[3] George Plekhanov, *In Defence of Materialism* (London, 1947), pp. 75–6.
[4] Compare Rosa Luxemburg, *The Russian Revolution* (New York, 1940) with the later reflections of Leon Trotsky, *The Revolution Betrayed* (New York, 1945). Both prophecy and reflection show a similar intellectualist, 'enlightened' attitude to the concept of proletarian dictatorship. In each, the moral question took priority: what should be the maximum price to pay for a socialist revolution.

Sorel went back to Machiavelli in seeing self-interest as an operative force in the political life of the nation, no less than in the economy, in the functioning of the State no less than in relations of production. It was likewise a service to political ethics that he drew the
consequences of this insight, the need for a socialist theory of government as well as a socialist theory of economy. The ledger would however be incomplete without a debit entry. For Sorel attributed to
wrong causes this conflict between private power and public power.
He saw it in the employment by socialists of the ideology and philosophy of Enlightenment rather than in the coming into being of new
objective factors, such as an increased rate of social mobility, the
growth of new market areas and the shift to government regulation
of economic fluctuations.

2. From the Philosophy of History to History as Myth

This analysis of the rise and fall of societies enabled Sorel to go
from objective to subjective history, from history as an unconscious,
objective process to history as a pliable, plastic agent of the imagination. We have already noted his marked preference for a Bergsonian
indeterminate view, in which the individual demarcates and works
for his goals, rather than for a Marxian explanation of social conflict
as an outgrowth of economic oppression. However, Sorel's indeterminism involves a quite clear commitment to a power thesis. Egoism,
violence and alienation are viewed as expressions of the primary urge
to seek personal fulfilment through political power.

The life-long resentment Sorel harboured towards utilitarianism is
etched in sharp colours. *Les illusions du progrès* is an unrelieved attempt to overthrow the critical rationalism upon which the Enlightenment ethic rested. From Fontenelle to Condorcet, he sees but a
series of vulgarizations and abstractions aimed at convincing men
that power urges can be mediated by rational understanding, by the
need for social co-operation. In contrast, Sorel develops a theory of
history founded on a unique combination of asceticism and power.
Unlike the Marxian notion of 'proletarian asceticism,' that of Sorel's
is a symbol of human sublimity and courage rather than a compelling
economic condition. He resurrected the asceticism of the Christian
orders both as an antiseptic to the corruption of labour under industrial capitalism, and as a perfect symbol for the future socialist man.

Eager to establish the alleged decline of capitalism as a consequence of a utilitarian ethic, Sorel followed Catholic historiography in its efforts to explain the decline of religious temper. Like Church spokesmen, he bifurcated the sacred and the profane, spiritual perfection and historical imperfection. 'Far from imposing a far-reaching reform on the profane world, the Church itself had become corrupted by imitating the profane world; it began to resemble an imperial administration, and the factions which tore it asunder were much more moved by an appetite for power than by religious reasons.'[1] This quest for power is constant amidst a sea of historical deviants. 'We can, by analogy, imagine what would follow from a revolution which brought our official Socialists of today into power. Institutions remaining almost where they are today, all the middle class would be preserved; the middle class state would dominate with its ancient abuses; if economic decadence had begun, it would be accentuated.'[2] The utilitarian ethic in which the Enlightenment was saturated, and which became a semi-official source of orthodox and reform socialism alike, would only hasten the decline of civilization. If it were a choice between Fourier's petty-bourgeois socialism, and the religious socialism of a Saint Jerome or Saint Ambrose, Sorel clearly would choose the latter for its sublimity.[3] Sorel's regard for Catholic institutions was, in its theoretical aspects, an outgrowth of both his and Renan's studies of the historical muscularity of asceticism. On the pragmatic level, it expressed a contempt for the pettiness and corruption of French bourgeois society, which Sorel shared in common with Catholic restorationists like Maurras and Catholic revolutionists like his friend Péguy.

Sorel, who laboured mightily to conceal his limited comprehension of economic theory, often fell prey to generalizations based on a fondness for the small handicrafts industries prominent in France throughout the nineteenth century. He tended to view the labourer as an essentially creative and artistic person. He never thought about the emergence of a highly mechanized industry which would transform the relationship of worker and machine. In his mind, the machine assumed a mystical, fetishistic superiority over men in advanced capitalism. It operated to cut down the creative imagination of the worker, making of him a stupefied and simpering appendage to a mechanical system of production. The years spent as an

---

[1] *Réflexions sur la violence*, p. 127 (111).
[2] *Ibid.*, p. 127 (111).
[3] *La décomposition du marxisme*, p. 49.

102

engineer did not make Sorel into a technocrat. To the contrary, this past training heightened his awareness of the limits of technics. The transformation of wage labour into a primary form of aesthetic creation was for Sorel the way in which socialism overcomes the contradiction between manual labour with its reputed servility, and intellectual labour with its reputed nobility.[1]

Sorel displayed slender awareness of the distinction between art and industry. His pragmatism failed to distinguish between products for use and artifacts for enjoyment. Aesthetic creation in its relation to the processes of production is complex. The arts involve their own specialized technology that is not necessarily connected with machine techniques. The fact that the labourer can have his physical energies replaced by machine equivalances allows, but of course does not assure, that the creative side of human beings can be fulfilled outside the process of production, and as a direct consequence of a decrease in labour time and labour energies. Involved in a moral and aesthetic stance suited to a pre-industrial Christianity, Sorel was prevented from having any clear-headed ideas about a society in which labour prevails. To call utopian every activity of historical diagnosis is to undermine the varied reasons why men act. Sorel sensed an acute imbalance in his position and was compelled to call into play a subjective doctrine of evolution.

Sorel is struck by the 'individualistic characters which are met with in armies,' particularly in the armies of Homeric kings.[2] He sees a similar variety of individualism in labouring groups: 'each working with the greatest possible zeal, each acting on his own account, and not troubling himself much to subordinate his conduct to a great and scientifically combined plan.'[3] Political sociology in France still witnesses appeals to a pre-technological socialism, in which the aesthetics and psychology of small handicrafts prevail. 'Community socialism, based on flexible decentralized institutions, seems better adopted to the individual's psychological needs, which, under it, can be harmonized with the use of modern techniques of organization and production.'[4]

Sorel's orientation assumes that small-scale industry is the best method of achieving higher productive standards. From a factual viewpoint, this can only be characterized as economic provincialism,

---

[1] *Matériaux d'une théorie du prolétariat*, pp. 43–4.
[2] *Réflexions sur la violence*, pp. 373–4 (268).
[3] *Ibid.*, p. 375 (269).
[4] Georges Friedmann, *Le travail en miettes* (Paris, 1956), p. 261.

since it flies in the face of an accentuated tendency towards greater mechanization and automation. The faulty assumption was that the relatively stagnant condition of French industry during the nineteenth century typifies industrial technology elsewhere in Europe and America. 'The organization of the workshops, the collection of raw materials, the disposal of the product—these were "trade and industry," not science. What is happening now is that modern industry is becoming scientific through and through. This does not mean that the other qualities of engineering, design, or commercial judgment are neglected, but that they are integrated in the fulfilling of a function that is becoming more and more definite and conscious.'[1] This is a description of an industrial transformation that Sorel neither envisioned nor desired. The practical character of economics was closed to him; it was only its classical vocabulary that he used.

Since the evidence of his own epoch contradicted an economy of the creative workshop, it is necessary to look at another source to explain Sorel's intense desire to retain an idealized individualism at the productive level. His primitive economic orientation obscures an essentially modern psychological insight into the relation of man and machine. Sorel was more concerned with the necessary condition for the humane application of labour than he was with maximizing industrial output.

His emphasis lay in the psychological perspective that labour, when provided with a certain emotional compensation in the work process, plays a fundamental role in the worker's general equilibrium, his adaptation to his social environment, and his physical and mental health. And since he assumed that labour had had such a role throughout history, in every social and cultural milieu, he further assumed it would always have a therapeutic function. He did not take note that the reduction of the work day, improved automatic techniques in production, added safety factors in work processes, growth in the size of the factory unit, would determine a new style of proletarian life. He failed to develop a perspective of labour in industrial society. He was left advocating an essentially anti-scientific theory of industrial technology.

Sorel sought to resolve the dilemma of the alienated worker, not in a scientific organization of social existence, but in a feudal socialism which incorporated the characteristics of early, aggressive capitalism. Nostalgia for ages when 'men were men' seriously handi-

[1] John D. Bernal, *The Freedom of Necessity* (London, 1949), p. 265.

capped Sorel's investigation of tendencies and processes of industrial society. Yet Sorel's conception of socialism involved an acceptance of the theory that the reorganization of society can only take place when there is an abundance of commodities. He was placed in the paradoxical position either of protecting the labourer's sense of pride in accomplishment against the invasion of mechanization and industrial depersonalization, in which case material abundance would be an impossibility, or of claiming that such an abundance is nonetheless possible in a handicraft economy. He chose to believe the latter, *ex cathedra*.

An antiquarian note crept into Sorel's theory of history. He understood the evolution of capitalist society in a dual way. On one side he was confronted with the need for a theory of progress. The progress of capitalism in his opinion consisted essentially in its technological achievements.[1] At the same time Sorel was desperately trying to establish a dialectic of growth. He wanted to establish decadence and devolution as integral parts of the capitalist economy. But where does one locate this devolution? Rousseau found it in the moral degradation of western civilization. Marx found it in the economic degradation of all class societies. Sorel's view, while scarcely an amalgam of these, represents a germinal effort to once again rephrase a theory of progression and retrogression.

The very achievements of capitalism in the sphere of science and technology foster indolence and cowardice in the dominant classes and mediocrity in the labouring classes. So emphatic is Sorel on this point that he accuses Marx of making 'the great mistake of underrating the enormous power of mediocrity displayed throughout history.'[2] The power of mediocrity is a negative influence. In their contentment with the *status quo*, labourers lend support to the cowardice of exploiting classes. If this were not so, *if the class conflict were always an active force*, a condition of permanent revolution would prevail. Social myths trigger action. Their institutionalization is the sole guarantee of a virile society and a permanent social revolution.

Finding nothing in the scientific enterprise itself to overcome this machine-induced psychology of passivity, Sorel turned for a solution to a personalized heaven, to an ascetic socialism rooted in the small

---

[1] *Les illusions du progrès*, pp. 276–81.

[2] *Ibid.*, p. 331. One must distinguish between Sorel's admiration for the active entreprenuer capitalism prevalent in the United States and the capitalism of Europe which he considered decadent.

handicraft industries. Faced with the dilemma of an advancing capitalist technology which was destroying individual vigour and passion, Sorel attempted to transform technique into a creative idyll by taking production out of the control of an indolent bourgeois class. His system of socialism amounted to a renunciation of further economic advances by transforming industrial technique from what it is, a scientifically rationalized enterprise, into what it most assuredly has not been, an aesthetic undertaking.

It has been remarked that Sorel nowhere criticizes the harsher aspects of life for the factory worker. Two reasons suggest themselves: one is that Sorel thought of the producer as a skilled artisan-craftsman rather than as an assembly-line worker; the other reason is that Sorel viewed industry as the goal of life, not as an instrumentality for achieving the ends of human existence. Sorel's *Stakhanovism* took the ascetic ideal as a moral and psychic necessity. The factory was to replace the monastery as the home of traditional ethical virtues. 'It would be extremely dangerous for the proletariat not to practise a division of functions which has succeeded so well for Catholicism during its long history; it would become no more than an inert mass destined to tumble, like democracy.'[1]

Antagonism for industrial society, for its sapping of individual initiative, also served Sorel as the basis for a critique of democracy as well. He did not see how industrialism could flourish without liberal-democratic relations. With his strange sympathies for royalism and such partisans of restoration politics as Maurras, Sorel's socialism became nostalgia. 'Nothing is easier than to give Christian asceticism a socialist tinge,' noted Marx prophetically. 'Has not Christianity declaimed against private property, against marriage, against the State? Has it not preached in the place of these, charity and poverty, celibacy and mortification of the flesh, monastic life and Mother Church? Christian socialism is but the holy water with which the priest consecrates the heart-burnings of the aristocrat.'[2] Indeed, it certainly cannot be said that Sorel's workshop therapy lacks theological supports. His answer to capitalism is the satisfaction of Christian values. While Sorel is not entirely out of sympathy with Marx's comments, at least at the level of theory, his view of Christianity is sufficiently distinct to mark him apart. His reasons for taking a positive view of Christianity invoke several parallel lines. First, the moral

---

[1] *Réflexions sur la violence*, p. 429 (298).
[2] Karl Marx–Frederick Engels, *The Communist Manifesto*, Chapter 3, Part 1a.

teachings of prophetic Christianity can be salvaged for socialist ends. Second, the only contact with ideas for most of the masses is through the Church and its emissaries and therefore it is necessary that socialism become identified as a movement as forceful and dynamic as Christianity. The organization of the Church can be a model for the organization of socialist society since both are free of the fetters of democratic corruption and yet retain high moral standards.[1] The faithful Christian becomes Sorel's socialist ascetic. The personalistic idea of growth becomes the common property of social Christianity and secular anarchism.

Sorel was within established precedent in viewing the real progress of capitalism as essentially the growth of the industrial system; but he failed to establish why this must be accompanied by a mediocre, passive personality. Even if we assume this to be an actual condition, how can one overcome the paradox of scientific creativity, human passivity? How can mass man achieve the goal of a dynamic and non-exploitative society? For Sorel, the resolution was fraught with grave difficulties. He recognizes the mass character of genuine social upheavals and yet he poses an empirical situation that cannot be overcome without recourse to the doctrine of the 'double truth,' a theory of the élite, a weeding out of the pacific and weak who 'are the ruination of the élite corps.'[2]

The rhythm of history was transformed into a social psychology. Given the tendency to scientific planning in industry and the legislation of social needs and wants, he viewed the future with trepidation. Industrial civilization breaks down primitive ferocity and replaces it with shrewdness. Following the plaints of conservative critics of capitalism, Sorel writes that 'robbery, deceit, and fraud increase in spite of legal repression more rapidly than brutal and violent crimes, like pillage, murder, and rape, etc., decrease. Egoism of the basest kind shamelessly breaks the sacred bonds of the family and friendship in every case in which these oppose its desires.'[3] In this situation it was Henrik De Man's *gegen der Strom* principle, the manipulator of myths, the individual who could resist the persuasive blandishments of industrial civilization, who was to become the source of social salvation.

The inescapably irrational social relations produced by a rational-

---

[1] 'L'église et l'état' in *La Revue Socialiste* (Aug.–Oct. 1901), pp. 131–51.
[2] *Réflexions sur la violence*, p. 430 (298).
[3] *Ibid.*, pp. 288–9 (214–15).

ized capitalist economy, and the resistance of men to becoming robots, Sorel saw the possible rehabilitation of modern society by an *avant-garde* proletariat. But the pernicious aspect in Sorel's position is that he was more concerned with making technology and industry capricious and irrational than with making man truly rational. This collapse of aims flowed from an unconscious inversion of heroics and history. Instead of pushing the psychological analysis of the conflict between creativity and mediocrity towards an analysis of history, Sorel sought to intensify the chasm separating human impulse from the social resolution of these impulses. By contrast, heroism can only spring from the individual.

The dualism of fact and myth in Sorel's system remains just as long as he retained a belief that everything must be considered from the standpoint of the laws of empirical history. In order finally to escape from the determinism and impersonalism of objective history, to inject a note of imagination into the historical record, Sorel attempts to overcome the dualism between progress and decadence by establishing a firm division between levels of history. In much the same way as Benedetto Croce, Sorel maintained that empirical history is only of the past, while the charting of future historical events is imaginative and mythological.[1] The unusual attention Croce bestowed on Sorel, a man of quite different temperament and interests than his own, was not motivated by sentiment. There is a close proximity between the philosophies of history of the two men. 'The relation between historiography and practical activity, between historical knowledge and action, establishes a link between the two, but not a causalistic or deterministic link.' Croce then adds: 'Action, however much ideally correlated with the historical vision which precedes it and conditions it, is so completely a new and different act, that it will in turn provide the material for a new and different historical vision. Therefore we can say that historiography, as regards practical action, is preparatory but indeterminatory.'[2]

Since Sorel rejects the possibility of a scientific interpretation of history, based upon empirical law-statements as they apply in the social sciences (on the grounds that such an approach resolves itself

[1] For an exploration of the relation of Croce to Sorel, see Antonio Gramsci, *Il Materialismo Storico e la filosofia di Benedetto Croce* (Rome, 1953), pp. 176, 242, 223–8. In general, Gramsci views Sorel as the French champion of an anti-historicist and relativist Marxism. It is this which relates the 'anti-theoretician' Sorel to the 'theoretician' Croce.

[2] Benedetto Croce, *History as the Story of Liberty* (New York, 1955), p. 179.

into a new form of utopianism) he is led to adopt a theory that history is a product and consequence of the self-directed energies of men. Since the present human activities cannot claim the sanction of empirical history, activities must of necessity be undertaken in the name of mythical residues men hold about the future society. What Sorel holds improper in the reasoning of utopians is not the arbitrariness of their goals, but an unwillingness to grant that such goals, when postulated as rational and realizable, lead to intense disenchantment with all forms of social action. The future history of man cannot be discussed as if it were in the nature of things to unfold by proclamation. Ideals men hold of the future are never fully realized in actual historical evolution, but this is neither sufficient ground for inaction nor evidence that belief is impossible. By a pragmatist critique of historical law Sorel hoped to clear the way for revolutionary activity without having to claim that such activity is the consequence of the social sciences.

The illusions arising out of the myth differ considerably from those of utopian fantasy. In the former instance, we are cognisant of the non-empirical sources of our action, whereas Sorel believed that the utopian, in his very stress on rational schematization of the future, is the most absurdly irrationalist. The social scientist calculates the irrational elements in action, whereas the utopian in ignoring these elements only acts out unconsciously the illusions fostered by social evils. Thus, mythological history distinguishes itself from utopianism in making no pretence that the ideals of socialism are translatable *en bloc* into the living tissue of society. This knowledge guards the advocate of mythological history from the rude disillusionments occasioned by the utopian interpretation of real history. For the myth believer, only action is total. Success as well as failure has always to be measured in relative terms, while for the utopian action is partial, but the measurement of such action is always total.

For this reason Sorel believed that although 'the historians of the future are bound to discover that we laboured under many illusions, because they will see behind them a finished world' this would be no sanction to quietude. For 'nobody can tell us today what these historians will know; nobody can furnish us with the means of modifying our motor images in such a way as to avoid their criticisms.'[1] The frequent counter-charge made against the positivist critics of historical determinism, to the effect that it is a sanction for personal

[1] *Réflexions sur la violence*, p. 219 (169).

and political inaction, greatly disturbed Sorel. He met this problem by shifting the function of historical exploration from facts to myths.

Sorel's anti-historical posture has ominous social consequences. Mannheim aptly expressed these consequences, no doubt unforeseen by Sorel. 'Historical events appear as a process only as long as the class which views these events still expects something from it. Only such expectations can give rise to utopias on the one hand, and concepts of process on the other. Success in the class struggle, however, does away with the utopian elements, and forces long range views into the background the better to devote its powers to its immediate tasks. The consequence is that in place of a view of the whole which formerly took account of tendencies and total structures, there appears a picture of the world composed of mere immediate events and discrete facts. The idea of a "process" and of the structural intelligibility of history becomes a mere myth.'[1] The critical factor is here perceived: a philosophy of history which steadily focuses on the immediate present and the generalized past tends to isolate itself from the sources which initially inspire a revolt against reason, namely, the need for progressive change in the social structure. In drowning the rational direction of change in the immediate felt need for change, goals become separated from instrumentalities; ends become myths and means become hypostatized.

3. Illusion and Reality in Human Progress

The criticisms Sorel offered of Enlightenment views on historical progress fell into two distinct categories: reason and responsibility. These two words gripped the eighteenth century with a tenacity that reduced theory into the commonplace. The Enlightenment was a revolutionary movement not because it preached the art of revolt, but because it urged the art of reason over and against the method of inherited dogma. Men like Helvetius, Condorcet and Holbach eschewed violence and revolution as activities of blind faith, tools of the ignorant mass. They registered the opinion that revolution is rarely, if ever, the way to real social equality and individual liberty.

Listen to the most radical anti-religious thinker of the age, Hol-

---

[1] Karl Mannheim, *Ideology and Utopia* (New York, 1953), p. 146. It should be noted that Mannheim's use of the term 'utopian' is like Sorel's use of the 'myth'; that is, the perception and intuition of the total framework of future society.

bach; note the extent to which he pits reason against revolution no less than against revelation as a means toward historical progress. 'Not through dangerous convulsions, not through struggle, through regicides and useless crime, can the wounds of the nations be healed. These violent remedies are always more cruel than the evils they are intended to cure.' Opposed to this is 'the voice of reason that is neither seditious nor bloodthirsty. The reforms which it proposes may be slow, but therefore planned all the better.'[1] This point of view was definitely not an eccentric aspect of Enlightenment thinking; it formed the core around which discussions of the future of society took place. Not Sorel's conservatism, but his implacable preference for revolutionary violence over legislative and educative reform stimulated his critique of the philosophy of Enlightenment and triggered his attack on any effort to develop a scientific sociology.

One giant of French Enlightenment who rejected the piece-meal and reform consequences of the *philosophes*' social outlook, Jean-Jacques Rousseau, did much to introduce the theme of social responsibility into Enlightenment discussions. Sorel was dedicated to the removal of Rousseau's theme which placed obligation for human fulfilment with the collective leadership of society. What in Rousseau's view occasioned such violent opposition? Rousseau placed the onus of failure to satisfy fundamental requirements of men on the shoulders of other men and not on providence. It is a societal guilt, not providential edict which frustrates man's noblest inspirations. But as Rousseau clearly knew, such a theory cuts both ways: for just as it exonerates God it also exempts man as an individual from primary responsibility for improving his lot. At the level of history Rousseau sensed that individual efforts to fulfil that which is properly a common social task is hopeless. The very idea of the social contract requires that we view 'the impulse of mere appetite as slavery, and the obedience to the law which we have prescribed to ourselves as liberty.'[2] Rousseau's idea of social responsibility for individual growth is a cornerstone of modern political and social democracy; and as such it came within Sorel's purview.

---

[1] Paul Henri d'Holbach, *Système social* (Paris, 1822), Vol. II, p. 345.

[2] Jean-Jacques Rousseau, *Du Contrat Social* (Paris, 1946), Egloff edition. Book I, Chapter VIII, p. 62. Rousseau's view of democracy is intensely disputed by the Locke–Mill view of democracy as the fulfilment of the individual through laisser-faire policies. See on this two-fold nature of democracy, J. L. Talmon, *The Origins of Totalitarian Democracy* (London, 1952); and Alf Ross, *Why Democracy?* (Cambridge, 1952).

Sorel first saw Rousseau's comments on civil society as a 'magnificent obscurity,' and then more seriously as a pernicious attempt to undermine the psychology of action and the impulse to violence.[1] Against the concept of the primacy of reason, Sorel offered the primacy of appetite; and against the idea of social responsibility, he offered the responsibility of the individual. The spirit of democracy and collectivism lurked behind every pronouncement of Enlightenment. It was this spirit that Sorel was determined to eradicate. Socialism minus philosophical enlightenment equalled revolutionary syndicalism.

According to Sorel, the difficulties in the Enlightenment conception of science arose because it considered nature as thoroughly determinist. 'Idealism and determinism fabricate a fictitious and deceptive continuity. Marx teaches us to seek historical continuity in what is really true, that is, in man equipped to change his nature.'[2] The Enlightenment was further burdened with an 'incredible scientific ingenuousness,' which led it to think of science as having as its primary aim 'forecasting the future with accuracy.' The *philosophes* were utterly predisposed to carry this over into the field of history.[3] The dogma of progress, which was an inference drawn primarily from Newtonian science, became the supreme illusion of advocates of a purely rational approach to historical events. It was this theory of history as eternal and predictable progress, common to aristocratic, bourgeois and reform socialist forces, on which Sorel centred his fire. 'The doctrine of progress as designed by the Encyclopaedists was a reflection and anticipation of the reform projects first instituted by aristocratic reformers and later carried out by the bourgeoisie.'[4] Reformism is thus not a peculiar aberration of a single class, but a characteristic of mediocrity and mendacity in all classes.

What is special and unique about the bourgeoisie is not its orientation toward reform, but the character of the reformist policies employed. It was the bourgeoisie which transformed reformism from a fashionable, if slightly eccentric aristocratic mode of conduct, into a first principle of politics. It went on to develop a philosophy of history patterned on the mechanical processes of the physical universe, but this served only to disguise its essentially conservative economic

---

[1] *Les illusions du progrès* (second edition), pp. 94–108, This contains Sorel's most complete statement on Rousseau's social contract theory.

[2] *Saggi di critica del Marxismo* (Palermo, 1903), pp. 79–83.

[3] *Réflexions sur la violence*, pp. 204–5 (159).

[4] *Les illusions du progrès*, p. 133.

policies. 'The theory of progress is the creation of the bourgeoisie and although it no longer employs it as anything but a smokescreen to disguise class domination and social monolithism, it dare not be criticized.'[1] The range of application of progress was withdrawn from society at large, and limited to technology.

Aside from its function as a pretext for middle class ambitions and as a ruse to arouse feelings of sympathy and harmony from the producers, the Enlightenment theory of progress suffers from its empty, tautological character. For on the one hand it says the obvious: that improvement in the material conditions of civilization steadily takes place; and on the other, it blurs the actually repressive dynamics of power relations by considering them narrowly.

The bourgeois Enlightenment was thus as Panglossian as the Leibnizian view that it so assiduously mocked. It never envisioned the possibility that a series of happenings, unforeseen even by a genius, might bring a halt to technological progress. It never admitted the possibility of catastrophe. For these reasons Sorel rejected the Enlightenment view of history. It rested on a philosophy that 'derived its immediate strength from its abstract criticism of society. When concretized it is seen to be a mass of opinions suitable to a class of professionals with growing class ambitions, removed from production.'[2] The force of Sorel's critique is but slightly mitigated by its vituperative quality. He was able to perceive that Enlightenment thought has a philosophy of history which is sentimental no less than rationalistic.[3]

A distinction has to be made between Sorel's critique of the illusions attending past theories of progress and the total denial of the possibility of progress as such. Sorel no more denied the reality of progress than Marx believed that the utopian content of early socialism was empty. Although Sorel's critique of the theory of progress is made with an eye to the past, his regard for Christian asceticism was more a search for an alternative basis of rational action, than a belief in the adequacy of Catholicism.[4]

Sorel claimed that his view represented a shift from ideals and fantasies which improperly assert historical sanction, to ideals and phantasms as simply stimuli to social action. Sorel's pragmatic ap-

---

[1] *Les illusions du progrès*, pp. 50–1.   [2] *Ibid.*, pp. 82–83.

[3] For a similar recent assessment of the doctrine of progress, see Georges Friedmann, 'Le Progrès: Dignité ou Déchéance, Liberté ou Servitude,' in *Frankfurter Beiträge zur Soziologie* (Frankfurt am/Main, 1955) Ed. I, pp. 279–92.

[4] *Réflexions sur la violence*, pp. 121–2 (107).

proach to history is satisfactory to a point because it does not assume imperial dominion over the entire realm of learning. Its inherent pluralism makes possible the acceptance of the vicissitudes of human events without developing a vast ideology to disguise such vicissitudes.[1] Yet real historical progress does exist, even though it assumes forms different from those charted by revolutionists. The basis of action are just these myths of the revolutionary thinkers. It is clear to Sorel that history is made by men fervent in their discontent with the present, rather than those intent on discovering the pre-determinate paths of history.[2]

Sorel's defence of history as myth is not an attempt to deny the operations of objective laws in human society. Rather, it represents a denial that such laws can be known with respect to future events. Sorel is not denying the reality of either physical or social laws, only the mechanistic idea that the social can be deduced from the physical. This belief in historical regularity emerges in Sorel's critique of the idea of national pride and proletarian patriotism. The attachment workers have in the nation, the class, or in the labour process itself, is not a voluntary decision, but a 'choice imposed by external conditions, and not freely made for reasons drawn from the nature of things. The character of historical necessity gives to the existing anti-patriotic movement a strength which it would be useless to dissimulate by means of sophistries.'[3]

Historical necessity can in no sense be employed as a legitimate reason for action. Empirical history is thus for Sorel an existential fact with no directive value, no more of a guide to action than physics or any of the biological sciences. Since action was integral to Sorel's entire edifice, supposed limitations of empirical history served as a saction for developing a normative basis for social action.

With all due consideration given to the qualifications and clarifications Sorel offered in developing a theory of the relation of action to history, several major weaknesses are evident in his standpoint. The fact that history has limitations does not necessarily sanctify acting on the basis of myths. The awareness of actual limits to historical perception may serve to expand our grasp of the potentialities and alternatives in given situations. The compulsion to act is no indication that men must always act on the basis of false consciousness or immediate wants. Action may, by virtue of facing its limits,

---

[1] *De l'utilité du pragmatisme*, pp. 188–9.   [2] *Ibid.*, pp. 190–2.
[3] *Réflexions sur la violence*, p. 165 (135).

be more realistic, more assured of reaching proximate historical goals.

Real knowledge, an estimate of both the conditions and consequences of a particular enterprise, is not only possible, but may well turn out to be the basis of successful action. Nor must it be inferred with Sorel that such action is always opportunistically motivated and insincere. The convictions with which one undertakes social action can be just as firm if based on scientific evidence or available sociological information as action generated by purely emotional attachments to myths. It is not dogmatism to assert that advocates of action based on rational understanding have a distinct advantage over those who act only on myths, for they can understand both the myths and the motivations caused by other factors. The great difficulty for the myth-maker is that, like his followers, he is bound to the myth *ex cathedra*. The great strength of the myth-breaker is in his ability to show that a course of action can more cogently be undertaken in consequence of empirical understanding. Sorel misunderstood his antagonism for the advocate of reason. He failed to distinguish between rationalism as a doctrine and the man of reason who seeks to understand all layers of belief and action. Since Sorel was no less a man of reason than any other scientist in search of truth, he was forced into the untenable position of denying in theory what he affirmed in practice—the ability to study irrationality in a scientific way.

Implicit in Sorel's dualism of empirical and metaphysical history is the idea that action undertaken on behalf of a universal and admittedly unattainable goal is more forceful and encompassing than action taken with limited but realizable aims. This idealistic notion emerges most forcefully when Sorel writes about great events such as the French Revolution. One might imagine, from what he says, that the Revolution was fought to prove that men are good, virtuous and reasonable as the *philosophes* maintained. The customary reasons for the Revolution, peasant impoverishment, bourgeois attempts at political emancipation from a moribund aristocracy, and the general decline within the aristocratic State and ideology, are not dealt with. Sorel's critique of Enlightenment and Jacobinism proceeds from an inversion of facts and ideas. In consequence, he sheds more light on his own contempt for the rational principles of the Revolution, than on the actual character of the various stages of the Revolution.[1] New

[1] James H. Meisel has made a careful observation that as early as 1889, in *Le procès de Socrate*, Sorel had the French Revolution in mind when he criticized

ideals and concepts, different in substance and appeal from those of the established social order, energize society only when social conditions make such intellectual reform necessary. To assume that an adequate theory of history or sociology cannot guarantee action is to make the unwarranted inference that no functional relation of ideas to action is possible in human affairs. Sorel's theory of ideas, in its desperate attempt to avoid ideological traps, succeeds at the cost of ignoring material conditions and relations.

Precisely because Sorel could not find anything to criticize in the mechanism of capitalist productive relations, except to argue that reform socialism could only retard the further evolution of this mechanism, he was unable to locate an empirical cause for the radical reconstruction of society. Subjective history was unable to appreciate the degree to which the response to pleadings of myth-makers and prophets is simply a consequence of existing inherited evils and not of prophecy.

In sum, although the real history of mankind gives no sanction to violence, it does explain why and under what conditions violence is possible. The limits of real history are no more a sanction for abstract mythologies than the limits of physics prove the reality of divine providence. He disdains the Enlightenment precisely because it was disinclined to point the way to action on the basis of any method other than science. But the Enlightenment was responsible for a supreme achievement. It showed men how to live rationally and radically without the assistance of either divine or social myths. Whatever corruption took place in later ages does not detract from this.

Sorel makes much of the false notions in defence of which actions are undertaken. But the false consciousness of revolutionaries is hardly their private sin. The ideas of revolutionary thinkers are, after all, more often 'right' than 'wrong,' if such terminology is to be employed. The assumption that the history of political theory is a series of brilliant but wrong guesses that provoked action rather than amelioration of existing conditions, is itself something of a myth. Reformers and revolutionists have sketched much of what became a reality perhaps centuries later. The free society has come to tolerate their reformers and visionaries precisely because the entire range of official and orthodox learning might be wrong.

'those famous dialecticians' for the ruin of the city and the popular antagonism towards its oligarchic leaders. For Meisel's observations on Sorel's approach toward the French Revolution see *The Genesis of Georges Sorel*, pp. 55–6.

To endow radical political philosophies with speculative content alone is to miss the point of popular response to radical appeals. They rely precisely on the degree to which radical solutions seem dictated by social conflicts. In several fundamental ways, therefore, Sorel understood neither the sources of human action nor the directive value of historical knowledge. The *apriori* certification of the theory of violence is due to Sorel's unwillingness to admit that violence is neither the only source of historical movement, nor necessarily that form of change sanctioned by empirical history.

4. History and Histrionics: The Role of Violence

We have seen that the social agent for Sorel is mythological history. Empirical disciplines simply record past progress, and by their nature cannot examine the mechanisms for changing things now. History becomes the transformation of past facts into present values. This is Croce's thesis, and it differs markedly from the French Enlightenment notion of abstract right based on objective laws. Sorel insisted that the lack of concreteness in such a theory of history is intrinsic to its rationalist presumptions, its inability to deal in 'particular terms alone; the only terms capable of evoking images that one can genuinely express without deception or self-deception.'[1] The translation of this sensuous truth involves action; and the motor-force of such action is violence.[2] The critique of Enlightenment rationalism reached its fruit in the doctrine of class violence.

Sorel drew extreme implications from the pragmatic open universe. Although American experience inhibited these implications, pragmatic doctrine offered no theoretical limits to prevent European irrational radicalism from working them out. The relevant tenets of pragmatism claimed that truth is related primarily to belief and not to cognition, that science offers instrumental values and not description, that an action-based social psychology gets things done while rationalist psychology only stimulates a new scholasticism. They indicated to Sorel that an instinctualist-pragmatic theory was an effective way of restoring optimism to a world which had lost its faith in pure reason and objective law. Pragmatism became the theoretical pillar of proletarian violence.

[1] *Les illusions du progrès* (first edition), p. 52.
[2] *Réflexions sur la violence*, p. 99 (93).

In the Sorelian system, violence tests the virility of people, classes and nations. The contempt in which he held the bourgeoisie of France bore little resemblance to the traditional socialist critique of the immorality of the wage system. The reverse is more nearly the truth. It was the lack of barbarism, the absence of significant appeals to violence, that Sorel considered the crisis in the bourgeois world. The bourgeoisie is castigated for accepting 'the ideology of a timorous humanitarian middle class professing to have freed its thought from the conditions of its existence.' Their pacifist ideal is 'grafted on the degeneration of the capitalist system while the race of bold captains who made the greatness of modern industry disappears to make way for an ultra-civilized aristocracy which asks to be allowed to live in peace.'[1]

Instead of pursuing the primordial characteristics of their class inheritance—tenacity, boldness and violence—the modern bourgeoisie has revealed its decadence by emulating theories of its predecessors, an effete aristocracy. Pacificism, reasonableness and compromise are the marks of contemporary middle class reformers in much the same way as they were characteristic of aristocratic reformers of the eighteenth century.[2] The upshot of this bourgeois mimesis is that, far from forestalling social disintegration, the rationalist illusion only serves to accelerate the liquidation of the bourgeoisie as a functional class. Thus pacificism is a symbol of decadence while violence is the supreme symbol of virility. This is the characteristic dualism of decaying capitalism from which Sorel anticipates a socialist synthesis.

The extension of political democracy, which most Marxists have conceded to be the major achievement of capitalist government, is considered by Sorel its ultimate weakness. With its 'return to an ideal of conservative mediocrity,' justified as democratic by 'the preachers of ethics and sociology,' any thought of the continued growth of capitalism has passed. By adopting the humanistic code, the middle classes ensure their defeat, and upset the balance of historical *ricorso*. 'An arbitrary and irrational element is introduced, and the future of the world becomes completely indeterminate.'[3] Progress of a predictable type depends on the vigorous pursuit of class interests. Any

[1] *Réflexions sur la violence*, p. 109 (99).

[2] *Les illusions du progrès* (first edition), p. 117.

[3] *Réflexions sur la violence*, pp. 115–16 (103–4). Note that Sorel here makes the effete code of humanism an *irrational* and yet negative element in that it introduces capriciousness into the formerly consistent class struggle—a strange criticism for a philosopher of social contingency to make.

efforts to vitiate such interests, by whatever class, compromise men and complicate the historical situation.

Such irrational elements are always present in history. Hence Sorel must conclude that history is to be studied psychologically. If only an idealized violence could validate historical predictions, it is evident that subjective distortions rather than objective laws govern the workings of human history. Sorel's theory of permanent revolution is a vision of the continuing moral purification of society, bringing history into line with morality. It is a position which rejects the assumptions of materialism in favour of pragmatism.

His deep concern with the philosophy of history notwithstanding, Sorel's wish to promote determinism in historical studies is second to his greater hope of promoting violence as the sole cleansing agent of human action. His thinking is dominated by the cathartic role of action. The equation of class violence with socio-economic virility leads Sorel into some very dark intellectual quarters. Proletarian violence awakens a creative response in the middle class, restoring the hard and fast separation of classes and a sense of the historical destinies of these two contenders. 'Everything may be saved, if the proletariat by their use of violence, manage to re-establish the division into classes, and so to restore to the middle class something of its former energy; that is the great aim toward which the whole thought of men—who are not hypnotized by the event of the day, but who think of the conditions of tomorrow—must be directed. Proletarian violence, carried on as a pure and simple manifestation of the sentiment of the class war, appears thus as a very fine and very heroic thing; it is at the service of the immemorial interests of civilization; it is not perhaps the most appropriate method of obtaining immediate material advantages, but it may save the world from barbarism.'[1]

The eccentricity of this position inheres in the belief that class conflict is waged by labourers not so as to achieve a greater portion of human pleasures through economic security, but for the purpose of maintaining the virility of those economic forces which deprive labourers of this very security and happiness. To assume that men fight to preserve the strength of what they are resisting is a logic that surpasses even sublime wisdom. Underlying Sorel's view is an instinctual psychology which declares the battle to be the thing. It is James' 'fighting instincts,' Nietzsche's 'warrior spirit' and Bergson's 'intuitive urge to battle' given a class-conscious coat of armour. The

[1] *Réflexions sur la violence*, pp. 130–1 (113).

position rests on a theory of human nature as aggressive, and a theory of society as regressive.

Sorel always manages to turn Marx inside out. His fear about the labour process is not that further technological developments under a capitalist economy will displace large numbers of producers, but that such basic material improvement will soften the workers, resulting in a catastrophic spiritual decline.[1] Civilization, as a consequence of its own material achievements, would ensure a halt to further progress in the social relations among men.[2]

The flavour of Sorel's psychology emerges most clearly in his concern with mediocrity. In the political arena, mediocrity reflects itself in the 'intermingling' of classes, 'in the democratic marsh.' It is, however, in the realm of individual psychology that this mediocrity is said to have its most serious effects, for Sorel's theory of historical evolution rests upon a concept of individual creativity. Those who lead a *Heldenleben* are the singular bearers of progress. He contends that the widespread advocacy of gradualism as a guarantee of socio-economic development rests on a fear of the apocalyptic path of history; a fear reflecting an inability to move beyond mediocrity.[3]

Platonic élitism rather than Marxian egalitarianism was the chief instrument urging Sorel to seek salvation in the producers. The ideology of Enlightenment, rooted as it was in the conditions of life of royal leisure, fostered a philosophic justification of mediocrity common to all non-productive and commodity consuming social classes.[4] Only the energies involved in the productive processes and its human agents could alone recreate the conditions of the heroic life. Like Bernard Shaw's *Major Barbara*, neither piety nor professorial pundits could overthrow the kingdom of mediocrity and hypocrisy. Only production, a connection to the sources of industrial life giving energy, can achieve such a monumental psychological transformation.

Sorel envisioned the proletariat as the human battering ram for overcoming the taboos and repressed longings inherited from the bourgeoisie. If the middle classes were what they pretend to be, the bearers of civilization, then the producing classes carried this civilization to its negation—to concrete freedom. The lower classes recreate the conditions of freedom by recalling the primordial, yet sublime,

---

[1] *Les illusions du progrès* (first edition), p. 277.
[2] *Matériaux d'une théorie du prolétariat*, p. 137.
[3] *Les illusions du progrès* (first edition), pp. 41–2.
[4] *Ibid.*, p. 78.

drives of pre-civilization, 'when all is instinct, creative and poetical in society.'[1] The overthrow of inhibition, of culturally conditioned fears and taboos, coupled with the directed release of instinctual energy, would be the source of proletarian revolt.

Like Le Bon, he envisions the moment of revolution as a phenomenon made possible by the coalescence of psychological factors. Revolution is the point at which individual psychology connects itself to universal history. Because of this, the study of objective factors alone can never yield a knowledge of when or how revolutionary transformations take place. In like manner, a purely subjective analysis is unable to cope with reasons why men choose one moment and not another to revolt and separate themselves from everyday prosaic existence.

Sorel's promulgation of proletarian violence represents more than a political tactic, or a messianic sense of destiny. It was a response to what he felt to be the major inadequacy of Marxian sociology: its failure to describe the subjective prerequisites of political action. His was an attempt to understand the story of human history at a new level. Like Machiavelli, Vico and Croce, what concerned Sorel most was the machinery of rule and revolution, rather than the objective economic causes. This primacy of the subjective in Sorel's system was largely responsible for his warm reception in Italy. The predominant theme of Italian political realism had always been the psychological power factors in politics and history.

Neither the refined rationalism of the eighteenth century *philosophes* nor the political liberalism of nineteenth century British empiricism, was considered by Sorel to be responsive to the irrational elements in political motivation. Sorel overlooked the fact that this was also the case for most varieties of continental and English conservative doctrines. The rationalist prejudice was thus shared in by the most diverse schools of thought. With the stark exception of the Italian political realists, socialism, liberalism and conservatism, showed a similar reticence to examine psychological motives in political action and in sociological theory.

The emphasis on a subjective philosophy of history is responsible for Sorel's perspective on the economic conflicts of past ages. They are viewed in symbolic, dramatic terms, rather than as valuable in themselves. The specific causes and consequences of a given conflict of economic interests was deemed of far less importance than the fact

[1] *Matériaux d'une théorie du prolétariat*, pp. 66-7.

I

that economic conflicts do exist. The struggle of classes formed the real content for Sorel; the resolution of class antagonisms was viewed as a temporary and transient form. However, even this real content, the struggle itself, is basically a psychological phenomenon. The historic resolution of antagonisms is ultimately determined by the psychological equipment with which the contending economic forces enter the fray.

Violence in Sorel's scheme is not an accidental aspect of social existence, an agency for eliciting changes. Violence forms the warp and woof of social structure. Violence is so central an agency in human affairs that every attempt to eradicate it only produces opposite results. 'Ever since social democracy has become the centre of government policy it has inculcated the adoption of pacific tendencies in worker–management relations—it has sought to modify bourgeois violence. But the contrary end has been achieved—economic antagonism and class violence have become sharper.'[1]

One task of revolutionary socialism therefore is to avoid the platitudes of Enlightenment and Utopia and to oppose the belief that revolutionary results can be registered without revolutionary violence. The revolutionary stance must 'realize in practice that which is actually true in Marxism; that concrete power is superior to all formulas—that the class struggle is the alpha and omega of socialism —that this class struggle is not a sociological concept used by intellectuals, but an ideological aspect of the social war, carried on by the proletariat against the entire citadel of industry. The syndicate is the instrument of the social war.'[2] The drama of class war is exceeded only by the purifying impact it has on the political arena. At times it is doubtful that for Sorel it was exceeded even by this.

Yet Sorel realized that drama turns to melodrama and then to disbelief if not linked to an objective anchor. He insisted that it is the fact of violence rather than preference for it that determines the pathways revolution must tread. Violence, precisely because it is disguised by a hypocritical bourgeoisie joined by an equally hypocritical reform socialist movement, is oftentimes not recognized by the masses. The task of recognition is buried deeper still by the ideological posture that violence which is covert and indirect is not violence at all. Coercion always assumes both forms: covert and overt, direct and indirect. Of the two, Sorel clearly indicates a preference for coer-

---

[1] *Insegnamenti sociali della economia contemporanea*, p. 343.
[2] *Matériaux d'une théorie du prolétariat*, p. 67.

cion that is straightforward. 'I have a horror of any measure which strikes the vanquished under a judicial disguise. War, carried out in broad daylight, without hypocritical attenuation, for the purpose of ruining an irreconcilable enemy, excludes all the abominations which dishonoured the middle class revolution of the eighteenth century. Social war by making an appeal to the honour which develops so naturally in all organized armies, can eliminate those evil feelings against which morality would remain powerless. If this were the only reason we had for attributing a high civilizing value to revolutionary syndicalism, this reason alone would, it seems to me, be decisive in favour of the apologists for violence.'[1] The choice before us, as Sorel sees it, is not between violence and pacifism but between types of violence. And sublimity, it would seem, demands that violence take its most integral form: open, shameless and defiant.

Sorel was captivated by the legendary Homeric conception of war to such an extent that even modern conflict is made to appear as a logical extension of good manners and dignified breeding. The ghastly features of scientific warfare were, it is true, far from reaching the refined stage of our atomic epoch, but nonetheless the contours of future warfare were clearly etched, even at the turn of the century. Explorations in chemical warfare, aerial bombardments, mechanized battalions were quite well known fifty years ago. Yet Sorel preferred to think in terms of the Greek myths. 'Everything in war is carried out without hatred and without the spirit of revenge.'[2] The sacrifices that war entails at both individual and institutional levels were justified by its cleansing effect on the body politic in general.

The force of this mock heroic approach to violence has still not been spent. The *fin de siècle* heroes of revolt somehow found their suffering ameliorated in the glories of warfare. Social alienation ceased with the call to arms. Sorel's relative inactivity during the war period signified an unresolved dilemma in his mind: should a wrong war be supported for the right reasons?

The unreality of Sorel's moralism in relation to the value of peace stemmed in part from a failure to appreciate the causal and factual elements in any ethical edifice. An ethic with limited ends must be defended no less than an absolutist morality. That it is tentative and subject to constant modification does not necessarily make it weaker. In the light of thermonuclear weapons, the archaic nature of the Sorelian position becomes manifest. For if war is no longer a matter

[1] *Réflexions sur la violence*, p. 435 (302).   [2] *Ibid.*, p. 161 (132).

123

of military personnel fighting according to rules of international law, but a matter of the survival of civilization itself, an ethic which can take this new factor into account must be judged far more potent than one which insists on repeating the legends of late romanticism in philosophy. When the idea of peace is placed in the broad context of human evolution, the dogmatism of Sorel's fixed moral system can be avoided. The desire for peace in a military context is not just a maudlin sentiment, it requires the kind of heroism Sorel attributed only to the warrior.[1]

Sorel differed from Nietzsche in that he had only a limited regard for violence between nations. The shortcoming of international conflicts is that they generally result in a compromise, a negation of the ends of violence, an incomplete victory. The idea of *Pax Romana* burned deep in Sorel's soul. The ability to carry on consistent and organized violence belongs only to that class which is not suffering from the utilitarian malady of mediocrity. In that class alone resides the will for 'the complete destruction of its adversaries.'[2] Forms of violence are determined by the historic functions of classes. For feudal barons, aristocrats, merchants and petty bourgeois, violence centres on who shall control State authority. But since in order to grow, the producers must abolish State authority and its power apparatus, the gravitational pull of proletarian violence takes the form of the general strike.

The myth of the general strike, a myth not of the strike itself but of the anticipated results of the strike, is the supreme weapon of labourers because it places the class conflict in the forefront of social life and civil administration. 'The idea of the general strike has such power behind it that it drags into the revolutionary track everything it touches. In virtue of this idea, socialism remains ever young; all attempts made to bring about social peace seem childish; desertions of comrades into the ranks of the middle class, far from discouraging the masses, only excite them still more to rebellion; in a word, the line of cleavage is never in danger of disappearing.'[3]

Aside from its immediate cathartic effects, proletarian violence has a two-fold consequence of the greatest importance. It is instrumental in the creation and development of a healthy political organism out-

[1] Cf. Irving L. Horowitz, *The Idea of War and Peace in Contemporary Philosophy* (New York, 1957), p. 49.
[2] *Matériaux d'une théorie du prolétariat*, p. 68.
[3] *Réflexions sur la violence*, p. 193 (152).

side the framework of the middle class State, and at the same time it acts as a decisive influence in obtaining social legislation favourable to the development of the proletariat.[1] The consequences of revolution are genuine reforms. The consequences of reformism are only false ideologies which are calculated to weaken the moral fibre of the workers. What these revolutionary reforms will be is indeterminate. All that can be said about revolutions is that they usually produce progress. The mythological element becomes transformed into utopianism when *apriori* assessments are made concerning the precise course of this progress. Of one thing Sorel is nevertheless certain. Without violence all talk about historical progress is utopian chatter, better left in the vocabulary of parliamentary ideologues.

Sorel's study of violence presents us with the paradox of socialism. On the one hand, violence is considered the characteristic of those uncorrupted by democracy and industrial civilization, the motor force by and through which primitive unconscious yearnings of producers fulfil themselves. But then such a view presents proletarian man as hardly a notch above pure animality. In consequence, Sorel became discomforted by the contrasting pictures of the proletarian as a virile animal and as a creative being who raises production to an aesthetic principle. Therefore, the proletariat in relation to production is considered to have the highest properties of consciousness and creativity. Can it be that these artists of production simply employ violence as a purely instinctual response to the complex, intertwined problems of modern society? Can a class which conducts its revolutions at the level of pure animality create the machinery for the maintenance and extensions of the highest fruits of civilized living? Then there are a different set of problems: can men who approach their work as excursions into the realm of artistic creation really be expected to repudiate sensitivity and sensibility, to storm barricades with mouths frothing and breathing fire, in the manner of a Bosch painting of Hades?

Sorel moved closer to the pragmatic view which construes progress as a consequence of the conscious choice and capacities of productive people. In his critique of Bergson's *Creative Evolution*, Sorel made clear his desire to move beyond a conception of history as something unconscious and oblivious to human wants. He wanted history to become the property of the thinking subject who is able to direct and control the forces of destiny—like Sorel's image of an American

[1] *Matériaux d'une théorie du prolétariat*, p. 132.

125

pioneer or politician.[1] That Bergson was unprepared to make a similar distinction, and therefore left the boundaries of history to the stream of consciousness, separated Bergson's metaphysics from a revolutionary standpoint.[2]

On whatever peg Sorel placed his theories, it tottered under the weight. The dual outcome of Sorelian syndicalism, its movement toward fascism and bolshevism, is a consequence of the unresolved polarities in his vision. The collapse of syndicalism as an organized political force, its movement toward authoritarian extremes of the political spectrum, was the inevitable consequence of the contradictory aims and ambitions of revolutionary élites on one side and revolutionary producers on the other. Élitist revolutions from above manipulate the herd impulses of the masses; they are bound to be different in achievements and consequences from spontaneous social revolution from below.

It was in the area of psychology rather than morals that Sorel made his ultimate attempt to resolve the dualism represented by an objective political sociology and a subjective philosophy of history. The fruitfulness of this effort does not lie in his ability to achieve a positive synthesis of history and politics, for such a resolution eluded him. What he did achieve was to take the first step in framing a theory of politics which insisted on the centrality of *irrational* human impulses and false ideologies in the determination of the social relations of men. In this sense, he was a forerunner of the sociology of knowledge.

[1] *De l'utilité du pragmatisme*, pp. 336–7.
[2] *Ibid.*, pp. 381–4.

V

THE PSYCHOLOGY OF ACTION

'*Our deepest sickness is in being divided, troubled by a thousand individual wills, by a thousand individual imaginations. We are crushed, we have no knowledge of our common aim, of our resources, of our centre.*'
Maurice Barrès, LES DÉRACINÉS.

SORELIAN thought moves inexorably from objective factors in the social structure to the influence of private and subjective elements at work in the inter-play of politics and economics. Whatever its consequences, psychological factors have become a major theme with variation in contemporary intellectual life. There has been a growth of consumption theories in economics, motivational and propaganda research in sociology, instrumentalist and atomistic epistemologies, operationalist theories of science, inter-personal psychoanalysis and non-objective art forms. Our vision of the world has gone from one extreme to another: from a mechanical universe that has no place for men to an anthropocentric frame of reference with little regard for the mechanical universe.

The peculiar interest in Sorel from the standpoint of contemporary theoretical issues stems from his contribution to the furtherance of that charged conception, the anthropocentric universe. Specifically, we must distinguish between his philosophy of unreason and his realistic political sociology. The task might be simpler, neater, if

Sorel merely employed the vocabulary of realism, or only used irrationalism as an eccentric pose. But neither of these premises are correct. Sorel strove mightily to be a rational sociologist of the unconscious, in much the same way as Freud was a rational psychologist of the unconscious. He became so completely captivated in the capricious way men appear to behave, he was unable to stand apart and separate the strands of determined behaviour from determining behaviour. Sorel's intellectual career demonstrates that a man can be thoroughly rational in criticism of institutions and ideas he disapproves of, and yet fall prey to self-deception and irrationality in the face of the greater task of constructing workable social and political alternatives.

The charge of anti-intellectualism, like the claim of irrationality, helps avoid rather than solve the paradoxes present in Sorel's thought. It is quite true that granting primacy to subjective and irrational factors tends to limit the uses one can make of causalist and determinist explanations of social events. Nevertheless, the study of just these subjective features in behaviour have become a central undertaking of the social sciences. A deterministic logic tends to ignore these critical, negative functions of scientific studies. It is the task of sociological scholarship to note the forces and factors which produce indeterminism in science, subjectivity in epistemology, or eclecticism in methodology; not to assume these poses as axiomatically given and proceed to the more technical questions.

The function of the social scientist and the philosopher is both critical and creative. To achieve the highest results they must normally exist together, in fused inter-dependence. Given this definition of the social scientist, it might be said that Sorel's critical and negative attitude was so overwhelming that he was not in a position to contribute positively to either philosophy or political sociology. The fragmentary character of Sorel's negative system has caused one critic to say that 'like a second-rate expressionist painter, Sorel combines all the shades of feeling but never succeeds in producing an integrated picture.'[1]

But this is precisely the sort of charge that would have to be levelled against the entire domain of historical sociologies and pragmatic philosophies. It is clear that they are infused with an overweening critical spirit. Efforts at fresh creation, of new generalizations in the

[1] Valeriu Marcu, *Manner und Machte der Gegenwart* (translated as *Men and Forces of our Time*) (New York, 1931), p. 242.

128

social sciences, are more often than not viewed as throw-backs to a past synthetic age. We live off the inheritance of past centuries of political realism: the legacy of Plato, Machiavelli, Vico, Rousseau and Marx remains very much the working tools of the present. It was a chief virtue of Sorel's political sociology that it started from the premise that a new synthesis is not possible without an honest reckoning of these great men, without understanding that the first stage in creating a modern political realism is criticism. Actual problems, juridical issues and political theories cannot just be drowned in the swift stream of history. The easy solution was the dangerous solution.[1] It was Sorel's vice that he never got beyond this first critical stage. Be that as it may, his psychological interpretation of politics remains a cornerstone of contemporary political sociology.

1. Political Mythology and the Higher Truths

Sorel wrote and lived in an age which was beginning to take cognisance of its compulsive, neurotic basis of action and forms of domination. Single-mindedness and a general overall rational purpose were absent in both the political life and productive systems of western Europe. It began to be questioned whether such rationality had ever been a political or economic fact. Mediocrity in politics, stagnation in the economy sought ideological relief in the inherited democratic credo. This ideological justification of mediocrity caused Sorel his most acute despair. He was joined in this by the leading thinkers of the continent. Freud came on to note that 'the neurotic is above all inhibited in his actions; with him the thought is a complete substitute for the deed.' The psychology of the primitive is the very reverse. Primitive virility which stemmed from the fact that 'primitive man is not inhibited, the thought is directly converted into the deed, the deed is for him, so to speak, rather a substitute for the thought.'[2] Extended by Sorel, this notion presented men with an alternative: either be irrational and act, or be rational and confess to mediocrity.

Sorel was anti-rationalist in much the way Rousseau was. Both feared the consequence of a society which, in its hypocrisy and

---

[1] 'Étude sur Vico,' *Le Devenir Social*, pp. 807–9. This early essay reveals the exactness with which Sorel took up problems in the history of political philosophy, and is one of his earliest efforts at a summary of his position *vis-à-vis* Vico and Marx.

[2] Sigmund Freud, *Totem and Taboo*, in *The Basic Writings of Freud* (New York, 1938), p. 930.

artificiality, had the effect of changing men from doers into knowers, and where this was not possible, in keeping head and hand firmly separated in the economic life. 'Socialist man' for Sorel was a healthy and viable hero: the prototype of the authoritarian personality with a cause, for whom no barrier is insurmountable. Against this, liberal capitalist society could only promote as a hero the happily alienated neurotic, inhabiting a private world in which material acquisition replaces ideals as the controlling principle of measurement. In this way Sorel's predominantly critical spirit grappled with the question of creativity. Creativity in political life would no longer be the preserve of ideologists of the State, but the preserve of proletarian men of action. Like the *Bourses*, creativity in politics would be a fact of social life and a common property of producing classes, and no longer the dreams of speculative metaphysics or the postulate of pseudo-scientific rationalism.

Sorel's vision focused on formulating a general theory of social psychology. His concern was with human action, its basis in life and the forms it took. Proletarian violence was an aspect and outgrowth of a general theory of motivation. Men do not act to preserve a stake in the Nation-State or any other political institute from which they are alienated and toward which they feel spiritually opposed. Nor is action a consequence of either transcendental predeterminism or of historical determinism. Nonetheless, the fact is that men do act. Historicism for Sorel is the false extension of scholastic logic and natural science into historical sociology. The psychological basis of the irrational compulsion to act thus formed the required synthetic stage in Sorel's *Weltanschauung*.

Galvanizing men into action is not a product of discourse, nor of considered analysis. It is the outcome of an appeal to imagination and intuition, which dramatizes the consequences of an act rather than offers a reasoned prediction of those consequences. This is what converts ordinary men into extraordinary practitioners of the art of violence and class war. Men must be nourished on the strength of kinship and community feeling: on the ability to act as a collective unit. We have seen how Sorel agreed with Bergson that, like philosophy in general, the catastrophic conception of socialism should be an undivided whole.

To act as a whole, a single unifying element must be focused upon. It need not have an objectively primary content as such, but simply the quality of making men cohere in common endeavour. This is the pragmatic value of mythology. Such a binding element is the proletarian general strike, in which 'there is no longer any place for the reconciliation of contraries in the equivocations of the professors; everything is clearly mapped out, so that only one interpretation of socialism is possible.'[1] The demands of *fin de siècle* radicalism for an end to practical and intellectual anarchy were in this way faced directly by Sorel.

On principle any myth would do equally well if it produced corresponding revolutionary results. The conscious application of such a social psychology by fascism demonstrates the consequences of an instrumentalism tied to intuitionism. Without regard for the accuracy involved in appeals to stamp out Zionist plots, communist conspiracy, bourgeois cosmopolitanism, cultural imperialism, the workability of these appeals can hardly be denied. Applications of a theory of action based on the propagandistic imagination abound. For various types of societies, whatever objective motives are disguised and blurred in Sorel's theory of action, the fact is that mass action has with increasing intensity involved an appeal to irrational factors. As it has been put in a recent study of this phenomenon: 'The use of mass psychoanalysis to guide campaigns of persuasion has become the basis of a multimillion-dollar industry. Professional persuaders have seized upon it in their groping for more effective ways to sell us their wares—whether products, ideas, attitudes, candidates, goals, or states of mind.'[2]

Sorel's anticipation of propaganda as a stimulus to activity through a vivid projection of discontent, has become a fact of modern politics. The increase in the modes and range of communication made possible by our technology has made political mythology a widely disseminated commodity. The hope of the rational philosophers, that communication would be a handmaiden of popular education, has turned into something less than a bright hope. The scientific study of motivation has shaken political sociology to the core. The halcyon days when the social scientist assumed moral purpose as an end have faded into bland empirical descriptions of what men prefer and not whether their preferences are good or evil.

The control of State power automatically implies physical dominance; that is, control over military power, the civil service and the bureaucratic apparatus. In addition it now implies a firm right to

---

[1] *Réflexions sur la violence*, p. 173 (140).
[2] Vance Packard, *The Hidden Persuaders* (New York, 1957), p. 3.

mould the minds of men, according to specific needs of State. Because communications have become so central, the first targets of control in revolutionary struggles are telephone and telegraph centres and radio stations. For Sorel, such interest in communication is a consequence of the single most effective commodity distributed by the State—mythology. It is the intellectual cement of the nation, resting on the need to carry out State policy by whatever means are designated. Because the class war has become ideological at all times, and physical only at rare moments, revolutionary movements must engender the same respect, indeed a greater respect, for revolutionary myths than the State can for its myths.

Both the State and the forces of authority and violence are faced with the fact that the men of reason and scientific curiosity may turn into a hindrance. The truth is that on the basis of a logical ordering of facts alone, few would be willing to act decisively, either in defence of or in opposition to the State. Reichenbach has shown in a splendid allegory that for ordinary men the limits of logic become a central cause for inaction, rather than action. 'I shall know it for certain? I see your ironical smile. There is no certainty. The probability will be increased and my posit will have a higher rating. I can count on a greater percentage of correct results. That is all I can reach. I can't get away from making a posit. I want certainty, but all the logician has for me is the advice to make posits. There I am, the eternal Hamlet. What does it help me to ask the logician, if all he tells me is to make posits? His advice confirms my doubt rather than giving me the courage I need for my action. Logic is not made for me.'[1]

Action, courage in the face of destructiveness, involves a conditioned appeal to fantasy rather than a response to the reality principle. It is Freud's death-instinct rather than the pleasure principle that comes to govern practice in advanced societes. Sorel came close to such a Freudian formulation when he noted that 'experience shows that the *framing of a future, in some indeterminate time*, may, when it is done in a certain way, be very effective, and have very few inconveniences; this happens when the anticipations of the future take the form of those myths which enclose with them all the strongest inclinations of a people, of a party, or of a class, inclinations which recur to the mind with the insistence of instincts in all the circumstances of life; and which give an aspect of complete reality

[1] Hans Reichenbach, *The Rise of Scientific Philosophy* (Berkeley, 1951), p. 251.

to the hopes of immediate action by which, more easily than by any other method, men can reform their desires, passions and mental activity.'[1]

The need for mythology is a necessary adjunct of any theory of history which at one and the same time demands a clear-cut command to effective human action. Sorel seems to be saying that men will not act if such action involves violations of their real or imagined interests, or if such action is presented to the mass as a scientific or intellectual necessity. Logical perspectives may place the value of a proposed line of activity in a contextualist framework that would only reveal its inconsequential or limited possibilities. Sorel assumes that men who doubt the universal significance of a proposed act will justify passivity. The many failures of revolutionary efforts do indeed strengthen the tendency to disillusionment. Arguments for inaction are generally quite sound from a logical standpoint. Yet it is just this which shows the absurdity of logical reasoning in human affairs. For the logically rigorous pursuit of limited premises would mark the destruction of social revolutions, which is exactly what Sorel felt the bourgeois intellectual, with his 'little science of sociology,' was urging upon men.

Myth is needed to overcome the probabilistic world of scientific fact. Ideology, the conscious representation of class interests, is the basis of social practice. Their ability to stimulate activity is the supreme measure of the worth of ideologies. 'It must be admitted that the real developments of the Revolution did not in any way resemble the enchanting pictures which created the enthusiasm of its first adepts; but without those pictures would the Revolution have been victorious? Many Utopias were mixed up with the Revolutionary myth, because it had been formed by a society passionately fond of imaginative literature, full of confidence in "popular science," and very little acquainted with the economic history of the past. These Utopias came to nothing; but it may be asked whether the Revolution was not a much more profound transformation than those dreamed of by the people who in the eighteenth century had invented social Utopias.'[2] Even a cursory glance at the writings of the *philosophes* would show how profound an idea Sorel has developed.

The differences between the illusions of thinkers and the reality unfolded in revolutions is a phenomenon not confined to the French

[1] *Réflexions sur la violence*, p. 177 (142).   [2] *Ibid.*, pp. 178–79 (143).

Revolution. Freund has indicated that the source of Sorel's dual attachment to bolshevism and fascism, Lenin and Mussolini, stemmed from his faith in the power of revolution to transcend the theoretical statements of scientists and rationalists. The concentrated power of the revolutionary moment drowns the multitude of words and myriad of hypotheses into a higher truth of *einem Wort und einem Mythus*.[1] The development of psychoanalysis has tended to support Sorel's belief in mythology as both the initial condition of fresh scientific speculation and, no less, the limiting condition of science. When Freud wrote that 'it may perhaps seem to you as though our theories are a kind of mythology . . . But does not every science come in the end to a kind of mythology,' he merely confessed what Sorel had been asserting all along.[2]

Sorel indicates the very rationality which yields science prevents action on behalf of human freedom. The myth alone is the source of freedom, for it alone is the stimulant to action. Because of this, it is not to be judged literally, on scientific grounds, for the degree to which it makes accurate predictions. '*It is the myth in its entirety which is alone important*; its parts are only of interest in so far as they bring out the main ideas.'[3] Sorel's mistrust of science is not so much a mistrust for the accuracy of its statements, as it is a fear that such objective statements will be made over into a political doctrine of resignation. The superstitious respect that ordinary people have for science intensifies a distinction between doing and knowing that results in a drugged passivity.[4] The predictions of science always assume some sort of equilibrium. It is precisely this which Sorel feels is unrealistic and sentimental; for the myth is that instrument called into play to upset equilibriums.

Having established the functional role of myths, Sorel moves on to the main discussion: what kind of myth is best suited to socialism? In a number of ways, the answer he gave was dictated by his personal history. Long before Sorel discovered the utility of the *Communist Manifesto* in educating labouring class circles, he considered the *New Testament* as the most valuable, commonly understood, guide to mass action. The apocalyptic myth, the suddenness with which sweeping social changes are brought about, was the common ground

[1] Michael Freund, *Georges Sorel: der revolutionäre Konservativismus*, pp. 277–8, 267–8.
[2] Sigmund Freud, 'Why War,' *Collected Papers*, Vol. V, p. 283.
[3] *Réflexions sur la violence*, p. 180 (144).
[4] *Matériaux d'une théorie du prolétariat*, p. 90.

of Christ and Marx. The apocalypse, with its sublime faith in inevitable success, stands over science, the way action towers above discourse. Just as it is the centre of Christian radicalism, the apocalypse is the basis of socialist radicalism.[1] The myth need not contain a single fact which could come to pass. Its importance inheres in its ability to give organization to the vague projections which each person has to make about life. The myth is stronger than a fact; it is a belief.[2]

The will to believe makes possible great social upheavals. Cartesian rationalism, the steady questioning of assumptions, the doubt which even turns into self-doubt, is a hindrance to creation. The rationalist insistence on truth as a prologema to practice, aside from its epistemological untenability, creates the grounds for conservatism. Doubt, when raised to a philosophic first principle, undermines the intuitive certainty of men. And it is the feeling that we have a prevision of the future that feeds the instinct for change. In this fashion, Sorel sought to unite pragmatism to the messianic strain in socialist thought.[3] Whatever was on Sorel's recommended reading list for sound revolutionists: the *Gospel* according to John, the *Manifesto* according to Marx, *Evolution* according to Bergson, or *Pragmatism* according to James—the ends of action never shifted: 'the instruction of the people, to initiate them into the heroic life, to combat the deleterious tendencies of utilitarianism.'[4]

The religious zeal of Sorel was never really destroyed. The Enlightenment aroused his orthodox Catholic sentiments perhaps as much as his political beliefs. The bitterness he felt toward Enlightenment is not that of a detached political thinker of different philosophic persuasion, but of the engaged, religious zealot. Socialism constituted a substitute and palliative for attachment to an institutional religion. It possessed the same qualities of action and the same core of beliefs. Both socialism and Christianity centred on the day of reckoning and resurrection. While revolution and regeneration will

[1] Although secular interpretations of the Christian apocalypse for socialist ends is now rare, it still manages to find its way even into the work of orthodox Marxists. See John Lewis, 'Communism, The Heir to the Christian Tradition,' in *Marxism and the Open Mind* (London, 1957).

[2] Support for the Sorelian theory of myth has come from naturalists of psychoanalytic persuasion, who see in mythological projection an essential ingredient in intense human experience. See Lewis Feuer, 'Political Myths and Metaphysics,' in *Philosophy and Phenomenological Research*, Vol. XV (1955), pp. 332-50.

[3] *De l'utilité du pragmatisme*, pp. 210-11.

[4] *Contribution à l'étude profane de la Bible*, p. vii.

burst upon the world with a suddenness predicted by the early Christians, socialism shares with Christianity an inability to detail the precise changes in the world, and cares even less whether the qualities of the apocalyptic vision will be fulfilled in empirical history. Socialism is neither utopian vision nor scientific discipline. It contains elements of both but its core is the practice of the heroic life. It is basically 'a body of images capable of evoking instinctively all the sentiments which correspond to the different manifestations of the war undertaken by Socialism against modern society.'[1] Bergson's *connaissance parfaite* becomes in Sorel's hand *l'intuition du socialisme*. Political action emanates from the shadow world of the unconscious.

Traditional Platonic élitism, because of its intense rationalism, found no overt support in Sorel's philosophy. Sorel rejected Plato's view that the leaders of society know absolute truth while the masses lack such scientific insight. The distinction is rather between those people who can discover the psychological tone of the masses and are able to translate these feelings into action by means of the myth, and those who are not capable of rising above the banality of utilitarian wants or needs. Leaders are not made by either the quantity or quality of knowledge they possess, but in virtue of how many men they can captivate and galvanize by the projection of a novel myth. The leader is the charismatic myth-manipulator, the mass are myth-believers. The useful lie serves to direct men into action and at the same time creates the basis of leadership. The reversal of rationalism is completed by Sorel to the last detail. The aristocracy of knowledge is to be replaced by an aristocracy of the manipulators of myths. His is an élitism based neither on social status nor intellectual achievements, but on the ability to arouse and sustain the passions.

The maker of myths, it was discerned by Sorel, can thrive and enjoy leadership status among the masses, not in simple virtue of his crafty ability to fight his way to such position. The primitive urges to physical activity must have had a mental reflection in the producers' mind. Primitive man was awed by the individual possessing perception beyond the immediately necessary. Such a man, emerging so differentiated, possessed the secrets of nature. His social power amongst the group enhanced his individual character. The truth-seeking or truth-possessing personality grew to full importance as a magician, performer of rites, impassioned tribal spokesman. With the maturity of personality in a highly complicated social structure,

[1] *Réflexions sur la violence*, p. 182 (145).

truth-seeking became more difficult than ever as a means of understanding existence. The myth-believer searches out its hero-types
with an even greater ferocity than the ancients. The authoritarian
demand for the renunciation of the self, with its corresponding
establishment of the ruler as Patriarch or God-image, secures civilization against the instability and flux of the horizontal society. The
magician who will weave with golden thread his rainbow-coloured
illusions emerges from the desire of the mass to gain security through
obedience as much as from his own shrewd use of available means to
gain from the masses this respect and devotion.

The fearsome feature of a transvaluation of élitist values is that
despite its intellectual impotence, it has become a major feature in the
political life of advanced societies. This inversion of the basis of
motivation from the rational, deliberating conscience to the irrational
unconscious is, as Sorel grasped, a critical theme of modern political
life. The interaction of deception and self-deception, and the connection of political action to mass neurosis, has been clearly etched
in the annals of historical events. The appeal to 'vote with the heart'
or to 'think with the blood' is simply the application in practical
politics of this psychological conception of the mythical motivation
of human beings.

The myth of the general strike leads inevitably to socialism itself
as a myth: 'Le socialisme est necéssairement une chose trés obscure.'
Not only do the mysterious qualities of human nature urge men to
seek and sacrifice themselves on behalf of socialism, but the contours
of socialism is itself a supreme mystery. The economic future cannot
be rationally comprehended in advance of present levels of the
organization of production and technology.[1] Sorel is not offering a
plan for delineating the degree to which socio-economic development
can be anticipated. Neither is he concerned with admonishing the
wise to observe the national or regional peculiarities of socialism.
To be sure, Sorel would grant that the complex of institutions and
events should be given a firm contextual footing. He is, however,
arguing not as a counsel on behalf of scientific caution, but along
quite different lines.

Sorel is saying that the mystery is not in the concrete parts of a
socialist society, but in socialism *qua* socialism. Socialism has a
motivational and manipulative value only because of its ideals; its
economic and political qualities are necessarily left in a state of

---

[1] *Réflexions sur la violence*, p 217 (167).

indeterminism and amorphism. Traditional socialist ideas on the necessity for extending brotherhood and equality were discarded by Sorel as being utopian and effeminate. His disavowal of any broadly anchored political movement for socialism isolated him from intimate contact with the actual policies and practices of socialist and labour movements. This in turn separated Sorel from policy-making problems of socialists: he considered problems of strategy and tactics as a political parallel to *la tour d'ivoire des philosophes*. What is therefore left of socialism is a body of sentiments permeating the historical atmosphere and having as its major focus the proletarian strike.[1] Even with these limits, the myth is a higher value than socialism, than the goal sought, since 'sentiments have their value independently of the reality of the object which excites them.'[2]

In part at least, Sorel was a socialist because he knew of no other constructive way of releasing libidinal energies. The sublimation of all libidinal energies, and their transference to the passion and practice of socialism, is ultimately all that Sorel means when discussing the positive value of socialism. It was not only bourgeois production which Sorel admired, but equally bourgeois virtues. Prudence, thrift, efficiency, sexual repression, love of family were esteemed. Sublimity produces virility. The Christian ethic was to become the storehouse of proletarian virtues. The bourgeoisie was doomed, not only by its class practices and policies, but by the collapse of these virtues into licentiousness and mediocrity. Socialism was needed, not so much to create a new and different society, as to pull traditional civilization out of the moral fires consuming the bourgeoisie.

The sense of impending doom haunted western Europe in the early years of the twentieth century. If Marx's 'spectre' was viewed as little more than romantic homiletics by nineteenth century bourgeois theorists, it was not so viewed by the theorists of this century. Spengler's *Der Untergang des Abendlandes* was a climactic reply to those of the bourgeoisie who continued to believe that this was some sort of Panglossian world, where vice becomes virtue simply by thinking so, and where the spectre of revolution disappears in the annual tally of profits. Sorel's outlook was a challenge to the bourgeoisie, no less than a pleading on behalf of socialism. Virility had gone out of the capitalist world. Sorel fashioned a socialism that was to bring it back—even if it took the proletarian mass to do it.

---

[1] *Réflexions sur la violence*, p. 50 (60).
[2] *Procès de Socrate*, p. 120.

Spengler shrewdly sensed this element in Sorel, a socialist 'of higher quality and conservative ways of thinking.'[1] They shared a belief that while logical analysis indicated the decline of western civilization, the world did not move according to logical analysis.

The indeterminacy of Sorel's socialism, caused initially by a rejection of the use of science in historical studies, became cloudier with his search for psychological anchor-points. An ambivalent approach is taken toward social structure. Past societies are condemned insofar as they failed to maintain themselves in power. Socialism becomes a word describing that social structure which comes into being after the collapse of the bourgeois State. The social inadequacies of a commercial materialist spirit stems from its own failure of nerve, not from proletarian poverty. Socialism lacks positive features simply because one cannot describe a system which still is awaiting the final demise of capitalist polity and ideology.[2] Socialism becomes a myth, because the positive values attached to it by the proletariat under capitalism are merely responses to the pressures of industrial civilization and in no sense a scientific tabulation.

The mythological conception of socialism was, from a factual viewpoint, a failure. People interested in the myth lost interest in labour, and people concerned with the fates and fortunes of labour showed no interest in the value of the myth. This apathy extended even to Sorel, who in 1910 could 'renounce socialist literature' for the concentration of his thought on the more profound religious, philosophic and aesthetic problems of civilization.[3] What is strange is not that Sorel, 'the metaphysician of socialism,' should want to deepen his knowledge, but that such a process required a renunciation of participation in socialist affairs. If the theoretical pillar of the mythological approach to socialism can drift away from the practical currents, what can be expected of the less well informed proletarian *bete-machine*? Sorel notwithstanding, the fact of the legalization of socialism had a greater magnetism than the myth of the general strike.

Sorel's heirs point up the problems the master left unresolved with

[1] Oswald Spengler, *The Hour of Decision: Germany and World-Historical Evolution* (New York, 1934), p. 133.

[2] For a sympathetic outline of Sorel's substitution of a psychological for a historical criterion in estimating socialism, see Sammy Beracha, *Le marxisme après Marx* (Paris, 1937), pp. 176–9.

[3] Cf. Pierre Andreu, *Bergson et Sorel* (*Les études Bergsoniennes*), Vol. I, pp. 225–6; Vol. III, pp. 43–78.

a touching poignancy. In the 'thirties they denounced the popular front led by Léon Blum as a new form of statism. The war decade saw the same men, Jean Luchaire, Marcel Déat and the brilliant Bertrand de Jouvenel, support Vichyism and later national socialism. As a result, the anarchist-syndicalist movement has become a speck on the ointment of French literature and life. A prosaic note, indicative of old age, has now appeared: it studies the economics of countervailing power in place of class power, it calls for the further integration of the European community in place of fervent anti-nationalism, and it concerns itself with the immediate problems of security and welfare for labourers rather than with the sublime myths evoked by the proletarian strike.[1] In short, it has become *religieuse avec politesse.*

The chronic ailment of doctrine has driven the sturdier Sorelians toward the standardized poles of political activity and expression. Sorel's career itself offered anticipatory evidence that syndical socialism could not support the weight of the theoretical burdens imposed upon it. It was unable to provide a meaningful solution to the individual-authority antinomy. It fostered psychological attitudes that invariably produced ambiguous and paradoxical results in politics and philosophy. Sorel was unable to end the abuse (even in theory) of political power that syndical socialism was supposed to eliminate. As Michels predicted, and as Sorel confessed, the anarchist-syndicalists fell to fighting amongst themselves. The socialist man of the *Bourses* seemed only to grotesquely reproduce the psychological ills of bourgeois society.

2. Science and the Inhibition of Social Activity

We have seen how by degrees, socialism became transformed in Sorel's hands from a political theory into a social psychology. The features of socialist production were to be merely a quantitative extension of the process of industrialization initiated under capitalism.[2] It was in the sphere of values that the change-over from capitalism to socialism would be marked. Socialism was to establish the supremacy of the man of action, the leadership of sublime heroes and individual virility as a general characteristic of socialized man. This

[1] Cf. Francois Sellier, 'Objectifs du syndicalisme,' in *Esprit* (December, 1957) pp. 833–44.
[2] *Matériaux d'une théorie du prolétariat*, p. 70.

view is hardly novel, having theoretical roots which go back at least to Sparta. Sorel shared with a number of socialists the idea that continuous social revolution could alone bring the Spartan type into prominence.

The implications of the Spartan conception remained nebulous, for the most part the exclusive property of *literati*. Sorel himself died before observing the applications of this anti-Athenian mentality by German National socialism. Nonetheless, the broad outlines of the psychology encouraged by authoritarian systems can be clearly perceived in his writings. The problems involved in separating the instruments of social change from the goals sought are clearly revealed in an examination of the virtues praised in this Spartan-socialist psychology. With Sorel, action, heroism and virility, categories for bringing about change, became deified. They become transformed into ends-in-themselves, separated from either the worth or consequence of a given action. On the other hand, they can be joined to an alternative system. Any social movement which requires heroism and virility for the attainment of its ends can adopt the Spartan ideal. The Soviet image of Stakhanovism was of this sort.

The fetishizing of the urge to activity, far from liberating men from dreariness of ordinary existence, creates the primary conditions of anxiety. Lacking concrete, historically verifiable goals, psychic instincts turn on themselves, inhibit effective action and become psychologically and socially regressive. Conflict, violence and struggle become human forces that can only be sublimated and not eliminated. Once the passions of men become hypostatized into eternal verities, the only thing left to do is to present 'equivalents' to war. This is exactly what happened in the political philosophies of James and Santayana. For Sorel, the equivalent of industrial war is class war.[1]

In rigorously working out the implications and logic of instinctualist psychology, Sorel reveals a basic link between political ambitions and neurotic repression. This phase of his thought deserves scrutiny because it reveals the behavioural psychology that underlies this *moraliste*. His general theory of action has two principal features: the first distinguishes action situations from non-action, the second

---

[1] For an examination of how this psychological principle of sublimation through positive equivalents works in James and Santayana, see Irving L. Horowitz, *The Idea of War and Peace in Contemporary Philosophy*, pp. 87–8, 171–7.

relates action at the social level to illusion and myth. To clear the ground, Sorel has to show the impotence of science as an instrument of social prescription.

The vindictiveness with which Sorel criticizes a sociology that views action as 'a work of pure reason, manufactured by indoor scientists attempting to solve the social problem according to the rules of logic,' indicates his complete dedication to an instinctualist psychology. 'We do nothing great without the help of warmly coloured and clearly defined images, which absorb the whole of our attention.'[1] Even prior to his acquaintance with James' writings, Sorel adopted a thoroughly pragmatic view of science. That is to say, first he separates the principles of action from those of empirical discovery, and then makes the action situation a problem of belief and science a problem of instrumentality. Sorel offers strong evidence for the epistemic kinship of intuitionism and instrumentalism. For in both cases, the quest for certainty led to an absorption of truth by belief.

His attack on sociology took the form of a critique of its overweening mechanism, its aping of Newtonian and Darwinian conclusions; its inability to frame social laws. He further reproached sociology for being captivated by a crude, picture theory of the world, as if cognition reveals an orderly functioning society that makes prediction automatic. Sorel was very much abreast of developments in the natural sciences. His scientific background equipped him to study the work of Helmholtz and Poincaré in mathematical physics, Claude Bernard's studies in experimental medicine, Francois Benoit's work in the development of architectural styles, and Bernard Brunhes' empiricist critique of materialist theories of physics. Sorel was one of the first men to see the vast implications for political sociology of the view that the traditional optimism of the scientific attitude was misconceived.[2]

The work of Poincaré in particular did a great deal to reinforce Sorel's adoption of a conventionalist rather than a cognitive approach to scientific knowledge. He was deeply impressed with Poincaré's marshalling of evidence to indicate that between the calculation of probabilities and the facts themselves is a deep chasm.[3] As Poincaré

[1] *Réflexions sur la violence*, p. 218 (168).
[2] The most complete statement made by Sorel on the subject of the impact of natural science on social thought is 'L'expérience dans la physique moderne,' in *De l'utilité du pragmatisme*, pp. 288–356.
[3] *De l'utilité du pragmatisme*, p. 318.

put the problem: 'To undertake the calculation of any probability, and even for that calculation to have any meaning at all, we must admit, as a point of departure, an hypothesis or convention which has always something arbitrary about it. In the choice of this convention we can be guided only by the principle of sufficient reason.'[1] The further elucidation of this notion by Poincaré, that the evolution of scientific thought depends in large measure on accepting fundamental physical principles as 'articles of faith' or as 'simple elements,' or as 'criteria of convenience,' which reside in the models of scientists rather than inhere as properties of nature,[2] was instrumental in the formation of Sorel's thoughts on the grounds of social action.[3]

Sorel sought to locate in the growth of scientific probabalism and relativism an adequate test for social practice, a way to measure and stimulate the probabilities of action of one kind rather than another. Sorel felt quite within the Poincaré frame of reference when he asserts that 'science makes no claim to know the real nature of things.' It simply 'confines itself to discovering relations which can be utilized for practical ends.'[4] This rejection of an absolute locus of scientific discovery became an essential aspect of Sorel's effort to establish a theory of sociology that would not be chained to a verifiability principle.

The limits of scientific prediction have generated widespread speculation on the part of scientists themselves as to the prescriptive value of their enterprise. If a science of society is not itself a sufficient cause of human action, what then is? For Mach knowledge hinged on the principle of economy, for Poincaré scientific activities depended upon the aesthetic intrinsic to scientific reasoning, and for Whitehead science and human life both depended upon the qualitative distinction between fact and value. Sorel's position came closest to that of Whitehead. Sorel located prescription, not in scientific statements, but in the emotions generated by mythology. The myth

[1] Henri Poincaré, *Science and Hypothesis* (New York, 1952), p. 210.
[2] Henri Poincaré, *Science and Method* (New York, 1952), pp. 15–45, 284–8.
[3] Recent scholarship indicates that, unlike Sorel, Poincaré himself did not accept the doctrine of total conventionalism. Further, that conventionalism is a necessary consequence of Poincaré's position, or that it can perform socially revolutionary theoretical functions, has no less been the subject of intense doubt. See Adolf Grünbaum, 'Carnap's Views on the Foundations of Geometry'; and Robert S. Cohen, 'Dialectical Materialism and Carnap's Logical Empiricism,' in *The Philosophy of Rudolf Carnap* (*The Library of Living Philosophers*. Edited by P. A. Schilpp) (New York, 1961. Publication pending).
[4] *Réflexions sur la violence*, p. 220 (169).

could best release man from the bondage of either a mechanical or probabilistic world view. Scientific statements could not effectively be used to challenge such a position, since Sorel had it on the authority of the leading scientists of the age, that science was itself bound to arbitrary models, to myths.[1]

It is clear to Sorel that if science cannot inhibit the forms taken by social practice, neither is science in a position to promote practice. It is therefore necessary to move beyond the orbit of science, beyond the probabilism of calculus, and locate the mainsprings of action in non-rational behaviour.[2] The very limitations of science in prescribing rational actions turns out to be a blessing, since it assures the autonomy of the myth in relation to scientific reasoning.[3] Science examines the properties of things, while mythology shows men how to function in a given situation. Social action is thus primarily connected to the myth.[4]

If men do not act on the basis of a rational sifting of evidence, on the basis of scientific propositions (irrespective of the epistemological status of these propositions), the basis of action must in the deepest sense be illusory and ideological. Contrary to the Marxian view, Sorel does not believe that false consciousness, the ideological standpoint, is injurious to the promotion of useful social action. Quite the contrary, ideology is the essential element in human consciousness that makes possible any sort of revolutionary practice. On this point, Sorel saw his relation to Marx quite clearly. Socialism divides itself on just this issue of whether revolutionary activity could be grounded on scientific knowledge, or was in fact a consequence of mythology and imagination. For Sorel, we either act on myths or not at all. We assume the value of fictions by acting as if they were the brute facts of experience. Belief instead of truth determines practice for Sorel. Victory in any conflict of social interests belongs therefore to the stout-hearted rather than to the sophisticated smart-headed.[5]

The standpoint of empirical prescription is scientism and not science. Now scientism is a metaphysical posture, of no more em-

[1] *Les préoccupations métaphysique des physiciens modernes*, pp. 48–57.

[2] *Le procès de Socrate*, pp. 9–10.

[3] 'Les theories de Durkheim,' in *Devenir Social* (April 1895), p. 3.

[4] For the best current American sociological presentation of the Sorelian view, see Harold D. Lasswell and Abraham Kaplan, *Power and Society: A Framework for Political Inquiry* (New Haven, 1950), pp. 116–25.

[5] A useful account of how syndicalism and Marxism cleaved on the question of science is Alfred G. Mayer, *Marxism: The Unity of Theory and Practice* (Cambridge, 1954), pp. 136–7.

pirical value than a theory of myths. That scientism 'corresponds exactly to the magical faith of the popular imagination' is indicative only that we are passing through an age of intellectual and political credulity, not that we are becoming more scientific in outlook.[1]

The value of scientism has to be tested in the same way as the theory of the myth: by how well it enables men to function in transforming society. This instrumental–functional standpoint is at the basis of Sorel's theory of revolutionary practice. Precisely because scientism counsels a magical faith in change as a product of laboratory techniques and scientific expeditions, it becomes a pernicious and dangerous conception when gripped by the masses. It is a fundamental source of working class quietude because it insists that mental gymnastics can do what physical struggle cannot do—transform the world. For this reason Sorel strongly believed in a theory of society that could move beyond sociological positivism and beyond scientific socialism. A theory of society must rest on a philosophy of human nature. In this way the intuitionist and pragmatic metaphysic came to be the controlling factor in Sorel's psychology of action.[2]

The critique of mechanistic and materialist theories of science complemented his critique of historicism. The view of history as a binding *diktat* on all men carried over into the area of social practice is a fatalistic interpretation of progress that stimulates an acceptance of things as they are rather than a struggle for things as they should be.[3] Historical dialectics, because of its pronounced monism, becomes a barrier to significant action. 'The attempt to construct hypothesis about the nature of the struggles of the future and the means of suppressing capitalism, on the model furnished by history, is a return to the old methods of the Utopists. There is no process by which the future can be predicted scientifically, nor even which enables us to discuss whether one hypothesis about it is better than another; it has been proved by too many memorable examples that the greatest men have committed prodigious errors in thus desiring to make predictions about even the least distant future.'[4]

A primary value of pragmatism for Sorel's outlook was its explicitly formulated defence of a pluralistic universe. The vanity of historicism, whether of secular determinist types or of theological pre-determinist types makes action pointless and real history an

---

[1] *De l'utilité du pragmatisme*, pp. 2–4.   [2] *Le procès de Socrate*, pp. 226–7.
[3] *De l'utilité du pragmatisme*, pp. 209–10, 338–9.
[4] *Réflexions sur la violence*, p. 176 (142).

appendage to scholasticism. Pragmatism as applied to historical events allows for the real study of the human adventure in ideas and acts. It separates *natural nature* (the physical universe) from *artificial nature* (the universe of human consciousness). For this reason pragmatism is demonstrably superior to both rationalistic and romanticist metaphysics.[1] Pragmatism is unlike either idealism or materialism in that it makes practice effective. It is the philosophy of human freedom. Sorel is the first European theorist to argue in detail that pragmatic freedom entails a commitment to socialism.

This critique of scientism and historicism, of the objectivity of the scientific enterprise and its worth in human affairs, consciously and clearly separated Sorel from Marx and the latter's doctrine of historical materialism.[2] Sorel sought to show that he was a socialist for precisely the opposite reasons as Marx. Sorel attempted to release the animal passions by means of myths—to set humanity free in the flame of revolutionary enterprises. Marx's aim was to realize through the struggle for socialism the specifically human impulses of men—the rational fulfilment and transformation of sensuous experience.[3] Between the two men stood the vast gulf of the place of reason in human affairs.[4]

3. The Heroism and Virility of Sublimity

'As long as there are no myths accepted by the masses, one may go on talking of revolts indefinitely, without ever provoking any revolutionary movement. This is what gives such importance to the general strike and renders it so odious to socialists who are afraid of a revolution. They do all they can to shake the confidence felt by the workers in the preparations they are making for the revolution; and in order to succeed in this way they cast ridicule on the idea of the general strike—the only idea that could have any value as a motive force.'[5] In this form, Sorel announced that since history is only a convention, the general strike is the best means of uniting the pro-

---

[1] *De l'utilité du pragmatisme*, pp. 460–1, 342–3.
[2] *Matériaux d'une théorie du prolétariat*, pp. 39–41.
[3] *Saggi di critica del marxismo*, pp. 52–5.
[4] Two very significant treatments of the emotional content of human liberation since Sorel are those of Herbert Marcuse, *Eros and Civilization: A Philosophical Inquiry into Freud* (Boston and London, 1955); and Norman O. Brown, *Life Against Death: The Psychoanalytical Meaning of History* (London, 1959).
[5] *Réflexions sur la violence*, p. 45 (57).

ducers. The complications of history are vitiated by the uncomplicated psychology of direct action. In a truly germinal sentence of the *Reflexions*, the ideological basis of the principles of revolutionary spontaneity are clearly etched. 'When the anticipations of the future take the form of those myths, which enclose with them all the strongest inclinations of a people, of a party or of a class, inclinations which recur to the mind with the insistence of instincts in all the circumstances of life; and which give an aspect of complete reality to the hopes of immediate action by which, more easily than by any other method, men can reform their desires, passions and mental activity.'[1]

The argument as to the scientific status of socialism clearly has no relevance to its value as a locus of immediate activity. Since science is itself presumed to be a blending of cultural factors, statements expressed in the language of science only offer a sophisticated mythology. The attempt to establish a determinist conception of history leads to procrastination and the decomposition of socialism. Sorel neither affirms nor denies the possibility of precise sociological appraisal of the causes of what appear on the surface as spontaneous events. For neither political structure nor economic classes alters the meaningfulness of the myth as the action centre.

A unique element in Sorel's position is that the labourers are exhorted not to heed the outcome of their instinctive activities. The class struggle expresses a deeper struggle: self identity through violence. The change from Nietzsche to Sorel on this point is from the glorification of racial interests to the edification of class interests. But neither Nietzsche nor Sorel accepted the ultimate ends of racialism or socialism. It is the purification occurring in the process of violent action which is of sole priority. The science of production is therefore not a concern of socialism, since capitalism already has taken care of this matter. Spared endless chattering over scientific considerations, 'people who are living in this world of myths are secure from all refutation.'[2] They are insulated from that sort of criticism which might lead to the consideration of alternative modes of behaviour.

From this it follows that, as far as the human attempt to improve knowledge of the methods and structural content of politics is concerned, it is a terrible confusion leading to passivity. There is much here that anticipates the existentialist *engagement*. The encounter with

[1] *Réflexions sur la violence*, p. 177 (142).   [2] *Ibid.*, p. 49 (59).

life has a meaning over and above the results yielded. The theory of myth is to take man beyond either optimism or pessimism, beyond either choices or absurdities. Success or failure in the revolutionary encounter does not lead to disenchantment because, in the first place, men acting upon myths are not concerned with the material results of their motivation, and second, the ends sought are from the outset recognized as convenient fictions.[1]

That this type of approach is secure from logical refutation is evident. But will social classes consistently submit themselves to a mythological position? Only by discounting empirical facts, the steady growth of scientific knowledge and the application of such knowledge to human needs, and negatively, the impotence of the myth as myth to sustain intense social action in the face of failure, only then can the Sorelian position be said to be beyond refutation. As Val Lorwin has indicated: 'It was not union leaders who would speak of the myth of the general strike. A myth announced as a myth loses its power to move.'[2]

Sorel repeatedly confused the ways in which social change occurs with the ways in which it should be brought about. Had Sorel attempted to make a case from empirical data that men act always and everywhere on the basis of myths and illusions, he would have had only to marshall the evidence supporting this thesis, and perhaps show the triviality of counter evidence. Or he might have chosen to consider the general theory of myth to be grounded in a Weberian ideal-type, in which case explanation of social changes could have been measured by the presence or absence of mythological or ideological factors. But Sorel preferred to weave an ingenuous, and sometimes, ingenious pattern of fact and fantasy, in order to save himself from that sort of withering criticism he tendered to others.

The individual labourer, no longer troubled over the technological deficiencies of industrial capitalism, nor disturbed by his lack of verifiable information about the world he inhabits, nonetheless assumes heroic proportions in Sorel's scheme for the reformation of society. This hero is roughly parallel to what is known in popular culture as the 'all around man.' He is a person who in the circumstances of ordinary life can respond calmly and adequately to the environment, and at the same time, a person who in the extraordinary moments of existence assumes the dimensions of the current illusions

---

[1] *Réflexions sur la violence*, p. 50 (60).
[2] Val Lorwin, *The French Labour Movement* (Cambridge, 1954), p. 36.

and idealism, and does battle for them.[1] The cult of the hero exemplifies in real history what the masses attain to only in imaginary history. What separates the hero from prosaic existence is the transformation of imagination into action. The Machiavellian image of the Roman *condottièro* was never far from Sorel's mind as the ideal type hero of the modern world.[2]

The fusion of mass consciousness with the actions of the hero, the identification of the former through the latter, becomes the primary criterion for establishing a mass revolutionary groundswell. Appeals to factual consistency or theoretical coherence necessarily fall by the wayside in such situations. The proletarian virtue is an ability to tame *fortuna* even when logical evidence points to defeat. The proletarian hero is a hero to Sorel precisely to the degree that he defies the advice of rational men. He serves as a model for the ordinary man under the sway of the sacred cow of science. He offers a dynamic alternative to the social elements who drown their creative energies in base sexuality and sensuality. The hero is a messiah, concentrating in his person the universal virtues. He is, in short, the human agent of the apocalypse.[3]

Sorel was locked in combat with the Enlightenment view of heroism as social. The French Enlightenment was the source of an activist social psychology that still forms the residue of modern naturalistic accounts of human nature. The heralded doctrine of self-interest was conceived of in terms of the broader social spectrum. Selfishness is not self-interest, but only foolishness. The moral consequences of the doctrine of utility were viewed as superior to all inherited moral credos, especially the Christian ethic. The *philosophes* were unanimous in considering social requirements as the centre of gravity of the 'law of self-interest.' During the greater part of the eighteenth century, no portion of the discontent sectors of the economy emerged to claim a special place for its own interests in contradistinction to the general interests; consequently, a hedonist materialism of sorts claimed its place as the common outlook of the age.

In its examination of heroic types, the French Enlightenment took the common-sense view that men are heroic, not as a consequence of divine or instinctual force to gain sublimity of character, but because objective events occur which periodically compel men to satisfy the

---

[1] *Réflexions sur la violence*, p. 177 (142).
[2] *Les illusions du progrès* (second edition), pp. 310–13.
[3] *Ibid.*, pp. 279–81.

149

requirements of self-love in selfless deeds. That great feats are a product of and response to special environmental conditioning was part of the common currency of eighteenth century ideology. It has remained so for the bulk of liberal philosophies since then.

Heroism as a special topic of conversation was deemed unnecessary in an age when the individual was not divorced from his environment, when a man could still be a *philosophe* and function as a social being. Voltaire and Helvetius dissected how it was that foolish men can do foolish things while cloaking themselves in the mantle of heroism. Only the ego divorced from the social whole could fall prey to the absurdities of the Spartan–Feudal model; for only such men concern themselves exclusively with the forms and manners of social practice rather than with the goals of practice. Wise men can be truly heroic in a way that is foreign to mannerism and subjectivism, by being acutely aware of the actual interests being served by acts of bravery. For the *philosophes*, genuine heroism involved moral honesty, an acceptance of the universality of *amour-propre* regulated by an understanding of the goals of society. This naturalization of what constitutes a moral act had the profound effect of separating the ethical from the religious. The *philosophes*, contrary to the popular prose and poetry of medievalism with its emphasis on courtly and spiritual honour, attempted to show how it was possible to live a heroic life and a naturalist life without recourse to sacred or profane myths.

The legacy of Enlightenment became part and parcel of the major intellectual controversies of the romantic movement. One group attempted to further rationalize the basis of human motivation by substituting history for hedonism as a prime mover. With Lessing, Kant, Hegel and Feuerbach, the general critique of feudal altruism made by the French was transformed into a historical survey of the phenomenology of morals. Religious piety was seen as anthropological inversion, aristocratic philanthropy a disguise for limiting the range of culture, revelation without education as specious dogmatism. Individual heroism was meaningful only when it connected itself to *Weltgeschichte* and *Weltkenntnis*; otherwise it was simply a false assertion of egoism against the province of reason.

The very rigour with which romantic rationalism pursued its themes produced the *Sturm und Drang* as a reaction. The individual was proclaimed as worthy over and above either the interests of society or the magical workings of history. The rationalism of both the *philosophes* and the early German romantics was guilty of acquiescing in the bourgeois world order. Goethe, Herder and Hamann, even before the eighteenth century was out, felt that this identification of reason with history involved an intrinsic conservatism. The *Stürmer und Dränger* resurrected feudal heroism, a love of the countryside, delight in the unsophisticated classes, an almost mystical faith in the peasant *volk*, and not the least, a sharp critique of the learned sections of the society. This early stage in the revolt against reason, a cultural-philosophical revolt, came to save man from society; from a slave society and slave mentality. Schopenhauer and Nietzsche forcefully argued that individualism implied heroism. They asserted that in the world of human passions, history, society and reason counted for little; and it is in this world of wills that heroes are made and fops are revealed.

In Sorel's post *fin de siècle* effort to recapture the Spartan–Feudal conception of human heroism, he came to identify with the philosophy of *Sturm und Drang*. He sought to demonstrate its values to a socialist movement that uncritically accepted Enlightenment and Romantic rationalism as the only revolutionary philosophic standpoint. *Blut und Boden* was for Sorel the required standpoint of true socialism. 'The German has been brought up upon sublimity to an extraordinary extent, first by the literature connected with the wars of independence, then by the revival of the taste for the old national songs which followed these wars, then by a philosophy which pursues aims very far removed from sordid considerations.'[1] Sorel's infatuation with the cult of heroism as it held sway in nineteenth century Germany extended to Wagnerian opera, which 'constitutes, in effect, a renaissance of the splendours of the barbaric festivals.'[2] Nobility was not dead, only the noble aristocratic classes were gone. Christian sacrifice was not dead, only the Christian Church as a revolutionizing force had perished. It was the proletariat which would make the virtues of antiquity and feudality come alive once again. The spirit of valour and virtue would overcome the mediocrity of a decadent, timorous and materalistic bourgeoisie. The primordial hero would come to the rescue of the proletariat, providing it with a set of values that would unleash its fighting instincts. In so doing, the hero would lead the masses to a victorious conclusion of the social revolution—without professorial guidance or professional socialist mis-guidance.

---

[1] *Réflexions sur la violence*, pp. 326–7 (238).
[2] *Les illusions du progrès* (second edition), p. 319.

151

The calculation of interests, an exclusive focus on material considerations prior to any action, is the product of an aristocratic Enlightenment and a useful tool to a moribund bourgeois industrialism. This materialism violates genuine heroism. 'When working-class circles are *reasonable*, as the professional socialists wish them to be, when conflicts are confined to disputes about material interests, there is no more opportunity for heroism than when agricultural syndicates discuss the subject of the price of guano with manure merchants.'[1] The machinery of the State also functions to stifle genuine proletarian heroism. Since the State is grounded in the private interest of a ruling class over all other classes, it can safely be assumed that it, too, will mouth the phrases of democracy only to disguise its decadent materialism.[2] 'We are,' concludes Sorel, 'very far here from the path of sublimity, we are on that which leads to the practices of the political-criminal societies.'[3] Materialism and emasculated religion become the intellectual foil of the bureaucracy and the State which is its ultimate support.

What then is the path of sublimity? In what way can we recognize that type of action that really conforms to true standards of morality? In answer to this Sorel identifies with Nietzsche. Like him, the sublime form of action is not simply action on behalf of a well-defined, experientially derived goal, but an act undertaken in the assertion of life itself. And life, Nietzsche informs us, '*is* precisely Will to Power.'[4] Sorel shares with Nietzsche a belief that the Will to Power is that intuitive élan which is ultimately responsible for real social progress. 'Let us acknowledge unprejudicedly how every higher civilization hitherto has *originated*! Men with a still natural nature, barbarians in every terrible sense of the word, men of prey, still in possession of unbroken strength of will and desire for power, threw themselves upon the weaker, more moral, more peaceful races, or upon old mellow civilizations in which the final vital force was flickering out in brilliant fireworks of wit and depravity.'[5]

Nietzsche holds that the master morality is nothing beyond a

---

[1] *Réflexions sur la violence*, p. 324 (236–7).

[2] Sorel's use of the term materialism is pejorative rather than philosophic. His estimate of materialist philosophy, both ancient and modern, is clearly conditioned by the evangelical criticism made by clerical philosophies.

[3] *Réflexions sur la violence*, p. 325 (237).

[4] Friedrich Nietzsche, *Beyond Good and Evil* (London, 1923), p. 226.

[5] *Ibid.*, p. 224. See also his *The Use and Abuse of History* (New York, 1949), pp. 34–42.

recognition that an antithesis between master and slave, creativity and depravity, growth and decay, is universally operative. Further, he implies that if man is to be idealistic in the useful sense, he must be willing to face the practical consequences of this subjective dialectic by living and dying within its terms. Sorel approaches Nietzsche's psychology with a deep feeling of intellectual kinship. The fierce, atavistic terms in which Sorel describes class conflict has a dramatic content closer to the irrational romanticism of Nietzsche than to the analytics found in Marx's nation by nation studies of class struggles. Victory or failure mean nothing to Sorel; the entire range of tactical issues never arise, the struggle is everything.[1] Sorel was too busy looking backward in time for a heroic archetype to give much attention to possible sources of problems in even the immediate future.

Sorel's hero-type differs from Nietzsche's in two respects, which, far from undermining their intellectual kinship, established it beyond doubt. First, Sorel extends the master-slave antithesis to the sphere of class relations, whereas, just as with Péguy, it was the myth of the nation that engrossed Nietzsche. Second, Nietzsche adopted a pessimistic attitude to the presence of true idealism in modern man and its social potential. Sorel reproaches Nietzsche for not seeing that 'the master type still exists under our own eyes.'[2] The interesting thing in this reproach is that the typical hero Sorel has in mind is not the labourer, but his chief antagonist, the virile capitalist. Nietzsche, we are assured by Sorel, 'would have been struck by the singing analogies which exist between the Yankee, ready for any kind of enterprise, and the ancient Greek sailor, sometimes a pirate, sometimes a colonist or merchant; above all, he would have established a parallel between the ancient heroes and the man who sets out on the conquest of the far west.'[3]

Sorel was philosophically antagonistic to materialism because of his conviction that heroism demanded idealism as an attitude. Sober epistemological reflection would have shown him that even the materialist can have ideals. The profane theology of the ancients lurked behind his rejection of positivism as a social pose. 'I am not among those who consider Homer's Archaean type, the indomitable hero confident in his strength and putting himself above rules, as necessarily disappearing in the future.'[4] So intent was Sorel in locating this Archaean type that he collaborated with almost every

[1] *Réflexions sur la violence*, p. 358 (258). [2] *Ibid.*, p. 358 (258).
[3] *Ibid.*, p. 358 (258). [4] *Ibid.*, p. 359 (259).

element in French life that declared its opposition to politics and the State. Revolutionism and Restorationism blended into a frenetic personal search for the happy hero-type. Sorel reproduces the Enlightenment search for the happy legislator, for a counterpart of the Archimedean lever that could lift society to a new stage. Even on the grounds where Sorel fought the Enlightenment most bitterly, he tended to reproduce its exaggerated dependence upon rational education to resolve the social struggles of the age. The hero-types are radically different (for Helvetius a judicious monarchical law giver, for Sorel an injudicious labourer law breaker), but their essential tasks, the reconstruction of society in ideal terms, remains unquestioned.

Whereas for the economy of the future, social structure is held purposefully vague, the psychology is precise, unbounding in the specificity of its characteristics. What in economics is utopian and materialistic, in psychology becomes pragmatic and idealistic; what in economy is a far-fetched concern with the future, in psychology is a hard-headed concern for the practical. The concern of Sorel is for the master type of rugged individualist, not with the collectivist type envisioned by Marxism. 'Syndicalism would be impossible if the world of the workers were under the influence of such a *morality of the weak*.' If the producers retained the inherited slave morality, 'the only difference which would exist between this sham socialism and capitalism would consist in the employment of more ingenious methods of procuring discipline in the workshop.'[1]

Sorel had a confirmed belief that true socialism must accept the heritage of capitalist industry. The challenge to the established order is in a different, more personal direction. 'It is not easy to bring into existence a psychology that is contrary to the mediocrity of present-day relations.'[2] The main focus of revolutionary activity is to transform an élitist mentality into a general morality. The cycle of experience and action is an unbroken chain for Sorel. Experience translated into action is the moral cleansing agent that makes socialism the ultimate search of the moral man.

Just as Nietzsche's myth of national or racial superiority results in the predominance of one nation over another, in like manner, Sorel's myth of class superiority, when it assumes the vocabulary of socialism, expresses the potential of realizing the superiority of the

[1] *Réflexions sur la violence*, p. 367 (264).
[2] *Matériaux d'une théorie du prolétariat*, p. 137.

producers over their adversaries.[1] Anonymity and mediocrity separate the proletarian from the heroic life and the master-type. As long as the masses are ideologically circumscribed by the slave role assigned them by metaphysicians, they cannot emerge victorious in the class struggle.[2] Sorel grants the possibility that talk of master-types is a pose, a psychological attitude rather than a fact of social history; nonetheless, since attitudes fundamentally govern social evolution, the simple act of faith in the myth of proletarian greatness is itself a binding value functioning as a springboard for future social revolts.[3]

The deeper Sorel becomes involved in the psychology of socialism, the shallower do his observations on other facets of social structure become. Not only is he little concerned with plotting the course of economic development, but he also tends to lose interest in the necessary institutional conditions for socialist consciousness. It is the producers, here and now, who become his exclusive concern. How they respond to the myth of social justice is of greater consequence than whether such a future is realizable. The doctrine that socialism is a supreme myth places a utopian flavour on his thinking.

The myth, which Sorel conceives of as the essential cleansing agent of the utopian false projective conscience, becomes simply an extension of utopianism. He is compelled to undermine the original meaning of the myth to the extent that he remains steadfastly opposed to an examination of the realizability of socialism. Gramsci put the matter quite succinctly: 'In Sorel two necessities were in conflict: that of the myth and that of criticism of the myth, since "every pre-established plan is utopian and reactionary." The solution was left to irrational impulse, to "chance" in the Bergsonian sense of "vital impulse," or to "spontaneity."'[4] Sorel's benefactor and friend, Croce, suffered from a similar polarity. However, instead of taking the form of the myth versus the anti-myth, it took the highly intellectualized form of historicism and anti-historicism.[5]

The mass of contradictions pervading Sorel's psychology come together in his concluding discussion of the nature of heroism. In the

[1] *Réflexions sur la violence*, p. 367 (264).
[2] *Ibid.*, pp. 351–2 (254).
[3] *Les illusions du progrès* (second edition), pp. 325–6.
[4] Antonio Gramsci, *Note Sul Machiavelli Sulla Politica e Sullo Stato Moderno* (Rome, 1953), p. 4. (Included in the selections from his works, *The Modern Prince and other writings* (London, 1957), pp. 136–7.)
[5] *Ibid.*, pp. 4 f.

last analysis, who is the hero? Is it the class of producers *qua* class, or the individual leaders of this class? Hidden élitist premises abound in Sorel's examination of the class conflict. The ferocity of this conflict, described in glowing colours, never really characterizes a class so much as individuals. Class allegiance is a voluntary act as well as an economic imposition. Obedience to the rigours of class struggle is a choice of the individual; a choice which stamps the individual producer as heroic. Sorel sets up an interesting equation of military conflict and class conflict. 'In the wars of Liberty each soldier considered himself as an *individual* having something of importance to do in battle, instead of looking upon himself as simply one part of the military mechanism committed to the supreme direction of a leader.'[1]

Individualism is viewed as some sort of self-regulating mechanism, the way *laisser-faire* formerly governed the entire national economy. The proletarian hero is urged to emulate his military prototype. The revolution is to be 'an immense uprising which yet may be called individualistic; each working with the greatest possible zeal, each acting on his own account, and not troubling himself much to subordinate his conduct to a great and scientifically combined plan.'[2] The preservation of individualist values of the past is so pressing for Sorel, that he did not consider the obvious weaknesses of purely spontaneous behaviour, whether in defence of country or of class. The organizational requirements of successful business or political endeavours just never crossed Sorel's mind. He remained thoroughly immersed in the guild consciousness, in the craftsman's attitude toward achievement. The mass man as hero becomes transformed into the craft man as hero. The heroic virtues are once again thrown back into the arms of a waiting élite.

Sorel's hero is more distinctive than he is distinguished, a victim of an inflated personality. This inflation cannot be curbed or channelled since the hero functions primarily in a mythical realm. Sorel ignored the possibility of examining the hero-type in terms of motivation as well as practice. For the genuine hero, no matter how distinguished, necessarily assumes human proportions under analysis. Scrutiny may turn up weaknesses of all kinds: the hero may in fact be driven by masochistic impulses; ego motives may underlie every attempt to storm new barricades. At a different level, neurotic compulsion may

[1] *Réflexions sur la violence*, p. 371 (267).
[2] *Ibid.*, pp. 374–5 (269).

be at the basis of the spirit of violence. Anxiety might convert one man into a coward, and unconsciously drive another into intense social activities. The myth therefore is not simply the worth of violence, but measures the Sorelian hero-type itself.

Sorel is careful to cloak the hero with anonymity. In ordinary life experience he is one among many. Only in the extraordinary moments of history is the hero type called upon to be the hero proper. Why he emerges, what prompts him to do the things ordinary men shy away from, this is not made explicit. Clearly, Sorel had no wish to face the fact that the hero is in reality a man and not a superman, a force shaped by circumstances no less than a force shaping circumstances. Every individual is potentially a hero, once the myriad of positive and negative psychological characteristics are taken into account. On the other hand, the mythological hero is not definable in human terms, and therefore is not properly a hero—since it is precisely human terms by which heroism is measured. The difficulty with Sorel's typology of the hero is that the feeling man replaces the thinking man as sole criterion. He is thus cut off from a knowledge of when to act or how to act—preconditions to action itself. An enduring platitude has it that the thoughtless man is more often the fool than hero. And even men of extraordinary ability are not so desirous of glory that they cannot distinguish between heroism and heroics.

Sorel's conception of the hero in history is perhaps the weakest link in his chain of intellectual armour. Literary feeling tones replace either his regard for the findings of social science, or his faith in the producers as a whole. Significant questions as to whether there is a psychology of classes or nations with clearly distinguishable features, or whether economic transformations can do more than modify primal psychic qualities, went completely unheeded. Since proletarian heroism is of a protean quality, and at any rate based on mythological aims, Sorel shifted his concern from the proletariat as an economic entity, to the proletariat as a tool with the potential of restoring vitality to a dying civilization. Producer values are pre-empted by Sorel not because they are proven superior, or even different than the personal values of other social classes, but because the proletarian is a creature in conflict. And for Sorel conflict is the prime basis of revolutionary change. The producer replaces the Greeks, Mongols, Huns, and Tartars as the force of historical creativity. They are the agents of *ricorso*, leaders in a new barbarism which will see the regeneration of social relations. Poetic licence replaces social enquiry as the basis of human belief. The myth of the hero is the enthralling crystallization of the unfulfilled dreams about nationalism and socialism, race and class. It is utopianism indelibly joined to the unconscious yearnings for infinite and absolute power.

Sorel's phenomenological psychology is linked up to his theory of historical development. Action is the personalized component of general progress. Heroism has its externalized counterpart in the grandeur of classical civilizations. The last stage, virility, has its objective reflection in the moral climate of the social structure. This interchangeability of subjective and objective categories, of psychology and culture, is largely derived from Vico. As in Vico, the last of these stages, virility, closes the circle. Action may be taken in defence of essentially outmoded and decadent causes, heroism may likewise be wasted in futile wars of national aggrandizement characteristic of disintegrating societies. But the capstone, the final test of the value of both action and the courage with which it is undertaken is determined by virility; the moral purpose of the enterprise and the personal qualities called into motion. Virility is that quality which distinguishes regressive from progressive societies, healthy from sick individuals. Sorel gives as an example of this the strength or weakness of the marriage bond, which is a symbol of general social virility or the lack of it.[1] However else one might wish to test virility, its presence in individuals determines the capacity for making social revolutions.

Along with Sorel's general loathing of the Enlightenment, he retained throughout his career a powerful Rousseauian strain. His conception of social change is essentially rooted in the antithesis established by Rousseau between the material prosperity of civilization and the corresponding breakdown of individual moral and psychological virility.[2] Both held that the mechanical features of life, technology, science and the industrial arts are, properly speaking, automatically progressive. The same cannot be said of the moral conduct fostered by material advancement; here the very replacement of the human will by the mechanical artifact is the prime cause for psychological regression. Because of the existence of this inverse relation between material culture and morality, individual virility is necessary to overcome this outstanding paradox.[3]

---

[1] *Les illusions du progrès*, pp. 299–300.
[2] *Ibid.*, pp. 288–9.   [3] *Les illusions du progrès*, pp. 289–90.

Virility is the supreme effort of the human will to transcend the alienated, paradoxical position in which capitalism places man and machine.[1] Sorel is not merely concerned with virility in terms of increasing the population or even the economic output of the nation. His basic concern is the use of immediate practice in the transcending of the paradoxical position of the producer under capitalism. Virility is the application of the human will to the major problems of the age. The translation of desire and will into achievement entails the directed expenditure of energy. This *élan* is social violence; the concentrated release of stored energies.[2] Those individuals who actually accomplish the transformation of virility into violence are *les hommes supérieurs*. The moral economy was there to ensure that virility would be expressed in terms of revolutionary myths rather than reactionary norms.

There is a powerful Christian strain connected to Sorel's description of the highest stage of proletarian psychology. For virility implies the ability of self-regulation amidst a cesspool of social corruption. Neither an élite of knowledge, nor one founded on material privilege, can lead men to the path of self-renunciation. And it is the renunciation of things of the flesh that entitles a man to enter the palace of the morally chosen. Sorel's social psychology showed every sign of turning into a socialized religion. Contentment with the mediocre, the technological, the factually verifiable, is the path to banal materialism. Just as the principle of the myth of apocalypse vivified early Christianity, so too must the myth of socialism illumine the modern revolutionary movement. Material considerations move counter to the myth. But this is precisely the value and meaning of virility. Its purpose is not to inform consciousness of the practical or scientifically demonstrable, but to show that action has sublime sources untapped by the practical and prosaic mind.[3]

A major stumbling-block to Sorel's theory of material renunciation as the basis of proletarian radicalization, is his failure to present any evidence that this is empirically the case. Super-sensualism may be just as compatible with revolutionary aims as anti-sensualism. The gratification of biological desires, of sexual impulses, may in certain cases be quite consonant with healthy social activity. Why the social strivings of men should be easier to attain in a climate of sexual

---

[1] *Les illusions du progrès*, p. 317.
[2] *Insegnamenti sociali della economia contemporanea*, pp. 42–4.
[3] *Les illusions du progrès*, pp. 326–9.

renunciation is not made clear by Sorel. The traditional Catholic view maintains that success of Christianity over the Roman Empire flowed from the superiority of its moral system. Yet the same success can be more readily explained on political and economic grounds. There is, after all, no evidence that the moral conduct of Rome was perceptibly more conservative in the days of Caesar than in the later rule of Diocletian.

The ethics of Enlightenment inspired a recognition of sensuality as an aspect of the human search for freedom and equality; the fulfilment rather than the renunciation of sensual gratifications became a basis for further social action. It was from this point on that Sorel dates the decline of bourgeois civilization. Yet in point of fact, it was just this period of history that began the real burst of industrial and scientific activity. Sorel's attempt to ground a theory of revolution on an ethic of repression is faced with the supreme task of proving that no other code of personal conduct is compatible with social reconstruction.

Sorel adopted a Pauline view of socialism which left the big issue of man's repression at the hands of society thoroughly unresolved. The Sorelian standpoint of concrete man would seem to require not only a theory of social emancipation, but also the individual's freedom from sexual repression. Sorel's anarchism was incomplete because in addition to being incapable of offering a serious alternative to the economic position of the producer under capitalism, he abandoned his anarchist theory of the individual in favour of a normative ethic tightly organized to promote the next stage in civilization at the expense of personal freedom of action. Sorel thus leaves us with the paradox of rejecting traditional forms of politics, while accepting the buffer of State politics, a theological-centred morality.

Why Sorel was intent on uniting a normative ethic with revolutionary action is subject to several possible interpretations: a reading of past events through Catholic historiography, a personal history which was marked by a pure marital love relation, a fear that sexual freedom would turn men away from social problems. While these are part of the total picture, I should like to suggest that the primary motive stemmed from Sorel's identification of sexual liberty with democracy, and in turn democracy with the plague of mediocrity. Democracy is the essential political form of moral mediocrity. Sorel sees this in Platonic terms as the rule of the lowest common denominator.[1]

[1] *Les illusions du progrès*, p. 333.

Sorel is extremely critical of those intellectuals, who for vested interests in the commonplace, praise democracy and look upon history as if it were some sort of epic poem. To imagine that the sophistries that are part and parcel of democracies are responsible for social greatness is, in Sorel's opinion, to fasten the producers with the banal abstractions of the Enlightenment. The sin of assuming automatic progress in society is the sin of platitudinists and democrats alike. In relieving the individual of real responsibility for social growth, democracy becomes the antithesis of socialism. The steady application of the human will in a heroic way, in a struggle to mould the world to the will, this is what socialism ultimately means to Sorel; and democracy can only sustain itself through the suppression of the heroic will.[1]

What stands in the way of proletarian success is not so much the economic power of the middle classes, but the power of its ideology to infect the whole of society. Sorel insists that socialism is not to be looked upon as some sort of higher democracy, for that could only mean a higher stage in the rule of mediocrity and an even greater voice to the bureaucratic elements in society. Socialist democracy is a contradiction in terms. It could only mean over-centralization socially, a hypertrophic bureaucracy and a managerial domination that would ensure the priority of technology over men. Precisely because of its thoroughness, Sorel feels that the proletariat would be estranged from its productive source even more than under past economies. The sense of participation and control having been removed from the producers, the consequences of socialist democracy would be a return to its former condition of atrophy and mediocrity.

Sorel's theory of socialism excluded democracy because he felt that there should be no place for mediocrity in the healthy commonwealth. Socialism was to transform every individual into an active, creative soul. It was to replace both Aristotle's idea that the basis of science and culture is leisure, and Helvetius' affirmation that the basis of science and culture is equality. Labour alone was viewed as the transforming agent. In this way, Sorel believed that economics passes into aesthetics, politics passes into morality and, at the ideological level, materialism is transformed into idealism. The qualities of socialized man are to be poured back into industrial and cultural invention. The man of the future is to take his synthetic *a priori*

---

[1] *Les illusions du progrès*, p. 334.

morality seriously, and thus become the human insurance that society will always be regenerated and renovated.[1]

The overriding difficulty in Sorel's psychology of socialism is that it never is really content to describe the psychological conditions of revolution or reaction. Sorel is torn between a confusion of descriptive and prescriptive elements. He not only maintains the purifying role of action, the grandeur of heroism, the value of a disciplined use of human libidinal energies, but in each case offers an intuitionist framework as the only morally correct posture. Psychology is made to issue into ethics unnaturally; for the initial origin of Sorel's psychology is not the behaviour of individuals, communities or classes, but an unexplored moral dogmatism. Like Proudhon, Sorel was captivated by an absolutist theological ethic unhampered by empirical considerations.

This is not to say that a connection between description and prescription cannot be established. Quite clearly, the purpose of description is to better guide the choice men make. Such inferences, however, can not be legislated by *a priori* considerations and at the same time claim the protective covering of scientific adequacy. There is a distinction between the scientific study of moral behaviour and the handing down of rules for moral conduct. Even empirically grounded psychological descriptions and definitions require modification so that they become widely applicable and at the same time logically consistent. Sorel, however, reverses the actual procedures involved in a scientific psychology. He starts with a series of moral postulates and social goals, and insists that the right mode of conduct is that which conforms to these postulates and goals. But the canonization of goals yields the feeling of moral certainty only to those accepting the goals, it leaves untapped the bigger question of the adequacy of the goals themselves. What is missing in Sorel is a theory for measuring means in terms of ends, and not just ends in terms of means—the common vice of those varieties of pragmatism that recognize only continuums, and not the origin or aims of values.

The long-range deficit in this pragmatic framework is the denial of the very end Sorel affirms most loudly, human freedom: the transformation of labour as social necessity into labour as a liberating ethic, from a repressive sociality into an unfettered individualism. The moral strictures in early Christian ethics, a justifiable response to an economy of extreme privation, becomes enshrined as the socialist

---

[1] *Réflexions sur la violence*, pp. 377–80 (270–2).

morality in an age of material abundance and individual freedom. The repressions inflicted on man in an age of social alienation are to be continued and strengthened in a social system which supposedly is to liberate the discontents from decaying institutions. As it turns out, Sorel's approach would only result in political institutions being relieved of their discontents.

VI

THE AGONIES OF
PRAGMATIC SOCIALISM

'Sorel did not write for a party or a class, he wrote for those men capable of the effort of free and personal thought . . . The example of Sorel, obstinately dedicated to the truth, is the highest of philosophy and the life we advocate. He sacrificed everything to his work and to his research: the honours and security at first offered by the bourgeoisie, for the honours and security of revolutionists that followed.'

Pierre Andreu, NOTRE MAITRE, M. SOREL

THE enquiry into the sociology of political ideas is a distinctive theme in contemporary thought. It differs in a fundamental way from either political philosophy or political sociology in that it is not a systematization of general ideas about consensus and conflict in the folkways of men, but rather an analysis of how and under what conditions ideas are shaped in the crucible of political rivalries and antagonisms.

In the actual functioning of social doctrines we can discern the anomalies and paradoxes which limited theoretical description, logical restructuring or statistical calculation of probabilities do not yield. This is not to say that the analysis of social ideologies in terms of their social and political involvements can become a substitute for empirical examinations as such. Nor can one evaluate the total inherent applications of Sorel's 'open-ended' sociology by reference to the way in which it functions in one situation.

It is clear that irrational radicalism functioned in different ways in

Italy during the consolidation of fascist power, in Russia during the period of revolutionary experimentation and in France during the halcyon days of the popular front. Precisely for this reason, the apparently anomalous, sometimes capricious behaviour of the Sorelian perspective under varying social conditions, there is a need to distinguish the sociology of political ideas from both political sociology and philosophy in general. Beyond this, there is a need to cope with the interaction of the sociology of knowledge and the politics of mass action. Sorel's thought exists at a level where its truths are subordinate to its functions. This forms the centre of our efforts to sum up the Sorelian legacy.

1. From Political Sociology to the Sociology of Politics

To tie together the plural aspects of Sorel's social thought is to impose unity on his thinking rather than demonstrate its actual existence. Even in the realm of ideals, Sorel was deprived of unity. His dual allegiance to the goals of Christianity and socialism gave his thought a conflicting evangelical fervour. Sorel inhabited a universe in which the object, society, became submerged in the manifold desires and instincts of the altruistic radical. His was a fragmented world of feeling, separated from the material sources and consequences of this emotional turbulence. One of the claims of Sorel's pragmatic socialism is that only the position of the individual saves ordinary men from political saviours and philosophical savants. Radicalism starts with the concrete individual and not with the construction of large-scale sociological systems. This attitude towards wholeness sharply separates the work of Sorel, and his most ardent champion, Vilfredo Pareto. Unlike the work of Pareto, that of Sorel's makes few claims upon nature or science. Engineering principles of statics and dynamics, mathematical equations for the circulation of élites, the systematic exhaustion of political myths and slogans, were as opposed to the spirit of Sorel's efforts, as the earlier efforts of Menger and Lafargue to predict the exact contents of a socialist society.

Politics is the practice of power. It is Sorel's judgment that political issues are resolved only through the efforts of a combined human will that is hardly sure of the adequacy of proposed plans. On such a view, doctrinal inconsistency is a virtue. For it indicates that men are actually grappling with politics as such. When people are in the midst of action, when they partake of the radicalizing myth of the age, they necessarily modify and even contradict their pre-conceived ideas. The pragmatics of social revolution replaces the axiomatics of official socialism. When this transformation is realized, we have proof that the class struggle has been joined with life.

When the only perspective recognized as legitimate becomes that which fosters the practice of a special power agency in society, then social thought becomes the child of caprice, subject to ideology and faith rather than objectivity and truth. The failure to distinguish between political sociology and the politics of sociology is itself a cardinal form of the ambiguous legacy. Plato distinguished between the search for truth, to be carried on by a trained élite, and the ideological techniques of power. The confusions of political theory after Plato consist primarily in the fact that the dualism of political truths and political beliefs became, in the hands of a man like Sorel, indistinguishable. He vacillated between a sociological analysis of society and a sociology of knowledge without distinguishing between the functions of each. That he stumbled on to a huge discovery that political realism consists in differentiating power-claims from ideological claims does not vitiate the fact that he was just as much bound by his position as those effectively castigated.

What follows in this chapter is an attempt to show the forms of this overriding ambiguity between political sociology and the politics of sociology, in Sorel. It is necessary to follow up Posse's work on the fragmentary picture resulting from a treatment of Sorel as a forerunner either of fascism or bolshevism.[1] A much more fruitful approach is to examine Sorel in terms of the dynamics of authority and coercion, force in contradistinction to violence.[2] The central task therefore, is a review of the major polarities in Sorel's social theories in the light of his theory of human nature. Particular emphasis will be placed on the forms in which the bifurcation of fact and fantasy were set: first to a commitment to a scientific sociology and second to ideological socialism.

[1] Ernst H. Posse, 'Sorels Fascismus und sein Sozialismus,' *Archiv für die Geschichte des Sozialismus und der Arbeiterbewegung.* Vol. XV (1930), pp. 161–93. See also an earlier essay, 'Georges Sorel,' *Zeitschrift für Politik*, Vol. XVIII (1928–9), pp. 742–61.

[2] Preliminary work in this direction was done by R. Heyne, 'Georges Sorel und der autoritäre Staat des 20. Jahrhunderts,' *Archiv für Oeffentlich. Recht.*, Vol. XXIX (1938), pp. 129 ff. On the same subject, see Sigmund Neumann, 'Georges Sorel,' in *The Encyclopaedia of the Social Sciences* (edited by E. R. A. Seligman and Alvin Johnson) (New York, 1934), Vol. 14, pp. 262–3.

It need be noted at the outset that when Sorel transformed his wish images into actual instruments for the conduct of men, he became guilty of falling into an ambivalent attitude toward ideology and utopia. He moved from a form of thought reflecting a partial, partisan picture of society, to an equally fractured representation of what this world must be like in the future. Sorel recognized that 'an ideological system is never perfectly coherent.' Yet he was only able to deduce from this, not the limitations of ideology as a form of social consciousness, but the impossibility of social knowledge as such, that is, as social science.[1]

2. Sorel and the Dilemma of Authoritarian Politics

The iconoclast in Sorel should make it clear that a study of his form of authoritarianism is not reducible to any single political or anti-political position. He combined concepts of élitism with proletarianism, organized action from above with spontaneous action from below, and the doctrine of political primacy was linked to a network of psychological and moral precepts. No single political movement could contain all these parts intact and long survive. What can be said of Sorel is that he attempted to fuse all the elements involved in a pure theory of authoritarianism, and to show how they provide a substantial critique of the political democracy offered by capitalism and the economic democracy promised by orthodox socialism.

Authoritarianism is not an ideology as such, since ideologies are the mental images and utopian projections of specific social interests. Since ideology has the generation of human action as an immediate aim, it cannot be viewed as a private or purely psychological *Weltanschauung*. There is no authoritarian ideology; there are ideologies in which authoritarian methods predominate. Authoritarianism may rest on élitist sentiments or moral doctrines, on the superiority of certain classes or certain codes of behaviour. Translated into Sorel's terms, this means that his authoritarianism was not cut from one piece of cloth, but was a composite of several ideological fabrics that

---

[1] This jump from the limits of social knowledge to a negation of social science is characteristic of a number of writers on Sorel, as well as Sorel himself. As examples, see Enrico Leone, *Il neo-marxismo, Sorel e Marx* (Bologna, 1923), written in the first flush of fascism in Italy; the work of the French Jesuit, sympathetic to Sorel, Victor Sartre, *Georges Sorel* (Paris, 1937); and the prophetic volume of James Burnham, *The Machiavellians: Defenders of Freedom* (New York, 1943).

clothed various social and political systems. These different ideologies shaded Sorel's thought despite his insistence on the uniqueness stemming from a voluntarist picture of the relation of ideas to action. Indeed, they even moved Sorel to positions sharply critical of existing extremist ideologies. For despite his unwavering faith in authoritarianism as a broad referential point for the critique of democracy, his belief that ideologies are tied to politics made him suspicious of their worth.

In Sorel's implicit critique of fascism, the differences between a general authoritarian frame of reference and a specific ideology of a political movement can be clearly seen. In opposition to the fascist view that 'only the State can ascertain and control matters of the employment and unemployment of labourers, and of the complex index of conditions of production and labour,'[1] Sorel relentlessly insisted on direct worker control of production norms to be exercised outside of the State mechanism. Management, ownership and operation of industry were all to be socialized. Fascism intensified the economic bureaucratization of society by maintaining and even strengthening class divisions.

The established economic order remained intact under fascism, with corporativism gaining the upper hand over syndicalism.[2] Even the *right* of labour to strike was taken away to be replaced by proletarian *duties* to the State. At the economic level the labourers were further alienated from the sources of creation. The intensification of bureaucracy, the development of a managerial class and a military caste, both revealed the deepening crisis of European capitalism. For Sorel, this lay in its inability to engage in the class struggle in a direct fashion. Fascism, once entrenched, tended to disguise rather than intensify the class conflict, suppressing the growing disparity of production and consumption behind a doctrine of *Pax Romana*.

From the standpoint of politics, fascism squared no better with Sorelian standards. It intensified the role of the State in the management of social and individual affairs, enlarging the operational scope of the inherited political machinery at the expense of labour. Alfredo Rocco, in an important policy-making statement, reveals the elevation of the State in no uncertain terms. 'The fascist state . . . has asserted its own dominion over all the forces existing in the country,

---

[1] *The Labour Charter*, April 21, 1927. Reprinted in *Making the Fascist State*, *loc. cit.*, p. 335.

[2] *Disfattismo Sindacale*, in *Critica Fascista*, June 15, 1927. *Ibid.*, pp. 338–9.

co-ordinating them all, incorporating all and directing all of them to the higher ends of national life. A series of laws reasserts this necessary superiority of the state. . . . Thus is being realized Mussolini's formula: "Everything for the state, nothing outside the state, nothing against the state.' "[1] Sorel's aim of suppressing the State as the ultimate expression of working class authority becomes inverted under fascism into a suppression of the producers and their extra-legal machinery for rule. In place of the elimination of class antagonisms, fascism was only able to crystallize this antagonism in the form of the patriarchal State. The Sorelian syndicate was an instrument of proletarian organization and control. The fascist corporation was an instrument of class domination by the method of the forced collaboration of economic classes.[2]

The consequences of fascism for proletarian violence and virility are equally at variance with Sorel's pronouncements. The much feared mediocrity of producer existence was only intensified under fascism; its potential heroes were liquidated before they were able to assume a leading role in society. Proletarian life increasingly became difficult and grey; even advocacy of socialism as a myth became subject to official suspicion. Resourcefulness, individuality and integrity, hallmarks of Sorel's proletarian hero, were ruthlessly stamped out. Fascism transformed the psychology of action from a felt desire into an official duty. Organized terror replaced spontaneous violence. The corruption of social goals was indicative of a general moral corruption in Sorel's sense. Proletarian life ceased to be virile; except for the biological continuation of the race, it served as a cowardly appendage of a timid middle class. The goal became the common sacrifice of industrialists and workers for the common goal of the country's future.[3] National rather than class aims became the focal point of psychological excitation.

The morality of violence as conceived of by Sorel was also at sharp variance with the practices of fascism. Sorel possessed an almost feudal sense of honour, extending to the conduct of violence. The fact of violence, not its aimless propagation, lay at the core of his thinking. The uses of violence were to further the manliness of the contending parties, not to destroy whole sections of the population who

---

[1] Alfredo Rocco, *La Transformazione dello Stato* (Rome, 1927). *Ibid.*, pp. 331–2.
[2] Cf. Franz Neumann, *Behemoth: The Structure and Practice of National Socialism* (New York, 1944), p. 194.
[3] A. S. Benni, 'Loyal Industrialists' (May 16, 1927), in Schneider, *Ibid.*, pp. 337–8.

M   169

were blameless or defenceless. Violence was properly a tool for creating the conditions of a masculine and sublime society, not a weapon to increase the political misery of society as a whole and the poverty of producers in particular. The fascist Leviathan only further served to deepen the gulf between the basic poles of authoritarianism: between *organized force* for the purpose of strengthening the State and liquidating the class conflict, and *spontaneous violence* calculated to rid society once and for all of the State.[1]

German national socialism was even more pronouncedly hostile to the Sorelian theory of a society of producers. A reading of the Nazi regime's labour laws enacted to legalize its economic policies, indicates just how great a variance existed between national socialism and syndical socialism. The first proposition states that 'in any business the employer as the Leader (*Führer*) of the business and the employees and labourers as Followers (*Gefolgschaft*), work in common for the promotion of the aims of the business and the common good of the People and the State.' The next in the series of labour regulations points out that 'the Leader of the business, as opposed to the Followers, decides all matters relating to the business insofar as they are regulated by this law.'[2]

These propositions violate the major principles of Sorel's society of producers: (1) the incompatibility of labour and management under capitalism; (2) the inability of the bourgeoisie, by virtue of its special and private interests, to work for the common social good; (3) the incompatibility of the mass to harmonize their interests with those of the State, that is, the impossibility of the State to act as mediator of class warfare; (4) the bureaucratic corruption of a society in which the State controls all industry and economic activities. In addition, a moral violation of Sorel's outlook is implied in the Nazi laws governing labour conduct. The very word *Gefolgschaft* implies a cowardly and effete psychology, since its root implies 'to behave' and 'to be led' as well as to be employed in a factory. Syndical socialism differs profoundly from national socialism in that in the former there are no business leaders over and above the leadership provided by producer organizations. National socialism for Sorel would have, at best, been excused as a new form of paternalism, but at worst, the acme of the

---

[1] *Réflexions sur la violence*, pp. 153–4 (127–8).
[2] *The Law for the Ordering of National Labour* (January 20, 1934). In Michael J. Oakeshott, *The Social and Political Doctrines of Contemporary Europe* (Cambridge, 1944), pp. 213–18.

force and tyranny of the bourgeois State. And neither paternalism nor statism would have been left unexpurgated from Sorel's social system.[1]

Since fascism suppresses the very idea of the emancipation of labour (that is in Sorel's terms, emancipation means the transformation of work from commodity production to an aesthetic principle) it violates the basic motivation behind syndical socialism.[2] The very phenomenon which Sorel most feared, the arbitrary political control of industry, produced in Italy the results he predicted. A reading of the remarkable editorial in *Critica Fascista* reads like a catalogue of sins against Sorelianism. 'That the corporate fascist system is a system of duties and not of rights, that the syndical representative is an instrument of the State and not of separate parties, that class interests have no emphasis nor claim because they are outside the corporate unity, these are three given factors that it still behooves us to engrave deeply into the minds of many syndicate organizers in the corporate state. And it may be opportune and preferable that the energies of the fascist party in which the predominance of spiritual motives is most active, be dedicated to this work.'[3]

The distinctions between fascist corporativism and syndical socialism may be summed up in a variety of ways, all of which indicate that no grounds exist for taking fascist spokesmen at face value in claiming Sorel for a political movement whose contours he died too soon to appreciate. Sorel insisted on the primacy of class struggle rather than national unity as the basis of a healthy society. The notion of direct worker participation and control of the economic means of production was absent in fascist economic pronouncements. Sorel's crucial distinction between types of violence, the force of the *politique* and the violence of the *anti-politique*, was dropped by fascism. Consequently any sense of socially beneficent, if indeterminate, aspects of violence, likewise fell into disuse if not outright disrepute.

Vast differences are also to be found in the relative psychologies of fascism and syndical socialism. For fascism, the authority of the labour–management coalition together with the State, was to ensure that social harmony which Sorel felt would flow from a voluntaristic association of workers. At the productive level, Sorel's *laisser-faire*

---

[1] *Insegnamenti sociali della economia contemporanea*, pp. 395–6.

[2] *Ibid.*, pp. 397–98; also *Réflexions sur la violence*, pp. 451–2 (310).

[3] *In Fondo alla Rivoluzione*, in *Critica Fascista* (July 15, 1927). Reprinted in *Making The Fascist State*, p. 339.

individualism was replaced by a strict disciplinarian conception of producer obligations. This was no less a transvaluation of values: from a theory of individual freedom to one of economic obligations. What finally ensued was a disparity between a critique of utilitarianism based on the socialist need for an aesthetic, altruistic basis of activity, to a critique of utilitarianism based upon fascism's need for a militarization and codification of psychology and morals.

While it may seem that we have here been labouring the obvious, it is just these factual differences that have got lost in the analysis of Sorel and his social influences. Pointing to these distinctions is an antidote to those critics of democratic persuasion who tend to equate all authoritarian doctrines without considering the concrete evidence. It is notoriously true that social systems such as fascism and national socialism had to make a desperate search for respectable philosophical antecedents as a means of inspiring confidence and action on the part of the producers and the intelligentsia. Sorel's doctrines were used to convince workers of the socialist aims of fascism, and to convince intellectuals that they need not be conscience-stricken at the devious course of Empire.

This is not to deny that Sorel's special form of the revolt against reason, against social science and philosophy as a purifying discipline, did not share points of contact with the anti-intellectual spirit of Italian fascism. The failure on Sorel's part to recognize the existence of a causal or consequential connection between means used and goals pursued, between violence and terror, emphasize in some measure his differences with the Italian neo-realism of Mosca, Gentile and Pareto. The ludicrous idea that syndicalism is somehow spared from sociological laws, from the methodological and structural implications inherent in a theory of labour, made Sorel an unwitting source-book of fascist ideas concerning the pathology of political power.

What we have projected as Sorel's critique of fascism necessarily has many points of contact with his implicit criticism of bolshevism. However, since Marx was both the original ground of Sorel's political philosophy, and because socialism had a much longer history both in fact and theory than fascism, the Sorelian critique of orthodox socialism carries a greater force and conviction than that of fascism. It may be objected that the terms orthodox socialism, Marxism and bolshevism are not interchangeable. This is not the place to contest or affirm their synonymity. What will be done is to distinguish those points of Marxian political theory which were accepted or rejected by bolshevism, and further, to overcome the points of friction between bolshevism and syndicalism in terms of Sorel's general estimate of Marx on one side and his critique of the Marxian legacy on the other.

Sorel was unmistakably an original and seminal mind. Although crudities are present in his effort to reconstruct the socialist vision, we must not overlook the fact that his was a revision of Marxism that rested upon revolution rather than reform. It was the decay of Marxist theory into a specious form of humanism that prompted Sorel to examine what, in Marxism as such, led to an internal decomposition of the socialist movement. The fracturing of the labour movement and the growth of schisms within the socialist movement made such probings inevitable. It is the quality of Sorel's line of criticism, no less than its distinctive position, that raises it above the ordinary discussions of the age.

With the possible exception of Harold Laski, the Anglo-American socialist tradition has been unable to produce a figure on a par with this admittedly minor continental. Characteristic of Marxism in the English-speaking countries is a barrier separating theories of socialism from the process of practical implementation. Such socialism has never had to consider the question of revolution in its immediacy and, as a consequence, could afford the leisure of dogmatism. It could accept the conclusions of socialist studies elsewhere without the dire consequences of trying such studies out in different soil. France presents a different picture. French technology stagnated. Its imperial conquests could not keep pace with its designs. Bourgeoisie and peasantry alike could not move beyond a psychology of individual proprietorship. In consequence of these and other factors preventing social mobility, the proletariat remained fairly homogenous as a class, at least in relation to capital. Its demands were generally unsatisfied by a too satisfied bourgeoisie. Therefore, throughout the present century revolution and restoration were the poles between which its political choices were being made.

Sorel was aware of these demands for a theory of revolution that would work. It became his cardinal principle that the intellectually mature, socially oriented individual should (but does not) focus steadily on the pragmatic assignments foisted on men by a decaying European civilization. Any purely theoretical focus represented to

Sorel a blurring of vision, and in consequence a barrier to revolutionary action.[1]

Sorel's theory of contingency led to the view that every age has to resolve the perennial problems of freedom and authority anew. There can be no categorical answer to the question of what the standpoint of revolutionary man should be. Only immediate, rather than historical, answers suffice. Sorel was reluctant therefore to accept traditional Marxian solutions to what he felt were steadily shifting social relations. Moreover, he doubted the efficacy of categorical generalities that offered no means of verification or disproof, and no way of separating tautological from empirical statements. The Marxists, in contrast to Marx, because they did nothing to acquire adequate methodological safeguards, became rationalists and utopians. The desire to retain doctrinal purity outweighed the instinct to make revolutions.

There were other, less profound considerations which entered into Sorel's refusal to stay within the boundaries of orthodox Marxism, the stance of European social democracy: his general pragmatic tendency to regard historical laws as mythological, and economic laws as conventions; his lack of familiarity with the earlier writings of Marx and Engels on psychology, anthropology and history; his personal alienation from the realm of politics and industry, hypostatized into a general rule of *anti-politique*. Thus, despite an undeniable personal integrity and a keen ability to centre on the need to re-work radical attitudes and appraisals, Sorel sacrificed precision at every juncture. Never too clear as to his own motivations, he transmitted these into his work in the form of unresolved paradoxes.

Whatever Sorel's inability to see the beam in his own approach, he had little difficulty locating the mote in the structure of orthodox socialism. He viewed his own variety of socialism as an ideal rather than a political system, and hence did not see the need to start with a philosophic synthesis. Socialism was made pragmatic. It was simply the best way to organize the practice of working class emancipation, irrespective of what followed that emancipation.[2] His critical acumen clearly overshadowed his powers of construction. He exaggerated the tendencies of the socialism of his own age to move toward liberalism and Statism. But in so magnifying tendencies, he curiously anticipated many of the shortcomings in the evolution of Russian Marxism,

---

[1] *Saggi di critica del marxismo*, pp. 229–30.
[2] *Matériaux d'une théorie du prolétariat*, p. 112.

which both critics and advocates of the Soviet system have since come to recognize as essentially sound.

The dictatorship of the proletarian State underwent a frontal assault at Sorel's hands. The idea, the phrase itself, created an anomalous situation, for the words proletariat and dictatorship represent alien poles in relation to each other. In this judgment, Sorel was thoroughly within the principles of Marx and Engels. 'The State is nothing more than a machine for the oppression of one class by another, and indeed in the democratic republic no less than in the monarchy; and at best is an evil inherited by the proletariat after its victorious struggle for class supremacy whose worst sides the proletariat, just like the Commune, will have at the earliest possible moment to lop off, until such time as a new generation, reared under new and free social conditions, will be able to throw on the scrap-heap all the useless lumber of the State.'[1] From this postulate of Engels' flows two possibilities: either the immediate end to State authority after the proletarian revolt, or the use of the State machinery by the revolutionists until such time as the threat of counter-revolt ceases. Sorel intuitively chose to believe the former position.

Orthodox socialism assumes that the means of proletarian liberation are the organs of the State and the capture of its complicated power apparatus. But what, Sorel asks, if this assumption is not made? Can a theory of revolution be framed in such a way as to allow the force of labour to storm the citadels of established power directly? Can a realistic alternative to working within the State machinery be found? These are the issues to which Sorel addressed himself; and in each case he sided against the *politique*. 'Experience has always shown us hitherto that revolutionaries plead "reasons of State" as soon as they get into power, that they then employ police methods and look upon justice as a weapon which they may use unfairly against their enemies. Parliamentary socialists do not escape the universal rule; they preserve the old cult of the State; they are therefore prepared to commit all the misdeeds of the Old Regime and

---

[1] Frederick Engels, *Introduction* to Marx's *The Civil War in France*, in *Marx-Engels Selected Works* (Moscow, 1950), Vol. I, p. 440. For contrasting views on the differences between Marx and Soviet Marxism on the question of State authority, see Hans Kelsen, *The Communist Theory of Law* (London, 1955); and Rudolf Schlesinger, *Soviet Legal Theory: Its Social Background and Development* (London, 1945). Kelsen, viewing matters juridically, sees the two as discontinuous and in opposition. Schlesinger, emphasizing sociological perspectives, considers Marx and Soviet theories of Law and the State as forming a natural continuum.

of the Revolution.'[1] This being the situation, Sorel insists that the only alternative to either State capitalism or State socialism is a distinctively anti-political social reorganization of life.

The origins and traditions of the State are directly opposed to the requirements of labour. In Sorel's eyes, the State has become not merely a form of class domination in past societies, but a veritable cancer on social structures as such. To assume that the cancerous nature of the State disappears when it transcends class lines is to further assume that internal ailments can be treated with bright words. 'Syndicalists do not propose to reform the State as the men of the eighteenth century did; they want to destroy it, because they wish to realize this idea of Marx's that the socialist revolution ought not to culminate in the replacement of one governing authority by another minority.'[2]

It is Sorel's opinion that legal or political Marxism has essentially the same view on State authority as the Enlightenment and the English and German advocates of civil society. They differ on who should rule and perhaps on methods for attaining political power, not on the worth of expressing domination through a State. Such 'State socialism' is really reactionary socialism, for it speaks 'of breaking up everything, but they attack men in power rather than power itself; they hope to possess the State forces, and they are aware that on the day when they control the Government they will have need of an army; they will carry on foreign politics, and consequently they in their turn will have to praise the feeling of devotion to the fatherland.'[3] Like present-day advocates of a world State, Sorel denied that the notion of national sovereignty, of the right of nations to self-determination, has any positive value to the producers as producers. Nationalism assumes a significance only when socialism becomes State socialism. The basic political notion of civil society, sovereignty, in this way becomes a symbolic representation of bourgeois mythology in proletarian guise. This, for Sorel, is the disastrous consequence of allowing professional politicians, twice removed from the labour process, to assume the direction of proletarian efforts toward the realization of the historic mission of social emancipation.[4]

The inevitable consequence of State socialism, as Sorel calls all varieties of political socialism, is that in reproducing the conditions of political sovereignty over the producers in the name of producers,

---

[1] *Réflexions sur la violence*, pp. 156–7 (129).   [2] *Ibid.*, p. 163 (133).
[3] *Ibid.*, p. 163 (134).   [4] *La décomposition du marxisme*, pp. 24–6.

nothing in the social structure is fundamentally altered. The alienation of producer and production, men who labour and men who
control, remains intact. The mores and morals of the governing caste
remain distinctly separate from those of the mass. In brief, the social
antagonisms characteristic of class society would remain in force in
post-class society. 'State socialism could accommodate itself to this
morality perfectly well. Since the latter is based on the idea of a
society divided into a class of producers and a class of thinkers
applying results of scientific investigation to the work of production.
The only difference which would exist between this sham socialism
and capitalism would consist in the employment of more ingenious
methods of procuring discipline in the workshop.'[1]

The tendency of orthodox Marxism is to confuse the elimination of
conflict in general with the elimination of the economic forms that
conflict takes under capitalism. What Sorel was hinting at, but was
never quite able to say explicitly, is that state socialism represents the
outright transformation of the power base from economics to
politics. Instead of a direct economic confrontation of owner and
producer, with the State under capitalism performing a mediating
role, State socialism confronts the labouring class with political
power as such. They must contend with the political force of bureaucracy, which is an independent social element that sees in socialism
the further strengthening of the State rather than the emancipation of
labourers. Bureaucracy becomes the standardized way of life under
State socialism. Men who under capitalism only managed the affairs
of industrialists and bankers now become the industrialists and
bankers outright. The bureaucratic element becomes the juridical and
executive branch of the new exploiters. In this withering critique of
political socialism, Sorel did not say whether the new bureaucracy
becomes a class in the economic sense; however, like Trotsky in later
years, he indicated that in its social functions it assumes at least the
obligations and power of a minority class.[2]

No less a significant place in Sorel's thought is his belief that
traditional Marxism failed to meet the test of social science: the
application of its findings to new events, and the consequent ability
to devise methods of analysis to meet changed situations.[3] Unlike
Marx himself, his followers used the methods of science to make long

[1] *Réflexions sur la violence*, p. 367 (264).
[2] *La décomposition du marxisme*, pp. 51–3.
[3] *Matériaux d'une théorie du prolétariat*, pp. 251–3.

range predictions from contingent events. Starting from the premise that everything was moving society to socialism, orthodox Marxism became Panglossian. Every attempt to point out that that optimism is false which rests on erroneous premises was met with intransigence. Orthodoxy had a vested interest in maintaining the gratuitous platitudes of Enlightenment rationalism. Legal Marxism maintained that it alone was able to fulfil the dreams of the *philosophes* so rudely dashed to the ground by the bourgeois State. The proletarian State would do better these pundits said. Guided by *laisser-faire* notions of the relation of economy to polity, these prophets, counter to Marx, refused to believe that the State itself was an intrinsic source of exploitation.

The dogmatic faith in historical inevitability, coupled as it was with the inherited strategy and tactics of nineteenth century German politics, made a broad commitment to Marxism untenable for Sorel. 'Time after time the theorists of socialism have been embarrassed by contemporary history. They had constructed magnificent formulas, clear cut and symmetrical, but they could not make them fit the facts. Rather than abandon their theories, they preferred to declare that the most important facts were mere anomalies which science must ignore if it is to obtain a real understanding of the whole.'[1] The corruption of the idea of socialism, its transformation into a species of social reform and political careerism, was a consequence of the sterility of secular scholasticism; of paying homage to classic texts rather than class needs.[2]

No longer did Sorel feel it necessary to consider Germany representative of revolutionary socialism. Bernstein and Kautsky, whose brilliance Sorel never denied, were nonetheless responding to the growing aristocracy of German labour. They saw the harmonious development of society as a necessary aspect of a more powerful and articulate labour force. Those who continued to focus attention on socialism in Germany did so, in Sorel's opinion, because they were seeking a theory of labour reform rather than a theory of labour revolution.[3] The latter orientation was to be found in a different type of revision of Marxism, one which paid attention to socialist content rather than literary form. Italian neo-realism was perhaps unable to boast of success in squaring the circle of reform

---

[1] *Réflexions sur la violence*, p. 69 (73).
[2] *La décomposition du marxisme*, p. 6.
[3] *Réflexions sur la violence*, p. 188 (149).

and revolution, but it had the obvious merit of opening up further enquiry along this line, rather than insisting that further study beyond the corpus of Marx's writings was unnecessary.[1]

The movement of Marxism from a theory of revolution to one of reform issued into a philosophic castration: an emphasis on the method of compromise at the expense of the method of violence. That socialism tended to take this transvaluation seriously, as Sorel indicated it would, has since been made clear by the theory of communism as the gradual unfolding of harmonious, non-antagonistic interests. Its advocates reproduced the standpoint of German social democracy, but simply reserved it for use at a stage in history when State control passed into the hands of political socialism. The evolution of bolshevism tended to confirm Sorel's worst suspicions. Texts rather than facts conditioned theorizing about problems connected with social and economic transformations. In this fashion, the danger arose that orthodoxy could become a new variety of utopianism. Bolshevik theory asserted that proletarian society is compatible with the political state. 'The utopians excelled in the art of exposition in accordance with these prejudices; the more their exposition satisfied the requirements of a school book, the more convincing they thought their inventions were. I believe that the contrary of this belief is the truth, and that we should distrust proposals for social reform all the more, when every difficulty seems solved in an apparently satisfactory manner.'[2]

This boundless revulsion for historicism and teleologism opened up two different paths for Sorel: an empirically anchored sociology, or a personalistic theory of society as a collection of random events. His rejection of scientific methods in the social sciences moved Sorel towards the latter; toward the adoption of a pragmatic theory of society and a positivist attitude toward science.[3] The idea of *praxis* replaced the principle of organized intelligence as the propellent notion in his doctrine of social change. Sorel was unable to resolve the question of whether ideas are part of the battle, aside from the battle, or above the battle. Should a sociological perspective function as an instrument of a class ideology, or should it function as a critical instrument of all ideologies?

Sorel's personal detachment from the mainstream of political life

---

[1] *La décomposition du marxisme*, p. 5.
[2] *Réflexions sur la violence*, p. 207 (161).
[3] *Saggi di critica del marxismo*, pp. 85–92.

suggests at least an emotional awareness of this major problem in the sociology of political institutions. His resolution of it, which in fact was a compromise effort to have both science and action, indicated an unwillingness to accept socialist aims as a basis for revolutionary activity, and at the same time, a reassertion to retain socialism as an end. 'The ideas of socialism cannot be kept intact by diluting the phrases of Marx in verbose commentaries, but by continually adopting the spout of Marx to facts which are capable of assuming a revolutionary aspect.'[1] Unlike Alfred Weber or Karl Mannheim, it was in terms of a theory of myths rather than in terms of the critical, economically *freischwebende Intelligenz*, that Sorel hoped for a resolution of sociological theory and revolutionary action. Let the myth prepare the groundwork for those social changes that will give future sociologists laws to develop, Sorel seems to be saying.

The theory of myths, having its roots in a psychology of the collective unconscious, stands in sharp contrast to orthodox Marxism. In direct opposition to theories of spontaneity, Soviet ideology, which in this instance may be taken as representative of traditional Marxism, maintains that unconscious social behaviour is the upshot of societies without planning. Consciousness of class ambitions is what, in this view, distinguishes socialism from previous social systems. Socialism requires neither the guidance of an intellectual élite, nor spontaneous mass movements which ignore the lessons of history. Indeed, Soviet Marxism has maintained that consciousness, in the form of struggle against traditional ideologies, is both the methodology for overcoming material antagonisms under socialism, and also the form of social development in post-class civilization.[2] Thus, class consciousness, rather than being an inhibiting ideological counter-force, is said to impose a degree of responsibility and organization on all members of socialist society that is capable of resolving the historic antagonisms of head and hand.

The differences between syndical socialism and bolshevism are joined on the question of history: for Sorel, consciousness can study past history while unconsciousness makes future history; for Lenin, consciousness makes future history on the basis of studying past history. In the course of an article on partisanship, Lenin takes issue with the Sorelian thesis that Western European socialism is oppor-

---

[1] *Réflexions sur la violence*, pp. 328–9 (240).
[2] Andrei Zhdanov, *Essays on Literature, Philosophy and Music* (New York, 1950), pp. 70–2.

tunity-oriented and not class-oriented. Lenin agrees with those socialists who, in terms of given historical and economic conditions, came to 'regard parliamentarianism and trade unionism as their main method of struggle.' That which Sorel berated as political treason, Lenin calls history. 'Marxism demands an absolutely historical examination of the question of the forms of struggle. To treat the question apart from the concrete historical situation is to betray ignorance of the very rudiments of dialectical materialism. At different stages of economic evolution, depending on differences in political, national-cultural, living and other conditions, different forms of struggle come to the fore and become the principal forms of struggle; and in connection with this, the secondary, auxiliary forms of struggle undergo change in their turn.'[1] It is clear that Lenin sees in history a protracted series of events, and not a compounded moment.

The relation of freedom to social authority was no less an insurmountable divide between syndicalism and bolshevism. This rupture has been put clearly by a Soviet historian of an earlier period. Little has since happened to alter the objections to a Sorelian theory of freedom. Among syndical socialists 'decisions are followed only by those who agree with them of their own free will. What is the result? The result is that, instead of a collective opinion binding on all members of the organization and carried out in practice, every member is "his own master," free to follow any view he chooses. The result is the cult of the individual, an aristocratic cult; the result is that at the critical moment, when the working class must act without delay, an endless discussion ensues, to the advantage of the enemy. The enemy gains if the working class has no one opinion binding on all who take part in the struggle. The enemy gains if every man acts for himself, as he thinks fit, and not as the general interests of the working class demand.'[2]

In Sorel's field of vision, such a standpoint undermines the aims of socialist freedom. It replaces the individual imagination of the revolutionist under a regimen of conscious necessities of the collective duties which are usually externally motivated. From the free creativity of the workshop, we end in the miasma of the shackling of individual needs by the supposed requirements of family,

[1] V. I. Lenin, 'Partisanskaya Voina,' *Sochineniya*, Vol. X; translated as 'Partisan Warfare' in *Marx-Engels-Marxism* (Moscow, 1951), p. 187.

[2] E. Yaroslavsky, *History of Anarchism in Russia* (New York, 1937), pp. 100–1.

community, state and nation. In this attempt to introduce a working notion of egalitarian democracy, socialism undergoes a hardening of the political and intellectual arteries that eventually transforms socialist society into despotism. For Sorel, the only assurance that the free will does not result in chaotic consequences is the freedom to exercise one's decision-making powers. The only total guarantee against the 'cult of the individual' is individualism.

Inasmuch as Sorel died before the tendencies of either fascism or bolshevism had asserted themselves, the distinctions drawn between Sorel's vision and contemporary forms of capitalist and socialist polity have only inferential value. Nonetheless, the fact that a logical projection of this type can be established indicates the varied forms in which the authoritarian mould might conceivably be cast. Sorel's own standpoint is clearly lacking a positive set of values, or even a manageable ordering of propositions. His is a political philosophy set against others, not in virtue of its liberal or conservative partisanship, but rather as a consequence of his idealized image of a spontaneous and free society. That clear distinctions are necessary even within the framework of authoritarian perspectives serves to indicate how complicated the question of lineage really is.

Despite the evidence indicating a sharp divergence between syndicalism and fascism, Sorel was yet able to describe Mussolini as 'an Italian of the fifteenth century, a *condottiere!*' Beyond this, he was also viewed as 'the only energetic man capable of redressing the feebleness of the government.'[1] Similarly, Sorel's unbridled praise of Lenin and the Russian revolution indicates his willingness to overlook many theoretical divergencies in the name of revolutionary action. Lenin is said to have been 'at once the greatest theorist that socialism has had since Marx and the head of a State whose genius recalls that of Peter the Great.'[2] This antinomous relation to modern forms of democratic capitalism at one and the same instant points to common characteristics in the origins of bolshevism and fascism, and the private, highly emotive reasons Sorel had for praising the practice of movements and ideas he had continually damned in theory.

The essential point is that Sorel's stamp of approval on radical European currents is more in the nature of self-approval. The events

[1] This comment by Sorel on Mussolini was first reported by Jean Variot and cited in Gaétan Pirou, *Georges Sorel*, p. 53. A good summary of the largely unverified comments of the two men on each other is contained in James H. Meisel, *The Genesis of Georges Sorel*, pp. 219-33.

[2] *Réflexions sur la violence*, p. 442 (305).

following the First World War did much to wipe out his pessimism and bitterness at the failure of syndicalist radicalism in France. Sorel's relationship to the earliest tendencies of fascism and bolshevism was therefore not an account of the actual interests and attitudes at stake in either the Russian revolution or the Italian counter-revolution, but an imposition or, better, a super-imposition of his political doctrines upon these momentous events. Why Sorel was compelled to seek salvation through other quarters, why it was necessary for him to seek vindication in the theory and practice of these alternatives to capitalist democracy, forms the final stage in this analysis.

3. The Paradox of Power and the Collapse of Pragmatic Socialism

The ambiguous relationship which the Sorelian vision had with existing political and intellectual currents of the early twentieth century was an inevitable outcome of a theory which employed sociology to establish political mysticism. But this was a general failing of revolutionary thinkers with roots in the *fin de siècle*. France underwent a series of three major revolutions between 1830 and 1871. All of them promised far more than they were able to deliver. The people participated in events that altered their economic position but slightly. The spectacle of empires and republics toppling could not forever disguise the fact that revolution in political forms of rule did not take the place of revolution in economic content. The defeat of the Paris Commune, the alliance of French and German economic masters to ensure this defeat, shattered old faiths and old loyalties. The ideal of socialism had for many revolutionaries in fact become an unworkable myth.[1]

The philosophic ground of Sorelism was to establish a doctrine of social revolution that could act as a bulwark against further defeats and further disaffections. The tragedy of Sorelism is not that it was replete with ambiguity, but that it was an ambiguity built into the structure of French society. The following examination of these internal deficits of Sorel's thought should not, therefore, be taken as an assertion of personal failing, but as representative of the helplessness of a France without common or consistent endeavour.

[1] For accounts of the 'legalization' of socialism, see the classic accounts of Edouard Dolléans, *Histoire du mouvement ouvrier, 1871–1936* (Paris, 1939); G. Weill, *Histoire du mouvement social en France* (Paris, 1910); and Paul Louis, *Histoire du mouvement syndical en France* (Paris, 1948).

In the economic realm Sorel's syndicalism had its most logical force. He made his direct appeal to the producers. Yet it was precisely in this field of economics that Sorel offered the least valuable counsel. The strictures of a theory which posited economics as a socialist *ding-an-sich* made the study of economics, as a science, at best a fruitless task. It led Sorel to view economic solutions as attempts to compromise the political struggle.

The structure of an economy was in itself not the main source of the class struggle according to Sorel, but simply the residue of material and technological progress. His position maintained not only that Marx's *Das Kapital* was unable to explain the actual phenomena of economic existence, but that in principle it was not possible for any economic theory to assume the posture of scientific explanation. All that is feasible is to establish metaphysical economy, not a scientific economy. The real world of industrial conflict came to be viewed as a shadow world over whose control men had very little to say.[1]

What is important in Sorel's economic position is his characterization of Marx's labour theory of value. Even before Max Weber in Germany, he claimed that Marx worked out his view as an ideal construction, with only limited practical applicability. Sorel held that Marx, like Ricardo before him, for the purposes of abstraction viewed society as a mechanical economy in which competition is always at a maximum. In such a situation, in which the tendencies of capitalism are always viewed as realized, one can readily infer the class struggle from productive antagonisms. However, in reality all such ideal types are blunted, and therefore the intensity of the class struggle has to be explained in more concretely political terms. The substance of Sorel's critique is that Marx tried to infer a social programme from the propositions of a supposedly pure science. And as we have seen in Sorel's philosophy of science, his view of scientific explanation rules out all attempts to chart the character of future societies.[2]

Sorel laboured to evolve a theory of politics independent of economic factors. He remained incapable of considering economics as a unified process of machine production and human labour sub-

[1] 'Sur la théorie marxiste de la valeur,' *Journal des Economistes* (March 1897), pp. 227–8.

[2] *Ibid.*, pp. 228–9. See also *Matériaux d'une théorie du prolétariat*, pp. 183–9, where Marx's ideal constructions are justified on political grounds rather than as economically true.

ject to scientific evaluation *precisely because it operated with abstractions*. Empirical generalization is replaced by a fragmentary moral codification. Technology becomes morally valuable, for it alone can make possible the abundance which is necessary for a State-less society; but shifts in economic control were more feared than valued. Sorel retained a fear that the proletariat, ground under by a machine technology, would become spiritually mediocre. Writing about the modern intellectual in general, Bertrand de Jouvenal offers a striking account of the dilemma underlying Sorel's position on economic theory and practice. 'The intellectual is really of two minds about the general economic process. On the one side he takes pride in the achievement of technique and rejoices that men get more things which they want. On the other hand, he feels that the conquering army of industry destroys values and the discipline reigning there is a harsh one. These two views are conveniently reconciled by attributing to the "force" of "capitalism" everything one dislikes.'[1] In economics one detects how, in his effort to escape from intellectualism, Sorel reproduces the intellectualist fallacies. In his attempted flight from abstract moral prescription, he merely carried moral abstraction to a politically sensitive area. His high regard for the modifications of Marxian economics by Bernstein, Kautsky and Croce did not extend to a faith in the revolutionary potential of Marxian revisionism. It had its roots elsewhere in a belief that these men inadvertently revealed that *l'esprit petit-bourgeois* is inherent in attempts to locate the source of revolutionary ferment in a pure theory of economics.[2]

In consequence, Sorel's revised theory of socialism left the producers with a voluntary choice of economic beliefs; but no one belief could be the focus of revolutionary activity since none of them could legitimately move from description to prediction. Sorel shrewdly perceived that since Social Democratic Marxism rests upon an economic interpretation of events, the rise of social reform was inevitable. The sanction of economic law made unnecessary a mobilization of the physical capacities of the proletariat.[3] The daily activities of the

[1] Bertrand de Jouvenal, 'The Treatment of Capitalism by Continental Intellectuals,' in *Capitalism and the Historians* (edited by F. A. Hayek) (Chicago, 1954), p. 115.

[2] *La décomposition du marxisme*, pp. 31–4; and *Matériaux d'une théorie du prolétariat*, pp. 145–51, offer Sorel's summations at the ideological and political levels of the political consequences of economic reformism.

[3] *Saggi di critica del marxismo*, pp. 63–71.

working force, strengthening of bargaining positions through better conditions of labour and higher wages and benefits, were not considered politically meaningful. On the contrary, the political destiny of the proletariat was to struggle directly against State authority, and leave political bargaining to those for whom it is a vocation, the intellectuals.[1] The locus of organized activity was to be separate from the economic scaffold. This bifurcation of economic and political levels ensured a permanent separation of Sorelian syndicalism from the main currents of labour activities.[2]

An analogous paradox prevailed politically. Although the domain of politics was central, it was political activity outside the organized modes of society as a whole. The purity of the radical movement was to be preserved by developing a political-governmental apparatus separate and in isolation from political parties. In this manner the philosophy of syndicalism issued into the path of minority revolution without real possibilities for assuming the actual leadership of society. This self-imposed restriction led to a situation in which syndical socialism could only prescribe violence as a means of achieving power. This prescription of violence turned into terrorism, since social conditions were not evaluated independent of proletarian mythology.

There is a clear connection between absolute terrorism and absolute pacifism, between Sorel and Tolstoy.[3] Both rest upon a total disregard of the political machinery of society as a means for achieving human emancipation. Both offer a heroic concept of history; for Sorel the hero is an activist in blind disregard for personal consequences, while for Tolstoy the hero also rises above concern for the private person by being concerned with his universal moral standpoint. Both men shared a mystical respect for those who worked with their hands, and in their revolutionary potential. Finally, both of them assume an eschatological moral tone, understandably so, since they share an apocalyptic vision of revolution and social change generally. This analogy surely does not prove that activism and

---

[1] *Matériaux d'une théorie du prolétariat*, pp. 98–9.

[2] This split of anarchism-syndicalism from the rest of socialist factions was accentuated not only by the internal legalization of socialism, but also by the parallel rights granted to the trade unions. On this point, see Louis Levene, *Syndicalism in France* (New York, 1912); and for the following decade, D. J. Saposs, *The Labour Movement in Post-War France* (New York, 1931).

[3] The link with Tolstoy was probably made through the anarchist writings of Kropotkin, which circulated widely in France at the turn of the century.

pacifism are without widely differing consequences. But it merely demonstrates that when consequences are severed from the means by which they result, political capriciousness blurred by moral absoluteness is an invariable effect.

The same type of paradox rendered Sorel's intellectual outlook hopelessly inept. Anxious to develop a lineage between himself and the past, Sorel employs sources for his outlook that were to replace the spirit of free enquiry with dogmatism, and possibly transform sociological knowledge into political prescriptions. It was a dogmatism of a special variety, since it rested upon a rejection of the possibility that the intellectual perception of man could set tasks and resolve them in a predictable manner. Indeterminism, in Sorel's hands, was more than a theory of physical probabilities and improbabilities; it became the approval for a revolt against reason, against the criticism of society. Intellectual instruments of criticism being denied to men, criticism had to take the form of action. But it was an action uninformed as to its material ground. This contradiction between action and intellect compelled Sorel to abandon the search for a philosophic expression of experience. The search for general laws governing the intersection of the State and of Morality was buried by Sorel along with romanticism. In its place was put a meta-theory of the politics of sociology: the political determinants of human knowledge and ideologies. In moving from the general to the special case, from politics as a science to politics as power, Sorel moved further away from an analytic view of society. By taking his interpretation of power politics as the only correct one, he cut himself off from his ultimate goal: a critical and non-ideological view of politics.

The critique of contemporary sociology became in Sorel's hands a criticism of sociology as such. Criticism of existing problems in the labour theory of value became transformed into a critique of economic science as such. Opposition to Enlightenment principles of reason and utility became crystallized into a denunciation of the critical capacities of reason. In this fashion Sorel steadily moved from a position as critic of the utopian into a convert of utopianism, from a critic of metaphysics into a metaphysician of socialism. This was a consequence of a political sociology that lost its autonomy and became caught up in the political exploitation of social science.

Any theory of minority revolution is inherently a theory of violence. The source from which this élite minority was to come was denied to Sorel, since on economic, political and intellectual grounds a cleavage between the mass of men and their leaders was to be bridged by the syndicalist movement. But the energy of syndical socialism spent itself almost as soon as the velocity of industrial development became pronounced. When the small scale workshop was replaced by the large impersonal factory, when the producer no longer confronted the owner in open and apparent contrasting needs and ambitions, at that point the needs of the producers also shifted. The organization of the bourgeoisie on a highly efficient and de-personalized basis made a counter-development in the labouring sectors necessary. Organization, rather than individual sublimity, became the need of the time. Revolutionary spontaneity came to be replaced by economic discipline. Politics and political practice became an imitation of the modern economic enterprise. Problems of organization, buried by Sorel as trivial, became central. The need for a scientific sociology, viewed as an intellectualist substitute for direct confrontation with the effete civilization, became the principal instrument for understanding man's relation to modern industrial society. Since society is no longer simple, i.e., man to man and intuitive, a science of society becomes necessary. The question of a collective response to the challenge of industrialism, seen as a re-actionary departure from morality by Sorel, has become an anachron-ism, not simply because of an internal deficiency, but because circum-stances have posed a set of problems for civilization that Sorel was unable to comprehend, much less resolve.

In its effort to break through the complicated world of bureaucracy and statism, to release men's energies from endless concentration on the formal requirements of repressive civilization, Sorel's thought only reduced itself to a clumsy form of moralizing. What is absent in his thinking is a recognition that the political regulation of morals in a complex society is impossible. To reject political control of every phase and stage of human values does not carry with it a rejection of the State and politics in general, for they may regulate styles in which individuality and individual moral judgments can be presented.

With Sorel's philosophy of society, political schism followed hard on the heels of theoretical paradox. Depending upon where the emphasis was placed, the Sorelian syndicalist found himself shifting allegiance to parties and movements representing powerful material interests. If the politics of direct and immediate action, the theory of revolutionary myths, the function of violence as the essential agent in cataclysmic social change, and the cult of the hero in history, in short, if the psychology of Sorel was emphasized, the follower was likely to become attached to fascism and corporativism. If his critique of capitalist economy, the need for a strict proletarian conscience, and a regard for the virtues of socialism are placed in the forefront, the likely result was for the Sorelian to move towards an espousal of bolshevism. Syndicalism was thus consecrated at opposite poles of the movement, away from liberal middle class civilization. In the sense that Sorel was a philosopher of negation such an outcome was not unnatural. But this fact undermined possibilities of a political sociology which would also be a revolutionary battle-cry. It undermines Sorel's standpoint as such.

The assumption that syndicalism could stand outside history and create the conditions of revolution in isolation from involvement in the currents of political organization, collapsed as soon as the contending economic forces of modern industrialism were confronted with a crisis situation. The weight of syndical socialism was generally thrown on the side of radical currents, even within the fascist movements. But separated as it was from political realities, fetishizing the role of political outsider, syndicalism contributed a discordant note to attempts at achieving a unified labour movement. This is not to say that possibilities of uniting currents and factions in European socialism were possible, given the hostilities of socialist and communist elements following the establishment of Soviet power. It is rather to say that syndicalism, following its credo of anti-politics, performed a political role nonetheless. It served to deplete the social forces aligned against reaction in France and the growth of fascism elsewhere in Europe. Given its propensity to regard the idea of permanent revolution subjectively, apart from the aims of revolution, Sorelian socialism offered few safeguards against the encroachment of authoritarianism. It paved the way for a new conservatism as clearly as the Terror made Bonapartism possible.

Sorel is a minor figure in the history of political ideas despite the fact that he treated major themes. This is because his outstanding critical acumen outweighed any sense of construction. Lacking this sense, Sorel was subjected to the caprices of syndicalist socialism.

Sorel's strength lay in his remarkable ability to pose the concrete issues of political life as they existed in the early part of the century. At no point did Sorel evade intellectual forthrightness. His was a failure of constructive intelligence. His followers, interpreting his failure to construct a political theory to be either the failure of society as a whole or a necessary element in a social science pragmatically conceived, soon gave up the attempt to go beyond him. Given a desperate climate, they were unable to cope with the issues at hand. The followers of Sorel, concentrating their fire on society as a whole, became critics without portfolio. They were politically rootless, *déracinés*. The upshot was a failure of nerve which isolated syndicalism from revolutionary social currents. Sorelism became dogmatic in a way Sorel was not. If Marxism had become the opium of the Marxists by the turn of the century, Sorelism had become the opium of Sorelians within a much shorter time.

I should like to state the results of this study in five propositions. They include not only the mute and paradoxical results of Sorel's outlook, but his achievements as well. The bifurcated poles of his thinking have provided modern political theory with its fundamental problems, the solution to which will provide a deeper insight into the nature of social class and the function of political power.

The essential field of human activity for Sorel is political activity. Yet the contents of his political sociology represent a denial that the existing frame of politics contains either the solutions or the problems of men.

The State which is the central organism of domination, the bureaucracy which is the human substance of the State, and the military which is the concrete power manifestation of the State, receive the most attention and the sharpest criticism at Sorel's hand. Yet the forces aligned against the State, against the organized political force of the ruling élites, are seen as developing outside and independent of the State. Political concerns are transformed into anti-political concerns. The negation of the State becomes the negation of politics itself. Since working class activity is not examinable without reference to established organs of control, problems of law and social order find no place in Sorel's pragmatic socialism. The destruction of the bourgeoisie, and of the State itself, may answer the problem of power under social systems of past ages, but it merely raises the spectre of power under socialism.

Sorel did not examine how syndical socialism is to function outside the framework of historically evolved political processes because his concept of the leader played the part of a *deus ex machina* resolving human anomalies. To have no programme became an asset. Élitism was not an accoutrement in Sorel's thinking, but a necessity. The problems of men have no solutions in truth, only in beliefs. And since democracy is considered a disguise of the struggle of classes, what is better than the method of authority to ensure the continuum of myths?[1] The problems of men were to be handled by an élite, who were in turn to be repaid with undeviating loyalty. Socialism would be a feudal moral economy of the future: the proletarian élite would be a guardian nobility, while the proletarian commoner would receive a guaranteed annual morality. Sorel thus transformed the issue of political emancipation into a form for relieving psychological anxiety in a universe of chance.

In a world lacking verifiable truths, there is no need to make a concrete analysis of the politics of socialism, and even less need to anticipate potential shortcomings in syndicalist organization. Sorel was convinced that his socialism would not reproduce the evils of the State because he unconsciously operated with a theory of permanent revolution. His future society had flux without structure, in the same way that the intuitionist has experience without nature. Structural analysis of socialism became unimportant, not only for the stated reason that such analysis reproduce utopian formulas, but for the more basic reason that structure stood in the path of social flux, permanent revolution. The place of tradition became vital to Sorel, not because he was a conservative socialist, but as a means to compensate for the liquidation of structure in social relations. Tradition became a cementing agent that man could feel without having to know. Unlike structure, tradition was not subject to experimental criteria. Tradition assumed mythological dimensions, informing men subjectively of where they had been in relation to where they now stood in the historical voyage. Where they are going was not so important as the fact of going. In the subjective experience of men, all is flux. Sorel hoped to reproduce in society a replica of this flux, which he conceived as irrational, by making revolutionary change a constant; he never halted to enquire as to the values in human terms of all this alteration. Pragmatic socialism, by conceiving the revolt against capitalism in terms of a sensation of change, as the vocabulary of change, left the underlying material culture intact. Political

---

[1] Sorel insisted that his critique of democracy was a necessary consequence of Marx's position. He considered socialist politics an attempt to compromise Marx by viewing socialism as true democracy and capitalism as false democracy. See *Matériaux d'une théorie du prolétariat*, pp. 191–2.

emancipation was to come about through the emancipation of men from their reason. Sensationalism, in the philosophic sense, rather than socialism, in the economic sense, was to be the ground of progress toward the gilded future.

The evidence for syndical socialism is said to rest upon the historical requirements of humanity, that is, upon the belief in history as an objective and verifiable process. Yet, the basis of mass action is asserted to be anti-historical, based on subjectively held myths and not history; upon a view of history as simply an extension of individual imagination and fantasy.

The elaborate working out of Sorel's theory of socialism rested on a study of the empirical history of both ancient and modern societies with their various changes and transformations in economics, politics and culture patterns. It was the role of force in objective history that first turned Sorel towards a generalization of historical experience. But in the very process of generalization, Sorel effects a suppression of historical experience. The descriptive elements which are at first said to form the foundation of a theory of progress are denied in his generalizations as having any real or organic bearing on either the course of human events or on prescribing what one's actions should be in a specific historical situation. From a historical basis Sorel draws normative conclusions. The myth serves to save mankind from eternal damnation. The growth of empirical knowledge of society becomes but a tool in examining the past only. The facts of history which initially serve to point out to Sorel that a break with class patterns of oppression is possible, is sacrificed upon the altar of eternal normative patterns and instinctual gratifications of heroism and power. Sorel's political sociology is ripped apart by his theory of society, which asserts that history shows how to resolve the problems of men, while the same theory denies that such a resolution is possible given the essentially contingent nature of human inter-course. The function of history as a science is to explain human events. But if such events are determined by arbitrary mythical forces, explanation is without predictive value. Hence for Sorel, a theory of socialism hinges upon a doctrine of antisocial human nature.

Sorel develops a psychology of action in order to realize the goal of human liberation. But since human liberation itself is merely a continuation of an action psychology, the aim of scientific psychology, rationality, is submerged in an instinctual pool. Human practice, Sorel's

192

basic prophylactic of civilization, in this way loses a sense of meaning, direction and value.

Sorel employs a psychological dimension for the purpose of uncovering the motor force of human desires to grow. However, the notion of growth involved an ambiguity, since no objective criteria were considered permissible by Sorel in defining growth through commonly accepted scientific forecasts. If the purpose of action is limited to the emancipation of the imagination, the *raison d'être* of revolutionary action itself becomes questionable. Whatever insights Sorel provided into the necessary mental and emotional equipment necessary for the conduct of the affairs of revolution, he could not break the bonds of that interpersonal rivalry which he placed at the centre of politics and culture. If action were central, then the goals achieved by socialism were necessarily transitory and of secondary value. If socialism were the focal point, then action was simply an instrument for reaching the goal, intrinsically no more valuable than other means, and certainly fraught with greater danger than other methods. Sorel's theory of psychology is not only circular, but any attempt to break the circle results in the disintegration of at least one major Sorelian concept: either the idea that action based on myth is the essential pre-condition for a non-neurotic society, or that socialism is in fact the goal of practice. Freud once noted that 'science is no illusion; but it would be an illusion to suppose that we could get anywhere else what it cannot give us.' It was Sorel's supreme myth that he could defy science and its methods and yet manage an escape from paradox. Action was his supreme illusion. It was to replace science in informing men of their goals. Yet the very nature of action was to prove in fact there are no empirically grounded social goals.

The polarities of reason and unreason, mythology and science, sociality and individuality, were contained in Sorel's inability to supply a set of basic values by which men might live harmoniously. The further he sought the basis of an integrated society, the more deeply committed he became to an irreducible alienation and atomization of the human situation.

In framing an alternative to capitalism, in offering men a set of values that would ensure against stagnation and decadence, Sorel is essentially unable to take a standpoint based on empirical content. The wholesale rejection of Enlightenment, as formulated by the aristocracy in the eighteenth century, as used by the bourgeoisie in the nineteenth century, and as appropriated by socialism in the twentieth century, committed him to an authoritarian programme that, in the process of rooting out old forms of social and political ills, offers no machinery for bringing about a workable alternative. Where does decadence or criminality begin? What are the criteria by which we can describe the one or the other? Sorel offers none. The basis of modern production, insists Sorel, requires a higher consciousness than that possessed by any other class than the producers. Nonetheless, the producers are exhorted to follow their unconscious yearnings, not their rational understanding. The workshop of the future is to witness the further expansion of a scientific technology. However, the society of the future is supposed to restore the armour of primitive myth. Sorel desires to bypass the State machinery to ensure the purity of socialism; yet labourers are encouraged to oppose regimen or directives of any sort. The more deeply Sorel struggled to achieve an appropriate ethic for socialism, the closer did he return to scholasticism for the sources of moral wisdom. While on the plane of material culture, the deeper he probed, the more committed he became to an idealist metaphysic divorced from scientific and technological developments.

Emancipation was itself a major stumbling block for Sorel. At one and the same instant, emancipation is conceived of strictly as political emancipation from the nation-State, and also more broadly as human emancipation from the uniformity and mediocrity of class relations and class existence. Yet at no point is Sorel able to show the inter-relation between political emancipation and human emancipation, between freedom at the objective and subjective levels alike.

The foundations of human emancipation require in Sorel's view a separation from concrete political goals themselves. Since concrete political aims are never realized in the form in which they are anticipated, and the functioning of history is essentially a mystery which does not yield its secrets in advance of the occurrence, any attempt to unite political and human emancipation is doomed on logical grounds. Human emancipation is conceived in terms of the myth, political emancipation in terms of the material basis of socialism. Instead of a unified description of politics and psychology, Sorel only succeeds in achieving a permanent dualism between action and theory. The theory of political emancipation becomes a mythological device for organizing the aims of producers. But it is only through the abandonment of political emancipation as a realizable goal that human emancipation becomes possible. Alienation, the reflection of human misery, becomes enshrined in Sorel's system as the permanent lot of men. Illusion and ideology, the nourishment of the happily alienated individual, replace science and technique as the basis of human integration. Sorel bequeathed a legacy of permanent disillusionment for those who take political liberation seriously. Permanent revolution, the political expression of pragmatic socialism, becomes transformed into permanent disenchantment.

The polarities, glaring at us from the pages of Sorel's writings, form the nucleus of the genuine problems of political theory because they are the as yet unresolved paradoxes of existing social systems. What is living, what is genuine in Sorel's thought, is the presentation of the real choices which men have in this world. For him the world is stripped of the cant of divine essences and the hypocrisy of a predetermined freedom. What is of lesser importance, what in effect is dead in Sorel's thought, are the particular choices he made on behalf of the life-force, the myth and élitism. Our century bears firm witness to the fact that a radicalism founded upon irrationalism cuts two ways: It might serve as a decisive antiseptic to the infections caused by our inherited rational middle class civilization, but it is no less a poison which cures the infection by destroying the patient—civilization itself. What suggests itself is that when radicalism revolts against reason, it undermines the historical foundations of radicalism itself. Irrationalism is a revolt which results in counter-radicalism. This is the political agony of Sorel's pragmatic universe.

BIBLIOGRAPHICAL NOTE

IT is my belief that a formal bibliography would have been super-erogatory. The footnotes provide ample indication of the range of original works I have employed. For those wishing to pursue matters more deeply, I suggest that they look into Paul Delesalle's 'Bibliographie Sorelienne' published in *International Review For Social History*, Vol. IV (Leiden, 1939). For the literature published on and by Sorel between 1886 and 1938, this is by far the most extensive single source, although mention should be made of the fact that the secondary sources listed are not nearly complete. Delesalle somehow failed to include the many books about political philosophy, social history and economic doctrines that contain chapters on the work of Sorel. But with this exception, Delesalle's compilation is extremely reliable and thorough. James H. Meisel's, *The Genesis of Georges Sorel* (Ann Arbor, 1951), and Irwin Pomerance's *The Moral Utopianism of Georges Sorel* (Columbia University Dissertation, New York, 1950. Unpublished), each contain a substantial listing of the Sorel literature printed after 1938.

The books on Sorel fall into various categories, which display revealing national characteristics. Serious work on Sorel in the United States has been a relatively recent phenomenon. Most of the material has been severely handicapped by attributing a dominant thesis to the very elusive Sorel. Thus, for Pomerance (cited above) and for the far more sophisticated essay by Edward Shils (appended to the American edition of *Reflections On Violence*, Glencoe, 1950), the theme of Sorel as *moraliste* par excellence is emphasized. For the former the moral strain is an advanced form of utopianism, for the latter it is primitive and tribalist. In Scott H. Lytle's work, *Historical Materialism and the Social Myth* (Cornell University Dissertation, Ithaca, 1948. Unpublished), which has the distinction of being the first, and perhaps still the most worthwhile dissertation, a historical thesis is evident. Sorel is divided into pre-Marxian, Marxian and post-Marxian periods. However, even the author seems to sense that such a laboured division compounds confusion rather than removes it. He thus places Sorel's constant shifting of political loyalties in the realm of motives, and does not feel that the historian's 'prudence' should invade psychological domains. Meisel's dissertation, from a literary point of view, from the perspective of how the materials were left disorganized and dishevelled, leaves much to be desired. Nonetheless it represented a high water mark in Sorel scholarship. The extensive use of Sorel's correspondence provides a remarkable picture of the unity through eclecticism that is Sorel's trademark. Meisel's untidiness is perhaps truer to the actual spirit of Sorel's method of work than any of the other dissertations. Certainly, if we are to judge by Richard Humphrey's *Georges Sorel: Prophet Without Honor* (Cambridge, Mass, 1951), which is a study in Sorel's anti-intellectualism, and in fact succeeds in placing Sorel in a far more tidy intellectual package than is warranted by the evidence, the choice would have to be made for the wide-open approach. From my own vantage-point, it is clear that I consider these needless polarities, resting on insufficient analysis of the meaning of key terms like rationalism, radicalism and revolution. The interesting survey by the American historian, H. Stuart Hughes, *Consciousness and Society: The Reorientation of European Social Thought, 1890–1930*, appeared too late to assist me fundamentally in my own labours. I am appreciative for those parallels which exist between our appraisals of Sorel and his milieu, and, at the same time, respect those judgments different from my own.

In England, attention has lagged considerably since the 'twenties. Basically, it was the conservative *literati*, men like T. E. Hulme in *Speculations* (London, 1924), and Wyndham Lewis in *The Art of Being Ruled* (London, 1926), who responded most vigorously to the Sorelian challenge. Both of these writers, to their lasting credit, saw the profoundly anti-Enlightenment and anti-democratic content of Sorel's socialism. They employed Sorel as a warning to the contented bourgeois, that democracy is neither the only nor necessarily the best suited form of government. However, this conservative anarchism was too concerned with utilizing Sorel as a vehicle for expressing its own aristocratic position to do much to illuminate the picture of Sorel. Up to now, the most able summaries of Sorel's political views have appeared in survey volumes. Alexander Gray's *The Socialist Tradition: Moses to Lenin* (London, 1946) offers a chapter on syndicalism which reveals a serious appraisal of Sorel and his early association with Lagardelle. A most penetrating account of the Sorelian legacy is contained in the work of a pupil of Ernest Barker and Harold Laski, Roger Soltau's *French Political Thought in the Nineteenth Century* (London and New Haven, 1931).

It was a German scholar, Michael Freund, who in his work, *Georges Sorel: der revolutionäre Konservativismus* (Frankfurt am-Main, 1932), gave intellectual substance to what the English *literati* had only been able to intuit. Freund was the first to set forth the actual dialectic in Sorel, i.e., the use of conservative theory for radical ends when dealing with problems of socialism and the future of the State, and the employment of radical theory for conservative ends when dealing with the weaknesses inherent in all present social and political structures. Through this mechanism Freund is able to build up a systematic account of Sorel's inner philosophical and sociological evolution.

The French literature on Sorel, which is by far the most voluminous, and has the most to offer for those concerned with a picture of Sorel's personal life and its trials and tribulations, at the same time is the least rewarding from the point of objective analysis. Upon the death of Sorel, a spate of volumes appeared on him which were uniformly favourable, and at the same time, singularly uncritical. Among the most informed are those of the Italian writer, Max Ascoli, *Georges Sorel* (Paris, 1921); Paul Perrin, *Les idées sociales de Georges Sorel* (Alger, 1925); and somewhat later, Jacques Rennes, *Georges Sorel et le syndicalisme révolutionaire* (Paris, 1936). The next generation witnessed an intensely ideological and partisan attitude either for or against Sorel's ideas. One need only compare Sammy Beracha's *Le Marxisme aprés Marx: Sorel contre le marxisme politique* (Paris, 1937) with Pierre Lasserre, *Georges Sorel: Le theoricien de l'imperialisme ouvrier* (Paris, 1928) to see that French intellectuals were no longer as concerned with Sorel as they were with problems of the rise of fascism in Italy and communism in Russia, and the attendant restructuring of political lines in France. The period after the Second World War has brought the beginnings of a balanced appraisal of Sorel's intellectual worth. With Fernand Rossignol's *La pensée de Georges Sorel* (Paris, 1948) this attempt at objectivity is clearly evident. And although Rossignol's position does not offer much new evidence or theoretical novelty, it indicates a cooling of passions that might possibly augur well for French evaluations of one of their most significant intellectual figures. Pierre Andreu's *Notre Maitre, M. Sorel* (Paris, 1953) is the most detailed estimate of Sorel's personal career (to the point of providing a list of what Sorel was reading in his engineering days), and perhaps represents the peak effort of Sorel's old associates and admirers to keep his memory firmly intact.

Sorel studies in Italy, where Sorel exercised his most profound influence, are rather skimpy. A large number of articles on him have appeared over the years, but no major work of any significance. The early works of Agostino Lanzillo, *Giorgio Sorel* (Rome, 1910); and F. Aguilanti, *Giorgio Sorel* (Rome, 1916) are not much more than slender guides to the reading of Sorel, offering no more than broad intellectual connections and historical antecedents. The rise of Italian fascism produced a liberal counter-attack to the advocates of Sorel's views in the Italian syndicates. Such writers as Gaetano Salvemini, *The Fascist Dictatorship in Italy* (New York, 1927); *Italian Fascism* (London, 1938), and even more pointedly, Gaudens Megaro, *Mussolini in the Making* (Boston, 1938), tended to take fascism at its word in claiming Sorel as a major intellectual precursor. However, this is by no means the measure of Sorel's influence in Italy. Perhaps the greatest honour has been paid to his memory there, since it is only in Italy that the major intellectual figures have actually employed Sorel's findings in their own work. Vilfredo Pareto, Roberto Michels, Benedetto Croce, and even Croce's dogged Marxian adversary, Antonio Gramsci, reveal throughout their writings the pervasiveness of Sorel's point of view and the deep respect in which it was held. Thus, I should say that the Italian scholars have by indirection done more to save Sorel from becoming merely an intellectual curiosity than any other group of thinkers.

It remains only to add my intellectual indebtedness to works of a larger scope. The several volumes of G. D. H. Cole's monumental *A History of Socialist Thought*, and Jean Maitron's brilliant *Histoire du mouvement anarchiste en France, 1880–1914*, set a social frame of reference for me without which I would have been unable to place Sorel in his larger milieu. Likewise, Roberto Michels, *Political Parties*, and Franz Neumann's collection of essays, *The Democratic and the Authoritarian State* (Glencoe, 1957) have been influential in shaping my ideas on the relationship of politics to economics and society as a whole. Similarly, I have drawn from Freud's 'philosophical' works, *The Future of an Illusion*, and *Civilization and its Discontents* in evaluating Sorel's social and individual psychology. I have saved for last an acknowledgement to the work of Karl Marx, whose critical acumen remains an essential beacon for understanding all subsequent socialist literature.

SUPPLEMENT TO BIBLIOGRAPHICAL NOTE

Several works have come to my attention since preparing the book for publication. They bear directly on main themes dealt with. The tendency to uncritically lump Sorel with Michels, Pareto and Mosca, particularly evident in James Burnham, *The Machiavellians, Defenders of Freedom* (New York, 1943), has left a distorted picture of Franco-Italian thought. A step toward rectifying this is made by James H. Meisel, who in *The Myth of the Ruling Class: Gaetano Mosca and the Elite* (Ann Arbor, 1958), clearly distinguishes Mosca from Sorel. The precise relation of Sorel to Nietzsche remains cloudy. Evidence that Sorel's appreciation of Nietzsche's work was genuine but derivative comes from Genevieve Bianquis, *Nietzsche en France* (Paris, 1929); and Hans Barth, *Wahrheit und Ideologie* (Zurich, 1945). Barth's comments are noteworthy in showing that indirectly, through the writings of Enrico Corradini, Sorel imbibed Nietzsche's message. The *apologie de la violence* shows a basic likeness to Corradini's *culto della morale guerresco*. Two works bearing on Sorel's mature view of Marxism are James Joll, *The Second International, 1889–1914* (New York, 1956); and Ralph H. Bowen, *German Theories of the Corporate State* (New York, 1947). From different directions they show the conflicting nationalist and internationalist tendencies within socialism. The thesis that the Second International collapsed in the wake of insularity and national chauvinism is central to Sorel's ideas on reform socialism. A partial list of 108 prominent collaborators accused by the French High Court following World War II, is contained in Saul K. Padover, *French Institutions: Values and Politics* (Stanford, 1954). Of those listed at least eight had pre-war associations with *le cercle Sorelienne*.

HISTORICAL NOTE ON
THE DECOMPOSITION OF
MARXISM

THIS study, which I prefer to think of as a unified essay, is a product of Sorel's most fruitful period of theoretical activity. *Réflexions sur la violence* discussed the nature and aims of human struggle for political and social emancipation; *Les illusions du progrès* separated the bourgeois tradition of Enlightenment from the socialist tradition of *praxis*; and finally, *La décomposition du marxisme* revealed Sorel at his maximum intellectual sophistication in dealing with the relationship of reformism to radicalism, Marxism to Marx. These works were all published in 1908, reflecting Sorel's keen concern with the general theory of socialism and the special applications of this set of beliefs to the Europe of his time. *La décomposition du marxisme* shows Sorel as a critic of sociological and philosophic theories which, once they were enshrined in the practice of partisan politics, became grotesquely transformed into inflexible dogma.

Sorel's critical acumen was not amiss. He characterized the situation in French socialism at the turn of the century with perspicacity and foresight. If we are to believe those intimate with French socialism, it is no less a characterization of the fractured French socialist movement today. Sorel's description of the *cléricalisation* of socialism, its transformation into a parliamentary agency for the *status quo*, remains the central theme in efforts to explain the debacle of French social democracy at present.[1]

The Decomposition of Marxism is no antiquarian document, written

---

[1] For a recent study of the French Socialist Party, *Section française de l'internationale ouvière*, offering parallels to the situation described by Sorel fifty years ago, see André Philip, *Le socialisme trahi* (Plon, 1957).

for the archaeologists of modern intellectual history. It has obvious flaws: its petty attacks upon some of the most devoted advocates of a socialist outlook; its unrelieved sectarianism; the infallibilistic assumption that syndicalism was alone able to save Marx from the Marxians; the uncritical regard for idealistic critiques of Marx's economic and philosophic doctrines; and a general disdain for the policy-making aspects of social regeneration. Nevertheless, this is a study that must be taken seriously. *The Decomposition of Marxism* is a scathing critique of the politics of orthodox socialism, its armchair attitude toward social change and its philosophic justifications for turning political pietism into political quietism. Sorel sought to show, not without acrimony, how Marxism became transformed from an instrument for probing the interiors of society into a theoretical pillar of existing society.

The projective fallacy usually made in reference to Sorel, that is, the notion that he somehow wrote as a forerunner of future authoritarian movements rather than as a spokesman for his own age, is in one sense an inverted compliment to his remarkable insight into the direction of socialist currents. Nonetheless, it must be said that Sorel possessed such critical acumen because he was deeply connected to French intellectual life while being separated from doctrinal narrowness. *The Decomposition of Marxism* was one of a number of speeches originally delivered in Paris on April 3, 1907, before an international conference of syndical-socialists. Among other participants were the leading syndicalist theoreticians of Europe. They were, furthermore, men of intellectual stature independent of their political commitments. Victor Griffuelhes, Arturo Labriola, Roberto Michels, Boris Kritchewsky and Hubert Lagardelle were not so much leaders in the economic struggles of the *syndicats* as they were men in search of fundamental social and economic understanding. While this detachment might have had defects, it had the distinct advantage of removing their perspectives from the requirements of propaganda.

The concerns of these men were very much focused on problems of minority socialism. They sought those tendencies in twentieth century socialism which pointed a way towards a 'renaissance,' to use Lagardelle's word, no less than a study of those social forces which created the basis for the doctrinal decomposition of socialism. Jacques Barzun has ably pointed out the meaning of this period in social practice and in political theory. 'When Marx's principal critics—Pareto, Sorel, Croce, Sombart, Bohm-Bawerk, Andler, Pantaleoni, Stammler and others—did come round to his general and special theories, they were obviously more concerned with finding answers to the problems that everywhere agitated than with getting rid of him as a menace. They could not foresee 1917, 1922 or 1933, and could hardly have dealt with Marx differently even if they had. Revisionism and Reformism had already begun to disarm the small socialist parties of the Continent, and as early as the mid-nineties Sorel and Andler could speak in a descriptive way of the decomposition of Marxism.' A bit earlier Barzun made clear that 'the turn of the century was not occupied with preparing Mussolini any more than with making way for Lenin. Its business in sociology was to examine, among other theories, those of Marx, Rodbertus and the Marginalists. And the interesting point to note is that the criticism of Marx's tenets came close upon the heels of their popularization.'[1]

The specific purposes of the Conference at which *The Decomposition of Marxism* was delivered came under three principal headings. As outlined by Lagardelle, they are the following: '(1) If the struggle of classes is the basis of socialism, we can say that all socialism is contained in syndicalism. (2) The most favourable national condition for the development of syndicalism is that in which the historical and political conditions permit the greatest revolutionary outpouring of proletarian energy, and its total rupture with the other classes. . . . (3) Syndicalism is free of all utopianism in the sense that it subordinates prospects for its triumph to the complex of conditions, and while waiting, it performs the role of a cleansing agent in the world.'[2]

Sorel subscribed to these propositions, but only in the broadest possible meaning. Already, by 1907, Sorel had raised doubts as to the efficacy of organized syndicalism to create the conditions of social revolution. Nonetheless, while the *abstractness* of Lagardelle's remarks on the *positive* pre-conditions for socialism allowed Sorel, and other disenchanted radicals like Michels, to share in the general enthusiasm for syndical socialism, the *concreteness* of the *negative* aspects, that is, of what syndicalism set out to overturn, had a far more direct and cogent appeal to Sorel. Lagardelle's fierce negativism and activism gave political expression to Sorel's pragmatic socialism very directly. 'No more dogmas or formulas; no more fruitless

---

[1] Jacques Barzun, *Darwin, Marx, Wagner: Critique of a Heritage* (revised edition, New York, 1958), pp. 213, 214–15.

[2] Hubert Lagardelle, *Bibliothèque du mouvement prolétarien (Syndicalisme et socialisme)*, pp. 3–8.

discussions on future society; no more compendious plans for social organization; but a sense of struggle that provides through practice a philosophy of action which gives first place to intuition and which indicates that the simplest worker engaged in the class struggle knows more than the most doctrinaire thinkers.'[1]

This was the battle ground chosen by Sorel to complete his critique and judgment of Marx and the Marxists. But his *Decomposition* was not so much a doctrinal disputation as a settling of accounts with scientism and historicism, materialism and determinism. Beyond this, his essay contrasts what Sorel believed to be the sociology of Karl Marx as illustrative of the revolutionary emancipation of labour with the official Marxism of bureaucratic political organization and philosophical atrophy. Only by facing this distinction between revolt and reform did Sorel hold out the possibility of a maturation of radicalism in the twentieth century. This is how it is still being conceptualized fifty years later. For it is yet the case, as Joan Robinson quipped, that 'Marxism is the opium of the Marxists.'[2]

The text used in preparation of this translation is the second edition of *La décomposition du marxisme*, published in 1910 as part of the collected papers of the *Bibliothèque du mouvement prolétarien*. A considerable number of technical problems presented themselves in the preparation of this English edition. They are herein noted to explain certain differences with the original text.

Sorel's notation system is inadequate for purposes of scholarly research. At times, as in quoting Marx's *Capital* or *The Poverty of Philosophy*, he omits a reference altogether; or, as is sometimes the case, references are made which are incomplete and inexact. The places and dates of publication are rarely mentioned; while references to titles often contain errors. In all cases I have endeavoured to give complete and correct citation to the authors and works cited in the text. Sorel originally prepared this study as a public lecture, and although he was in general given to the practice of broad references, I do not think it violates the spirit of his effort to use a more exact notational system than the one originally given.

Where possible I have indicated the existence of an English language edition of the references. Either the English reference replaces the French citation altogether, as in the case of the writings of Marx

[1] Hubert Lagardelle, *Bibliothèque du mouvement prolétarien* (*Syndicalisme et socialisme*), p. 8.
[2] Joan Robinson, 'Would You Believe It,' in *On Re-Reading Marx* (Cambridge, England, 1953).

and Engels; or in works which are less well known, they are given in both French and English editions, with page references to both editions, as in the case of Croce and Ostrogorski. A third method used is to cite the English edition in brackets with page references to the French edition only, as in the case of Renan's writings. There are several reasons for this last procedure: the unavailability of the French texts, which were oftentimes translations from another language, or alterations and revisions in the English text which transform the meaning of the edition cited by Sorel sufficiently to make a textual transposition unwieldy and perhaps inaccurate.

Any material added to the footnotes, not in the original text, has been bracketed and initialled. In general, with few exceptions, I have tried to let the text speak for itself. One of the attractive qualities of *The Decomposition of Marxism* is that, despite its general immersion in the French political controversies of the era, the meaning of Sorel's commentaries requires little editorial elaboration.

Grammatically, only one type of change has been made. Sorel's use of the semi-colon has been generally superseded by the current form of keeping ideas distinct by separating them with a period. Other than this, the position of phrases, no less than the content, has been kept as literal as possible without destroying the literary qualities of the work, such as they may be.

I. L. H.

Translation of

THE DECOMPOSITION
OF MARXISM

by

Georges Sorel

CONTENTS

CONTENTS

INTRODUCTION

FOR a long time socialist writers have believed that Marx created a body of doctrines through the medium of which three results could be attained: to demonstrate that the attacks directed against capitalism by the working class are the irrefutable consequences of a scientific analysis of production; to base upon philosophy the next anticipated revolution, which would replace capitalism with communism; and to find, in a re-investigation of history, appropriate principles with which to guide with certainty the politics of revolutionary parties. In Germany the Marxian system was regarded as being above criticism. The weakness of the arguments utilized by German university professors against Marxism justified to a certain extent the conceit of its partisans.

In a book published in 1886 which, according to Charles Andler, made him (Anton Menger) a 'scientific authority,'[1] the eminent Viennese professor reproached Marx and Engels for not having described the world whose advent they anticipated: 'I consider,' he said, 'the description of a perfect social state not only to be entirely scientific but indispensable, if the socialist movement is even partially to achieve its goals.'[2]

It is evident that, in Austria, the word *scientific* is still understood in an archaic sense, no longer current in France. There is no way to create a total picture of the future without resorting to fantasy or even absurdity.

'No critique of existing institutions, however precise it may be,' he continued, 'is justified until the possibility of a better state has been adequately demonstrated. Nations will never resolve profound social problems unless a socialist theory of public law has been developed

[1] Anton Menger, *Le droit au produit intégral du travail*, in the *Bibliothèque Internationale d'économie politique* (Paris, 1900), p. 1.
[2] *Ibid.*, p. 150.

211

according to ideas based on experience.'[1] Does the author confuse socialists with students, whom he would expect to pass an examination? Without waiting for his permission, the working classes have entered the struggle against existing institutions. They are not preparing a critique but a revolution. The owning classes through their publicists fabricate theories of public law aimed at justifying their machinations. These are the publicists of bourgeois weakness, who transform a very real war into an ideological discussion—with whom serious interpreters of the proletarian movement are not much concerned.

Marxists have carried their wickedness to the extent of not taking into account the principles which were regarded as essential to socialism by Anton Menger: he cannot decide whether, according to their doctrine (i.e., Marx and Engels) 'it is the right to the entire product of one's labour or the right to exist which should form the basis of future juridical organization.'[2] In 1886 Marx's statement on the Gotha programme was not yet widely known. If our author could have suspected that, according to Marx, after the social revolution wages should be determined according to principles borrowed from capitalism, he would have eliminated Marx from his list of socialist writers. It would in fact be impossible to be a socialist if the formulation of one's opinions did not conform to the classifications established by a professor as notable as Anton Menger.

In accordance with their taste for bibliographical research, German professors busied themselves extensively with the exploration of the presumed sources of the outlook of Marx and Engels. The latter having declared that his associate had regenerated socialism by introducing both the theory of surplus value and the materialist conception of history,[3] Anton Menger attempts to prove that Engels was badly informed on the early socialist writers;[4] that William Thompson was the actual originator of the theory of surplus value;[5] that one must be an 'ignoramus or a charlatan' to attribute to Marx a doctrine he had borrowed from his predecessors, who at times even surpassed him in 'profundity and penetration.'[6] It is common knowledge how

---

[1] Anton Menger, *Le droit au produit intégral du travail*, in the *Bibliothèque Internationale d'economie politique* (Paris, 1900), p. 157.

[2] *Ibid.*, p. 144; also pp. 147–8.

[3] *Ibid.*, pp. 113, 138. Menger does not search for the sources of the materialist conception of history, which seems to him false, but which he knows most inadequately.

[4] *Ibid.*, pp. 74, 133.   [5] *Ibid.*, pp. 78, 114, 137–8.   [6] *Ibid.*, p. 3.

much discussions concerning scientific precedents engender violent polemics and how incapable they are of clarifying principles.

The sterility of German criticism has been established by a writer of deep feeling and eloquence Benedetto Croce, who congratulates Werner Sombart for having broken, in 1894, with the habits of his University colleagues, and for his honest attempts to penetrate the most profound thoughts of Marx.[1]

It must be recognized that, in terms of criticism, Marx's system presents considerable difficulties which have nowhere received a didactic exposition. Benedetto Croce writes that: 'It is not surprising that *Das Kapital* has been regarded, at one time or another, as an economic treatise, as a philosophy of history, as a collection of sociological laws so-called, as a moral and political reference book, and even by some as a bit of narrative history.'[2] One must search out the meaning in Marx's thought. It is an undertaking containing multiple opportunities for making errors. Often too much weight has been given to brief reflections that occur in the midst of statements which 'interpreted strictly, are erroneous; and yet appear to us, and indeed are, loaded and pregnant with truth.'[3] A veritable mountain of interpretation is necessary when Marx's hypotheses are presented, since at times they appear in satiric form. In short, we find here and there graphic illustrations, the exact meaning of which seems long ago to have escaped the Marxists, only now acquiring their full value, now that revolutionary syndicalism so clearly reveals to us the character of the class struggle.

The attitude of Marx's disciples has contributed greatly to rendering all criticism of his outlook sterile. And it certainly is. Normally criticism is made for the purpose of further developing the outlook of the master, rather than as a study of the outlook *per se*. But one finds that the Marxists, instead of expanding upon the original effort, have surrendered themselves to so many fantasies that serious people have generally not considered them to be authoritative interpreters of Marx. He has, consequently, remained shunned.

No one has considered, for example, that historical materialism

---

[1] Benedetto Croce, *Historical Materialism and the Economics of Karl Marx* (New York, 1914) (translated by C. M. Meredith, with an introduction by A. D. Lindsay), p. 54 (99). [The reference in Sorel's text is to the French edition of Croce's work: *Matérialisme historique et économie marxiste* (Paris, 1897), p. 99. In all cases the bracketed page references are to the text Sorel uses.—I.L.H.]

[2] *Ibid.*, p. 49, cf. also pp. 78–80 (94, cf. also 129–32).

[3] *Ibid.*, p. 79 (130).

might consist of the paradoxes, pleasantries or naivetés of Paul Lafargue's writings on the origins of law, morality and religion.[1] Marx would never have dreamed of saying that 'pantheism and the transmigration of souls of the cabala are metaphysical expressions of the value and exchange value of commodities.'[2] Astonished at how little attention was paid to his discoveries, Paul Lafargue declared that, due to the ignorance and prejudices of bourgeois historians, socialists have a 'monopoly' on historical materialism.[3] Kautsky had published in the official journal of German Social Democracy almost all the nonsense which Paul Lafargue has presented as applications of Marxism. He has given these articles his complete approval, which contributed in no small way to the opinion that the Marxian school is ridiculous.

While competent men made a sharp distinction between Marx and his disciples, these disciples arrived at the belief that their master should, in the history of human thought, occupy a totally extraordinary position. Marx was considered, for example, to be the only man who deserved to take the place of Hegel in the role of sovereign arbiter of philosophy.[4] Thus, Charles Bonnier wrote, in 1895: 'A reproach frequently made to socialists is that neither Marx nor *Capital* has yet found a successor; this merely proves the inability of our epoch to understand the history of philosophy any more than the philosophy of history. Just as Hegel did not find a successor until the middle of the century, so the successors to Marx and Engels will not

[1] The masterpiece of its kind is, I would say, the article on 'The Myth of the Immaculate Conception,' printed in *Devenir social*, May 1896. The author does not speak otherwise of the virgin, except for original sin, but of the virginal birth of Christ. He tells us in the last lines that a council 'of a majority with one voice, the English Christian, based upon *the ancient myth of the immaculate conception of woman*, decided that woman should have a soul like man.'

[2] *Devenir social* (August 1895), p. 477. Benedetto Croce has extracted many of the errors committed by Paul Lafargue in the article on Campanella in which this beautiful discovery is published; we can add to the latter (to Croce's comments): the author mistakes the word Sephiroth, which is feminine plural, for masculine singular. [The complete text of Lafargue's analysis of Campanella can be found in *Die beiden ersten grossen Utopisten*, in *Vorlaufer des neuren Sozialismus* (Stuttgart, 1895), Bd. I, pp. 469–506.—I.L.H.]

[3] Paul Lafargue, *La methode historique de Karl Marx: Le déterminisme économique* (Paris, 1907), p. 4. Read in the note on page 14 the amusing reflections on 'the ridiculous metaphysics and ethics of Justice, Liberty and Country, which pervades academic and parliamentary discourse, electoral programmes and mercantile phraseology.'

[4] For something more than analogies between Marx and Hegel, cf. Benedetto Croce, *op. cit.*, pp. 81–5 (133–6).

appear until the epoch of capitalism is ended.'[1] While waiting, one must resign oneself to the sterility of the Marxian school. Even more singularly curious is Paul Lafargue's last sentence: 'It is rash to meddle with the work of these two giants of thought (Marx and Engels), even to place it beyond dispute. Perhaps only until the transformation of capitalist society will socialists of both worlds be able to do more than *popularize* their economic and historical theories.'[2]

These sentiments of religious piety, so naïvely expressed by Paul Lafargue, appear to have been shared by a great number of Marxists and to have prevented them from following the excellent advice of Benedetto Croce, in 1897: 'the task of Marx's followers ought to be to free his thought from the literary form which he adopts, to study again the questions which he propounds, and to work them out with new and more accurate statements, and with fresh historical illustrations.'[3] A great independence of spirit would have been needed to carry out this programme. Marxists preferred to make résumés which seemed to Benedetto Croce to be more obscure than Marx's original text. In a large portion of Marxist literature, one notes a constant effort to reproduce the phrases of *Capital* in such a way that we are often led to believe that the writers in question are more familiar with the compositional techniques of the liturgists than with modern scientific method.

Thus the Marxist school was found to be characterized by fantasies clearly alien to Marx's system and by a rigidity arising from servility. The doctrine was always given the appearance of remaining intact in the midst of universal flux because, more and more, real life retreated from it. Ten years ago one would have been able to compare Marxism to an ancient tree whose tough bark enveloped a worm-eaten heart. It was then that Andler announced that the moment had come to write the history of the decomposition of Marxism. However, at that point Bernstein made a courageous attempt to revive the tree, whose end was not as near as the French professor thought.

Marx had written *Capital* on the basis of observations made in England. But during the thirty years following its publication many great changes took place in English industry, politics and in English life generally. The best means of rejuvenating Marxism seemed to be

[1] *Devenir social* (July 1895), p. 370.
[2] *Ibid.* (April 1897), p. 290.
[3] Benedetto Croce, *op. cit.*, pp. 66 ff. (114).

to pick up the enquiries at the point where Marx had left off and to complete *Capital* in terms of the development of the English working classes. In the preface to his book, Marx had told the Germans that it was necessary to seek in the birthplace of capitalism for the fundamental tendencies that characterize the present régime; he had written the following vague and paradoxical sentence, so often reproduced as if it were a magical historic law: 'The country that is more highly developed industrially only shows to the less developed, the image of its own future.'[1]

To the observer of contemporary England, the most striking phenomenon is trade unionism. Bernstein, in considering it as the form of syndicalist organization that is a necessary consequence in all countries that walk the capitalist path, considered himself faithful to Marx's most sacred principles. But the official representatives of the Marxian school were not bold enough to recognize, thanks to the principles they considered holy, facts contrary to the thesis of the class struggle. The object of trade unionism is to settle amicably the conflicts between employers and workers. If one must generalize: it becomes impossible to say that the mechanism of capitalist production aggravates industrial conflicts to the point of transforming them into class struggle. Bernstein's old associates, not understanding how he could have set himself the task of observing reality in order to complete the work of his master—instead of making, as they did, résumés of résumés—thought that such a scandalous situation must have very unwholesome causes. They accused Bernstein of having been bought by the capitalists, and they treated him as badly as the Middle Ages had treated the excommunicated. I do not here want to emphasize further this deplorable chapter in the history of Social Democracy.

Bernstein, convinced that he had remained faithful to the spirit of Marx, attempted to explain how the development of Marx's doctrine had led to results sharply at variance to the theses taught by the Marxian school. He was led to ask himself whether Marx's primitive system did not contain contradictory principles, among which he would find those which would correspond to his new conceptions. In 1899 he proposed a theory to which, it seems to me, due consideration has not been given.

According to him, two principal currents have developed in

[1] Karl Marx, *Capital: A Critique of Political Economy*, Vol. I, translated by Samuel Moore and Edward Aveling (Chicago, 1906), Preface, p. 13.

modern socialism: 'One, *constructive*, continues with the ideas of reform expressed by socialist thinkers; the other receives its inspirations from popular revolutionary movements and, in fact, aspires only to *destroy*. In terms of the possibilities of the moment, one appears to be *utopian, sectarian,*[1] *pacifically evolutionist*, the other as *conspiratorial, demagogic, terrorist.* The nearer we approach the present, the more categorical the watchword becomes: on the one hand, emancipation by *economic organization*, and on the other, emancipation by *political expropriation*. . . . Marxist theory attempted to combine the essential elements of the two currents. . . . But this combination did not signify the suppression of the antagonism; it was rather a compromise, such as Engels in his work, *The Condition of the Working Class in England*, proposed to the English socialists: subordination of the specifically socialist element to the politico-radical and the social-revolutionary element. And, however Marxist theory may have evolved throughout the years, it has never been able to rid itself of this compromise, nor of its dualism.'[2]

This manner of conceiving things filled Kautsky with indignation. Soon after, he answered that Marx had reconciled Utopian socialism and the revolution into a higher unity (!); that, therefore, there was neither dualism nor compromise; that Bernstein's supposed discovery aimed only at the destruction of the revolutionary spirit of Marxism which gives it life. The only dualism which could be recognized in Marx's and Engels' activity inheres in the fact that they were, at one and the same time, men of science and men of struggle: the man of science weighs the positive and the negative features before reaching a decision, whereas the man of struggle is obliged to act without necessarily having had time for lengthy reflection. 'It is not to appraise with the impartiality of history, but to infer from the duality of their functions, the contradictions in their theories or even their intellectual mistakes.'[3]

Kautsky was convinced that Marx had so ably utilized the researches and theories formulated before him that he had attained

---

[1] Sectarian in the language of Marx means doctrinaire. Cf. *The Alleged Secessions of the International.* (*Les prétendues scissions dans l'internationale.* 'Circulaire Privée du Conseil Général de l'association internationale des travailleurs.') (Geneva, 1872), p. 24.

[2] Eduard Bernstein, *Socialisme théorique et social-démocratie pratique* (Paris, 1900), translated by Alexandre Cohen, pp. 53–4.

[3] Karl Kautsky, *Le marxisme et son critique Bernstein*, translated from *Bernstein und das sozial-demokratische program; eine antikritik*, Stuttgart, 1899, by Martin-Leroy (Paris, 1900), pp. 68–70.

scientific truth. To consider that Marxism had simply joined two con-tradictory systems was to admit that there was something incomplete about the doctrine. Not for anything in the world would Kautsky have uttered such blasphemy. According to him, social democracy would have committed a grave error if it followed new paths leading in uncharted directions, instead of applying its collective intelligence to defending the principles it had accepted as positively true.

Bernstein's ideas were received most favourably by those who wished to see Marxism escape the rigid mould in which Kautsky wanted to keep it. In pointing out the lack of consistency of the sys-tem, Bernstein demonstrated the necessity for seeking new equi-libria, unstable and provisional as they might be, among the funda-mental tendencies of modern socialism. Thus, life was introduced into a doctrine which was, until then, condemned to sterility. None-theless, it was a decomposition of Marxism.[1]

In France the study of syndicalist organizations has led to the question of whether or not there is a reason for examining the de-composition of Marxism on grounds other than those which Bern-stein had considered. What Marxism has borrowed from earlier socialist currents is most striking. Nonetheless, Marx has added something which constitutes what I shall call the *Marxism of Marx*. This part was concealed for a long time because there were not yet enough workers' organizations that corresponded with its outlook; and Bernstein did not recognize it because he knew only England and Germany well. I propose to show how I conceive of this new way of viewing the decomposition of Marxism.

I

Formation of utopias — The pre-1848 social reforms —
Entrance of the workers to the petty bourgeoisie through
producer associations and trade unionism — Social peace
according to Vidal and Considérant

(a) THE writers known as utopian constantly appeal to sentiments of justice when they preach social reconstruction. In all actual organiza-

---

[1] Bernstein asserted, to the great chagrin of his old associates, that the final aim is nothing and that the movement is everything, *op. cit.*, p. 278. He thus pene-trated the true spirit of contemporary philosophy, in that he does not trouble

218

tion there are situations in which established law offends opinion; it cannot be otherwise. However perfect a juridical system may be, it cannot be applied perfectly in all cases, no more than science can be perfectly equated to nature. Apparently, universal identification can be created only by introducing flexibility to a system whose characteristic is rigidity: introducing the arbitrary in law and empiricism in science. When public opinion is strongly felt in unusual cases, it demands a change of juridical decrees with the objective of eliminating the discord that disturbs it. It is in this way that reforms come about, with a view to increasing respect for law and consolidating the existing system.

For example, although our matrimonial legislation is based on the ecclesiastical doctrine of marriage, which proclaims the indissolubility of sexual union, it has had to admit that certain cases require marital separation. In our time, men of letters have insisted so strongly on the inadequacy of separation that France has adopted a divorce law which seemed necessary to many people in order to increase the respect due to marriage.

Since it is particularly men of letters who influence public opinion and point out misdeeds resulting from the application of certain laws, it can be said that there is always, along with the justice of the jurists, a romantic justice, highly arbitrary and paradoxical, on which all men who like to imagine social change can draw. The utopians are not aware that contradiction is the condition of the historic movement of law. They see therein the proof of an error residing in the principles that govern society. They sought to create a completely logical world. But their opponents do not hesitate to point out that utopian projects would produce consequences which frequently offend our sensibilities, when they do not offend prevailing customs. A minimum of reflection would suffice to show that it cannot be otherwise, because a society would be made up of madmen if its ideas did not conform in general with prevailing custom.

The arguments of reformers appear much more substantial when they rest upon details because they thus lose the paradoxical character of utopias. The analogies through which they picture the world are easier to accept insofar as they appear reconcilable with a great number of existing interests. A time must come then when schools of

himself either with a point of departure, or with a starting point for changing things, but rather with the forces which, at each instant, are able to generate the movement in the sense that he conceives it.

social thought, impelled by the desire of obtaining an ever greater success, limit their ambitions to propagating the idea of reforms. It is then that they will be able to capture public opinion most vigorously.

The successors to the great utopians of the nineteenth century were men who abandoned the early aspirations of the founders for reform, that is to say, for the adoption of a conservative attitude. À propos this subject, let me draw attention to a striking page in Proudhon's letter of January 1, 1842, to Considérant entitled 'Warning to Proprietors.' By that time Fourierism had fully matured. As Proudhon explained so well: 'Fourier declares, and he has confirmed it by his example at the early stages of study and experience, it is necessary to place oneself completely outside the conventional ideas of civilization and break sharply with all its notions of pre-established harmony. One may say, to proceed by a grand sweep. What! This enormous labour of humanity is to be negated, history is to have no meaning, all progress is to be reduced simply to a long series of deceptions! You yourself, sir, do not think in this way; unless I mistake the meaning of this article on *General Politics* which has made such a deep impression, and in which you show yourself to be profoundly socialist because you deal with the themes of present day society.'[1]

Sometime before the 1848 revolution, François Vidal, who became one of the most outstanding men of the Luxembourg Commission, concluded his celebrated book on the *Redistribution of Wealth* with reflections which clearly reveal the consequences brought about by the many utopias developed in the last thirty years: 'The real question today boils down to determining how it would be possible to partially neutralize the disastrous consequences of our economic institutions; to examine the role that could be played, in 1846, by means of our laws, our mores and our prejudices, of principles of association and applied organization, as palliatives for the relief of poverty, for the amelioration of the condition of those thousands of our fellow creatures who can only await the future with patience, nourishing themselves with illusions, who want to earn their livelihood by work and who could produce far beyond their needs if their labour were well utilized, if they were provided with—on a loan basis—an advance and the necessary tools. Here, we are indeed far from the land of the

---

[1] Pierre-Joseph Proudhon, *Oeuvres* (Paris, 1866–83), Vol. II, pp. 55–6. In effect, Fourier would proceed like all utopians to impose his paradoxical ideas on the contemporary world.

utopians! Thus stated, the problem is found to be singularly specific and from the heights of the ideal we fall sharply back to earth, to the dominion of reality and necessity. It is altogether another world. But after all, it is the one in which we are condemned to live: we must resign ourselves!'[1]

We have just seen how a seemingly necessary evolution from the utopian to the practical is brought about. This evolution can still be regarded as moving from imagination to intelligence, from the romantic to the legal, from the absolute to the relative, from simplicity to complexity.[2]

Social reformers expected to lead all parties to an acceptance of their projects. Vidal claimed that the most intelligent economists were shaken, that there was talk in the official seats of power and organization, that the negative doctrines of the so-called liberal school were abandoned. 'Socialists do not in the least want to transform society with one blow, to overthrow the world; their aim would be to convert it.'[3]

(b) Vidal aimed to find the means of furnishing the workers with the necessary tools and financial credit. It was, then, simply a matter of better organization of labour. This had already been the objective pursued by all utopians since Fourier and Saint-Simon—but on an infinitely greater scale.

Fourier thought that he had found the means of making the workers more attentive to their work; Saint-Simon wanted to install the most capable specialists in charge of all enterprises. Later it was thought that the workers' associations (known today as producers' co-operatives) would provide the practical solution to the economic problem. For a long time profit-sharing as a means of creating a superior economic order was advocated. This was to assure large-scale industry the advantages arising from the shift of interest on the part of old workers tied to the success of their employers' business. It seemed to many people that profit-sharing would succeed where the workers' association seemed incapable of prospering.

Today the manufacturers of social reforms would be well advised to admit that the labour–management contract contains a mysterious property analogous to that which Louis Blanc attributed to the

[1] François Vidal, *Répartition des richesses: ou, De la justice distributive en économie sociale* (Paris, 1846), pp. 471–2.

[2] Georges Sorel, *Insegnamenti della economia contemporanea. Degenerazione capitalista e degenerazione socialista* (Milan, 1907), p. 97.

[3] François Vidal, *op. cit.*, pp. 464–5.

producer associations which Proudhon ridiculed so vehemently. The workers, by the sole fact that they would negotiate through the syndicate as intermediary, would acquire a higher status in the economic world; they would become less proletarian and they would have a right to higher remuneration. The *syndicat* has sometimes been compared to a banker who, the more that industry is equipped with powerful machinery and the more that it can create super-profits, the higher he raises his expectations. The labour–management contract would then be a kind of joint stock company sustained on one side by man-power; and on the other, by the commercial code of money.

If trade unionism really produced the results that its defenders attribute to it, it would have a double consequence: it would develop a sense of responsibility within the worker, and it would give him a juridical status more nearly approximating the traditional status of the owner. Thus there would be economic and juridical progress: it would then no longer be true to say, as Marx and Engels said in the *Communist Manifesto*: 'The serf, in the period of serfdom, raised himself to membership in the commune, just as the petty bourgeois, under the yoke of feudal absolutism, managed to develop into a bourgeois. The modern labourer, on the contrary, instead of rising with the progress of industry, sinks deeper and deeper below the conditions of his own class.'[1]

(c) It was the gravitation (of the producers) toward the bourgeoisie that particularly impressed Paul de Rousiers on his trips to England and America. I believe that this impression is at the basis of all his favourable judgments of trade unionism. In his view the English government pursued a wise policy in appointing trade union secretaries as justices of the peace and thereby facilitating the creation of a labour aristocracy that enters into the framework of established society without difficulty.[2]

In the previously mentioned work, Vidal expressed very clearly the conciliatory intentions of his contemporaries: 'The socialists do not press for social war; on the contrary, they would like to avoid it; they call for reforms in order to avert revolutions. Far from provoking hatred among classes, they preach concord and order.'[3]—'Read the popular newspapers; they all preach peace, order, union, tolerance,

[1] Karl Marx and Frederick Engels, *Manifesto of the Communist Party*, in *Selected Works* (Moscow, 1950), Vol. I, p. 43.

[2] Paul de Rousiers, *Le trade-unionisme en Angleterre* (avec la collaboration de Mm. de Carbonnel, Festy, Fleury, et Wilhelm) (Paris, 1897), p. 309.

[3] François Vidal, *op. cit.*, p. 465.

true charity; they all try to raise the morality of the people, to develop in them heart and intelligence, the noblest qualities; the most generous sentiments; they all nobly proclaim the respect due to existing interests; they all curse laziness and glorify work. The newspapers edited by the workers have transformed the proletarians, they have done more than all the professors of morals! Those workers, formerly ungovernable and impatient with all authority, now understand the necessity for order, hierarchy and discipline.'[1]

Thus, socialists of the time assumed the role of professors of social peace. The same approach is found in the *Democratic Manifesto* (*le Manifeste de la Démocratie*) published by Considérant.[2] The author hinted at possible means of bringing about the disappearance of the causes of economic conflict to his contemporaries. He wanted a gradual substitution of law in place of force, work in place of war. He expected to see the coming of a *democratic and Christian* regime which had as yet been known only in an abstract form, in the proclamation of liberty and equality. It was a question of removing an oligarchy which crushed not only the proletariat but even the bourgeoisie and already dominated the government.[3] 'Fortunately the ranks of the bourgeoisie are extensive and understanding is growing among them. Concern for the material and moral poverty of the working classes and the necessity for providing a remedy is becoming clear to them. Philanthropy only disturbs and inflames them. Besides, the bourgeois classes begin to see that they *are no less concerned than the proletarians* in the introduction of guarantees in the industrial system and in resistance to the encroachments of a financial aristocracy.'[4]

Contemporary writers concerned with social reform have not added a great deal to what the old socialists had said.

They have only replaced an apologia for the guild association with an apologia for trade unionism. Perhaps they are even less scientific

---

[1] François Vidal, *op. cit.*, p. 467. The author demands of the government protection of the poor classes, 'from control by the large socialist movement which is readying itself.' It ought to reclaim for the labouring classes 'guarantees against the all-powerful entrepreneurs of industry, against the abuses of competition. But, alas! power itself is at the mercy of the manufacturers and merchants. ... It is no longer power. Ministers debate while merchants lead them.' This is, in fact, what we could today call a programme of social royalism.

[2] This document has been reproduced in the review, *Ere nouvelle* (February 1894).

[3] *Ere nouvelle* (February 1894), p. 172.

[4] *Ibid.*, (February 1894), p. 172.

than their predecessors, because the Utopians expected that all their plans would yield a large increase in production, whereas contemporary reformers are much less concerned with economic progress. It might be said that in this respect the Utopians came near to Marxism; but they differ in their belief that it is necessary to make plans for directing industry while Marxism believes that industry directs itself very well.

II

Struggle of the poor against the rich — The Blanquists — Invention of the party system — The popular State and its machines — Recollections of the Revolution: relationship established between the fuedal regime and capitalism — Incorporation of the proletariat into the bourgeoisie by government authority.

(*a*) WE come now to the second element found in modern socialism, the revolutionary element. For a long time the idea of revolution was identified with the idea of a struggle of the poor against the rich. This struggle is as ancient as the civilized world; it destroyed the Hellenic cities. It does not seem to have been very much modified in the course of time. It constitutes a rudimentary form of the class struggle, with which it is often confused.[1]

Here justice is no longer invoked, but there is an entire body of literature consecrated to projecting the beauty of the victory of the poor. The Utopians' concepts of romantic justice are often incorporated into this literature. What is essential here is to give to the poor an absolute confidence in their own strength. To attain this result the traditions of submission, inculcated in them since infancy, must be conquered. This is to be done in two ways: first, by destroying the prestige of the ruling classes, and then by exalting the virtues of the poor. Revolutionary pamphlets and newspapers must never fail to point out all incidents that may reveal the rich to be odious,

---

[1] I am describing, for example, what the social democratic Hollander, Rienzi, (van Kol) constantly engages in as a result of this confusion, in *Socialisme et Liberté* (Paris, 1898). [Sorel is referring to Henri Hubert van Kol, who wrote under the pseudonym, Rienzi. He is not to be confused with the Italian popular leader, 'the last of the tribunes,' Cola de Rienzi.—I.L.H.]

ridiculous and shameful. According to Robespierre and his friends, because the poor live closer to nature, virtue is easier for them than for the rich. This unique metaphysical generalization is often found in contemporary works by would-be Marxists.[1]

Before 1848 the idea of a revolt of the poor was terrifying. For example, Considérant said, in the *Manifeste de la Démocratie*: 'What would become of civilization, what would become of governments, what would become of the upper classes if the industrial feudality which extends over all Europe heard the great cry of social war: "Live working or die fighting" one day stirring the countless legions of modern slavery to action? Indeed! If the wisdom of governments, if the intelligent and liberal bourgeoisie, and if science does not at last perceive this possibility, the movement of European society will be directed toward social revolution, toward a European *Jacquerie*.'[2] Later in the study he pointed out the danger of communism, 'violent, plundering, revolutionary and, furthermore, illusory,' which seduced the imagination by its extreme simplicity: 'These formulae are very simple and comprehensible to the starving and plundered masses. Moreover, they appear to be perfectly just, as long as society denies to them the right to work; the right to work is more sacred than property rights—the latter derive from the former.'[3]

(*b*) The men who, throughout the nineteenth century, considered themselves the most authentic spokesmen of the revolutionary tradition, the true representatives of the poor and the most determined partisans of street fighting, those who were called Blanquists by Bernstein, were no less determined than was Considérant to prevent any return to barbarism. A *Jacquerie* type of movement was definitely not their ideal. Bernstein saw very clearly that, in judgments bearing on them, one becomes too concerned with secondary aspects of their tactics. The Blanquists could not be described as being essentially conspiratorial; the manner of gaining power was of no interest to them; in their eyes, to possess power was to resolve all difficulties.[4] The creative force of a revolutionary political party in power is enormous, and many have thought it to be limitless. Such a party, once in control of the government, is much stronger than a conservative

---

[1] H. H. van Kol (Rienzi), *op. cit.*, pp. 242–3.

[2] *Ere nouvelle, op. cit.*, p. 166.

[3] *Ere nouvelle, op. cit.*, p. 170. Considérant makes an allusion here to his famous article on the 'Theory of the Right of Property' (Théorie du droit de propriété), which appeared in *Phalange* (May 1839).

[4] Bernstein, *op. cit.*, p. 50.

party in power would be, because it has no conflicts to adjudicate. Economic conditions were regarded as dependent phenomena.

Thanks to the intervention of a party which would lead the revolution, the historic movement acquires a new and totally unexpected pace. We no longer have to deal with a poor class acting under the guidance of instincts, but with educated men who evaluate the interests of a party just as stock-market speculators evaluate the strength of their business holdings.

Political parties are coalitions formed to obtain advantages that can lead to control of the State, whether or not their promoters are driven by hatreds, whether or not they seek material profits, whether or not their only ambition is to impose their will. However capable party organizers may be, they will be able to organize only a small general staff, which will be given the responsibility of winning the discontented masses, filling them with distant hopes and urging them to make immediate sacrifices. The party, in the event of success, will make great concessions to them. It will pay for services rendered with economic, juridical and religious transformations, the repercussions of which could greatly exceed expectations. Very often the party leaders who disturb society belong most deeply to the aristocracy which the revolution is going to overthrow. These men, not having found the means of seizing power through their own class, have had to recruit a faithful army from the classes whose interests are in opposition to those of their kinsmen. History indicates that it would be misleading to suppose that the motives so often attributed by philosophers to the promulgators of revolution were in fact those that made revolutions.

When events are long past, the passions which had guided the first actors in the drama seem negligible in comparison with the great changes which have happened to society and which one seeks to place in relation to the mysterious tendencies of the masses.[1] Generally, contemporaries have seen things in reverse order and have tended to be rather more interested in the rivalries which had existed among the general staffs of political parties. It must always be observed, however, that in our time such great value has been accorded to ideologies that each party is obliged to parade about its doctrines. The boldest politicians could not maintain their prestige if they did

[1] For Fustel de Coulanges, the common masses are the true historical agents who advance the interests of the world. Cf. Paul Guiraud, *Fustel de Coulanges* (Paris), p. 202 and pp. 207–8.

not arrange to strike a certain balance between their actions and the principles they are supposed to represent.

The introduction of political parties into a revolutionary movement puts us at a great distance from primitive *simplicity*. Those in revolt had at first been intoxicated by the idea that their will would encounter no obstacle, since they were the majority. It seemed evident to them that they had only to appoint delegates to formulate a new legality in accordance with their needs. But what happens is that they accept the leadership of men who have other interests distinct from their own. These men really want to do them a service, but on condition that the masses deliver the State to them, the State being the object of their cupidity. Thus the instinct of the poor to revolt can serve as the base for the formation of a *popular State* composed of the bourgeois who wishes to continue bourgeois life, who retains bourgeois ideologies, but who appears as the representative of the proletariat.

The popular State is led more and more to extend its tentacles, because the masses become harder and harder to dupe when the first moment of the struggle has passed and it is, in the meanwhile, necessary to sustain their ardour during time of calm. This calls for complicated *electoral machines*[1] and, consequently, the granting of a great number of favours. By constantly increasing the number of its employees, the government aims to bring into existence a class of intellectuals having separate interests from the proletariat. This strengthens the defence of bourgeois forms against the proletarian revolution. Experience shows that even though this civil servant group has a most feeble culture, it is completely submerged in a bourgeois out-

[1] Ostrogorski has given many interesting details on the functioning of American political machinery in his book on *Democracy and the Organization of Political Parties* (translated from the French by J. Clarke) (New York, 1902) (*Démocratie et l'organisation des partis politiques*, Paris, 1899). Read especially Chapter VI of Book V. He gives the following definition of a machine: 'A mass of men arranging themselves hierarchically, bound to one another by a devoted staff, but on a mercenary basis, and preoccupied solely with the satisfaction of their appetites in exploiting the fortune of political parties.' (Fr. ed., Vol. II, p. 347.) [Cf. English language ed., Vol. II, pp. 367–98 for an exposition of this point.—I.L.H.] It would seem that in New York, Tweed who had been 'boss' of Tammany Hall, after he was convicted of monstrous theft, had kept the esteem of New York's poor, who considered him a victim of the rich. (Fr. ed., Vol. II, p. 401.) Always the ancient struggle of the poor against the rich. ('The boss Tweed, when publicly convicted of monstrous depredations and sent to prison, lost none of the esteem and admiration in which he had been held by the lower orders of New York; they were convinced that Tweed had fallen a victim to the nefarious designs of the rich, he who was so kind to the poor.' (Eng. trans., Vol, II, p. 429.)

look. We may also note, from many examples, that if a revolutionary propagandist penetrates the governmental apparatus, he becomes an excellent bourgeois with great facility.

One could then say that by a kind of paradox, men of politics who regard themselves as the true holders of the revolutionary idea are the conservatives. But after all, had the Convention been anything else? Has it not often been said that it contained the traditions of Louis XIV and prepared the way for Napoleon?

(c) For a long time memories of the Revolution dominated socialist propaganda. For example, they attempted to identify capitalist profits with seigneurial rights and tithes, which the bourgeoisie formerly suppressed without indemnity. They did not neglect to draw attention to the fact that many bourgeois fortunes originated in the sale of State property, negotiated under conditions exceptionally favourable to the purchasers. They sought to make it clear that the popular State could draw its inspiration from these memorable examples for the purpose of liquidating capitalism cheaply.

The revolutionary politicians did not discuss property from the same point of view as the Utopians. The latter were always preoccupied with the organization of work, whereas the politicians saw only profits to divide. Their conception was one of intellectuals who find it difficult to consider property as a means of production and who regard it rather as a title of possession. Law should (as it so often did in ancient cities) ration wealth by imposing enormous charges on it which would provide appropriate resources for making the life of the poor more satisfying. Economic problems are thus found to be relegated to the background, whereas the *decrees of the heads of the State* come to the fore.

What had the ancient legislators wanted? To maintain enough citizens in the city able to bear arms and defend national traditions; we would say that their ideal was bourgeois. And the men of the French Revolution, what had they wanted? To greatly increase the number of well-to-do property owners. They created a bourgeoisie whose power is still not exhausted. Could not the popular State, in drawing its inspiration from contemporary economic necessities, result in completely analogous consequences? The redivision of profits can, of course, be done indirectly by means of social legislation which takes into account the conditions of large industry; by the creation of arbitration machinery which permit trade unions to take constant action on paper; by the replacement of small consumers' goods estab-

228

lishments by public services in the area of food supply; by exploiting municipal housing for workers; by the replacement of small money-lenders' usury by loan societies; by finding fiscal resources in heavy taxation of the wealthy classes in such a way that the financial harvests produced by industry are put to democratic use. Thanks to those procedures the workers can become petty bourgeois,[1] and we thus arrive at the same conclusions as before: the incorporation of the proletariat into the bourgeoisie.

III

Dualism in the Communist Manifesto; revolutionary measures and theories bordering on the utopian — Bernstein's fears concerning the political ability of social democracy — Abandonment of Marxism by the politicians.

THE dualism pointed out by Bernstein appears indisputably in the provisional measures that the *Communist Manifesto* proposed to adopt in the case of victorious revolution. In 1872, Marx and Engels, in re-editing their work, spoke of the need for minimizing the importance of these practical recommendations; but it is also peculiar that, in the prefaces edited in 1872, 1883 and 1890, no indication is to be found which could orient the readers. I suppose that they themselves were aware of the duality of the system and they dared not make lengthy incursions into the field of practical politics because they were fearful of shattering the edifice.

In his commentary on the *Communist Manifesto* in 1901, Andler does not seem to have thoroughly examined the source material. He would have done well to take Bernstein's theses as a point of departure. He classifies the propositions into juridical, economic and pedagogic. I can hardly see the point in attaching the label of juridical to those measures which resemble the conquerors' orders for the destruction of the vanquished on the day after victory: expropriation of land holdings and the appropriation of ground rent for State

---

[1] It is in New Zealand that one finds this search to realize in legislation the means of making workers part of the petty bourgeoisie. All conscientious observers have been aware of this.

expenditures; graduated taxes; abolition of inheritance; confiscation of the goods of émigrés and rebels. These so-called juridical measures would, furthermore, have for their object the ruination of all interests deprived of protection by the law, and the suppression of all private rights after one generation. It must not be forgotten that law, like science, considers things as if they exist eternally. Therefore I do not think that one can really give, without being guilty of serious misrepresentation, the name, juridical, to statutes whose application is so very limited in duration.

The other propositions are clearly borrowed from utopian literature: centralization of credit; State administration of transportation; nationalization of an increasing number of factories and land improvement according to an overall plan; work compulsory for all, and organization of industrial forces, especially for agriculture; rapprochement between agriculture and industry; public [non-clerical— I.L.H.] and free education for all children and a joining of education and material production.—It is not clear to me why Andler puts this last project into a separate category classified as pedagogic, since it obviously belongs to work organization.

The Communist Manifesto offers the widest analogies to utopian literature, to such an extent that it was possible for Marx to have been accused of plagiarizing Considérant's *Manifeste de la Démocratie*. Not only are phenomena often presented similarly, but observations are made which are temptingly easy to identify with those of the utopians. For example, at the end of the first chapter one reads: 'And here it becomes evident that the bourgeoisie is unfit any longer to be the ruling class in society, and to impose its conditions of existence upon society as an over-riding law. It is unfit to rule because it is incompetent to assure an existence to its slave within his slavery, because it cannot help letting him sink into such a state that it has to feed him, instead of being fed by him.'[1]

To my knowledge the postulates employed by Marx and Engels in *The Communist Manifesto* have yet to be precisely determined; their verbal imagery has been able to be interpreted on one hand, as nearly that of the utopians, condemning the bourgeoisie in the name of eternal justice, and on the other, as containing an incitement toward a revolt of the poor.

However, the *Manifesto* does not include a formulation having as marked a Blanquist aspect as that to be found at the end of *The*

[1] Marx and Engels, *loc. cit.*, p. 43.

Poverty of Philosophy: 'The antagonism between the proletariat and the bourgeoisie is a struggle of class against class, a struggle which, carried to its highest expression, is a *total revolution*. Indeed, should it be surprising that a society founded on the opposition of classes should culminate in brutal *contradiction*, the clash of body with body, as its final dénoument? . . . Till then, on the eve of every general reshuffling of society the last word of social science will always be: Combat or death: bloody struggle or extinction. It is in this form that the question is inexorably put.'[1] At the beginning Marx and Engels were so favourably disposed toward Blanquist ideas that in 1850 they considered the Blanquists to be the true proletarian party since, according to Bernstein: 'The French proletarian party was, in 1848, comprised of the workers grouped around the Luxembourg Commission.'[2]

In examining the situation of the Socialist Party in Germany, Bernstein was alarmed to see how inferior the ability of this party was, in terms of the role that it might be called upon to play in the event of violent revolution. He did not think that one could yet see the passage of power to a radical bourgeoisie, as in 1848. It would be the extreme Parliamentary left, in other words the socialist group, which ought to assume all responsibilities.[3] This perspective prompted him to some highly pessimistic reflections: 'The sovereignty of the people, even when legally proclaimed, does not in the least make the people a genuinely determining factor. It can place the government in a position of dependence on those toward whom it should be dominant: civil servants, professional politicians, newspaper owners. . . . The dictatorship of the proletariat means, wherever the working class does not already have at its command strong economic organizations and wherever it has not yet acquired, through apprenticeship in autonomous workers' assemblies, a very high degree of moral independence—the dictatorship of club orators and the literati.'[4]

In order to prepare socialism for the accomplishment of the mission incumbent upon it in the event of revolution, a study must be undertaken of problems long neglected by Marxists. 'The social question which presented itself to the utopians in all its grandeur, as a

---

[1] Karl Marx, *The Poverty of Philosophy* (New York, n.d.), p. 147. 'Le combat ou la mort, la lutte sanguinaire ou le néant. C'est ainsi que la question est invinciblement posée.' These two last sentences are from George Sand.

[2] Eduard Bernstein, *op. cit.*, p. 51.

[3] *Ibid., op. cit.*, p. 60.   [4] *Ibid., op. cit.*, pp. 297–8.

political, juridical, economic and moral question, has been concentrated and condensed into a question of the workers.'[1] The moment had come to correct and complete the work of the utopians, profiting from the experiences of half a century. This led to a *decomposition of Marxism*, since, from that time on, Blanquist assumptions could no longer be entwined with studies made of administration and practical politics.

While Bernstein tried to concentrate the attention of German socialists on portions of the doctrine they had neglected, the natural work of party evolution led socialist leaders to the abandonment of the Marxian point of view, all protecting their wish not to change a thing. On December 5, 1899, Bebel delivered a speech in Berlin in which the purest theory of State socialism was presented. He even dared to return to the State-subsidized co-operatives that Marx had condemned in his letter of 1875 on the Gotha programme.[2] However, Bernstein continued to be viewed as no less a heretic, in order to appear ever faithful to the old revolutionary hopes which remained dear to many workers (especially in Berlin) and in order not to give a weapon to the anarchists, so despised by Social Democracy.

The German socialist politicians were of the opinion that there was absolutely no further need to concern themselves with the research which Bernstein urged them to undertake, because a deputy, like a marquis of the *ancien régime*, is a man who knows everything without needing to study anything.

But is Marxism solely what Bernstein assumed it to be? This is what must be considered. Is there not something in it other than the quoted formulas, whose value seems to be more and more open to question? Could this (Marxism) not be a philosophical concept applicable to the clarification of social struggles rather than a collection of political precepts? This is what we shall examine briefly by confronting the utopians and the Blanquists with some of the fundamental elements of Marxism.

[1] Saverio Merlino, *Formes et essence du socialisme* (Avec une preface de Georges Sorel) (Paris, 1898), p. 244.

[2] German social democracy is officially Marxist, but it has always beautifully harboured its Lasallian tendencies. It is because of this that the *Gotha Programme* had been adopted in 1875, in spite of Marx's criticism. His communication did not have the same effect as it did in 1891. The Lasallian spirit became dominant to the degree that the socialists were able to obtain electoral successes. These electoral gains proved fatal to State socialism.

IV

*Differences between Marx and the utopians — No juridi-
cal critique of private property — Sophisms of Thompson
and Pecqueur — Organization of production achieved by
capitalism — Stabilization of wages through economic
equilibrium — Future work based on usages inherited from
capitalism.*

(*a*) ACCORDING to many contemporary writers, Marx left a large gap
in his work by not creating a theory of property. Professor Anton
Menger said, for example: 'He lacks the necessary complement to the
theory of surplus value, in other words, a *juridical critique of private
property*, of the means of production, and the use value of things and,
consequently, a more profound examination of the right to the integral product of labour.'[1] Many young academics who look upon
Marx as a 'dead dog' have used this solemn judgment pronounced by
the Austrian professor as a point of departure for juridical critiques
of property. All of this pseudo-scientific literature consists of a collection of obscure sophisms, devoid of any interest, unworthy of the
honour of a refutation.

I believe that Marx is to be warmly congratulated for not having
entered on the path he is reproached for not having followed. I regard
his attitude as being of capital importance. No criticism can be made
of his economic system from this point of view. Any author who
makes a juridical critique of private property will place himself outside of Marxism. It is necessary to make this decisive affirmation at
the beginning of our enquiry.

Otherwise how could one undertake the task to which Menger
urges us? With such a task in mind one must seek a basis in the principles of modern law. But are these not based on the existence of
bourgeois private property? However little one might approve of the
principles of historical materialism, such an enterprise appears to be
merely a tissue of sophisms. Menger did not see the absurdity of the
enterprise because he was not completely aware of the relationship
existing between ideological superstructure and economy. But for a
Marxist this lack of connection alleged by the utopians, and still
alleged by some philosophers without a philosophy, is nonsense.

It is indeed true that no ideological system is ever perfectly

[1] Anton Menger, *op. cit.*, p. 138.

consistent. Within the law there always remain decrees of past ages that can be correctly explained only through the medium of history and which, if isolated, could only yield fantastic interpretations. On the other hand, there are exceptional laws that have been introduced under the capricious influence of a powerful man; they form islets that the jurist seeks rigorously to delimit. In short, political circumstances exercise their influence from time to time on jurisprudence and disturb the work of the doctrinaire. Subtle minds can utilize these sporadic elements to illustrate a theory of the *natural* rights which should exist among men; and, basing themselves on this theory for judging existing law, they can criticize it or declare meaningless those parts which are not in agreement with their theories.

This is a method suitable for the seduction of those minds that are more concerned with logic than with history and economics. In effect, in their eyes there is no essential difference whatsoever between diverse juridical elements. Since no means exist of admitting all these elements into any system, each of us has the right to offer a construction which will be as valid as any other, provided that it can be illustrated with examples. The absence of any consideration of the economic substructure impressed itself in the most vexatious way, because there is no way to choose in a philosophic manner. The Marxian method does not permit such fantasies.

Most often, Sophists who have 'destroyed' property by deductive reasoning have proceeded even more arbitrarily. They begin with vague formulations which they borrow from ordinary language and in which various analogies are made with juridical terms. The Ricardian theory of value will most immediately produce sophisms relative to property. Professor Anton Menger who finds the English socialist, William Thompson, so superior to Marx says: 'Like a great number of English economists, and Ricardo in particular, Thompson takes as his point of departure the idea that *work is the only creator of exchange value*. From this economic fact he draws the conclusion that he who has created value by his labour should receive the integral product of his labour.'[1] But how this passage of economy into law has operated is what Menger neglects to explain. This must seem to him to be too simple to warrant his pausing, but it is, nonetheless, very difficult to justify.

I believe that Thompson's reasoning can be reconstructed as follows: by hypotheses one considers an equalitarian society in which

[1] Anton Menger, *op. cit.*, p. 76.

the productive instruments are in the hands of people whose sole function is to supervise them and who receive a caretaker's remuneration for this service.[1] If it is admitted that the only *source* of created wealth is the worker's labour, no one except the worker has a valid claim to these riches. But it must be demonstrated that this reasoning is juridically valid for our society; and one must not play on the meaning of the word *source* in either everyday use or in legal terminology.

Pecqueur presents his conceptions in a much more developed form; thanks to this author's somewhat naïve frankness, it is easier to follow the flow of his ideas: 'All material wealth is due to work combined with matter, or rather to the intelligent energy of man acting upon matter. . . . *Matter is given to us collectively and equally by God*; but work is the man. St. Paul has said that he who does not wish to work does not have the right to eat. The social and political economy of the future is found in embryo in that sentence.'[2] It can be easily surmised that from these premises must follow communist conclusions or inferences of an egalitarian communist nature; but the author would not have regarded these premises as self-evident if he had not already decided to condemn the capitalist regime.

Pecqueur answered Rossi, who had said that he who administers his fortune wisely, saving part and contributing to production with his capital, must not be called indolent, as follows: 'To produce is to work; to say that capital works in our place is an absurdity. . . . In order to be genuinely productive one must give of one's self. Capital is *matter* that creates nothing without man's labour;[3] for all wealth comes from labour. Capital cannot work in place of man; even though the materialization of capital might act as a person, moral and gifted with spontaneous activity like man, it still could not substitute for man in society. For in the matter of labour not even a man can substitute for another man. Personal presence is absolutely necessary.'[4]

---

[1] Anton Menger, *op. cit.*, p. 177. They can at most receive wages equal to that of the best paid worker in Thompson's utopia.

[2] Constantin Pecqueur, *Théorie d'économie sociale et politique; ou étude sur l'organisation des sociétés* (Paris, 1842), p. 497.

[3] The distinction between *dead labour* or capital and *living labour* has penetrated Marxian literature through the *Communist Manifesto* which had borrowed extensively from contemporary popular literature.

[4] Constantin Pecqueur, *op. cit.*, p. 512. According to Edouard Drumont, work is a punishment which everyone must submit to in his own personal way. (Cf. *Libre Parole*, September 1909.)

GEORGES SOREL

Production is everyone's duty and each producer is a functionary. All are equally necessary to society and all should be equally regarded, if they work with an equal will.[1] As for trying to demonstrate the legitimacy of such a system, it is impossible. Marx has truly done well in not involving himself in this labyrinth of sophisms.

(b) The utopians were convinced that capitalism was no longer in a position to direct a productive base which has become too large for individual direction. Such a conception seems very strange to us today, because in the past half century we have seen industry perform prodigious tasks, although prior to 1848 we had considered it to be in quite a rudimentary state. It is difficult, then, not to regard the utopians as having been naïve. But one must take into account the alteration undergone by capitalism itself, in order to appreciate fully the change that has taken place in ideas.

At this point I recall that one of Marx's most essential theses concerns the passage of commercial and usury capitalism to industrial capitalism; the latter is the most fully developed form of bourgeois society. In the utopian epoch industrial capitalism was still subordinate. At the beginning of his articles on The Class Struggles in France, Marx observed that under Louis Philippe's reign the government was in the hands of what has been called the financial aristocracy (bankers, stock market and railroad tycoons, coal and steel magnates, timber owners and a part of the large landowners), whereas the industrial bourgeoisie was in the opposition. More specifically it shows the role of Grandin and Faucher, who were actively struggling against Guizot, as representing industrial interests.[2] In England, somewhat the same situation existed. In a note to Chapter XX in Volume III of Capital, Marx said that the merchants were allied to a landowning and financial aristocracy against industrial capital (for example, Liverpool as against Manchester and Birmingham) and that: 'The complete rule of industrial capital was not acknowledged by English merchants' capital and moneyed interests until after the abolition of the duties on corn, etc.'[3]

Formerly capitalist enterprises were directed by men lacking scientific knowledge, because they (the enterprises) were conducted like commercial or usurers' businesses. It was alarming to confirm the

[1] Constantin Pecqueur, op. cit., pp. 583–6.
[2] Karl Marx, The Class Struggles in France: 1848–1850, in Selected Works, loc. cit., Vol. I, pp. 583–6.
[3] Karl Marx, Capital: A Critique of Political Economy, Vol. III (Kerr ed.) (Chicago, 1909), translated by Ernest Untermann, pp. 385 f.

236

discrepancy that existed between the ability of factory directors and the science of the times. Today science has made enormous progress but it is no longer unknown in any of its aspects to the engineers who direct the workshops. The problem that had been of most concern to the utopians is thus found to be resolved by contemporary capitalism. If there are still exceptions it is because the industrial regime has not completely triumphed everywhere and because finance still exercises its evil influence on a number of businesses.

The problem of the organization of the workshop seemed no less difficult than that of its direction. The Middle Ages had bequeathed practices of great brutality among the journeymen. It was, then, natural that factory discipline was severe. Furthermore the foremen had to sustain a daily war against the ill will of the workers, who could not easily accustom themselves to carrying out the functions of complicated machinery that demanded close attention and required rapid physical movement. There was a bitter struggle, especially in England:[1] certain industrialists looked upon the older

---

[1] It seems to me that Marx has not given a clear idea of this state of things in *Capital* (cf. Vol. I, Chapter XV, Section IV, 'The Factory', pp. 457–66). Andrew Ure, from whom he borrows his principal ideas, reports that the first mechanical spinning mills failed because John Wyalt had too gentle a nature; Arkwright succeeded thirty years later because he had 'the energy and ambition of a Napoleon.' (*Capital*, Vol. I, p. 404; and Andrew Ure, *The Philosophy of Manufactures; or An Exposition of the Scientific, Moral and Commercial Economy of the Factory System of Great Britain*, London, 1835. (*Philosophie des manufactures*, Paris, 1836, Vol. I, pp. 21–31). On the brutality of the old English wool workers, cf. Andrew Ure (French ed., pp. 13, 267–71).) During Marx's epoch there had been great changes.

[Sorel's claim that Marx borrowed 'his principal ideas' from Ure is not substantiated by the texts. Indeed, Marx used every occasion to ridicule Ure's philosophical economy. He is clearly hostile to 'Dr. Ure, the Pindar of the automatic factory' (*Capital*, Vol. I, p. 458). Marx mocks his ideas on the 'central machine, from which motion comes not only as an automaton, but as an autocrat' (pp. 458–9). He further fails to understand how Ure can call Arkwright 'noble,' since he was 'the greatest thiever of other people's inventions and the meanest fellow' (463 ff.). Marx is likewise not especially taken with Ure's plea for 'order' in industrial production (p. 404). It is true that Marx based much of his analysis of 'Machinery and Modern Industry' on the empirical findings of Ure, but it is manifestly clear, Sorel's claim notwithstanding, that he shared neither Ure's economic standpoint, nor his technocratic notions. As Engels notes in his synopsis of *Capital* (*Engels on Capital*, New York, 1937, p. 75), 'in capitalist production, economizing labour through developing productive power by no means aims at shortening the work day—the latter may even be *lengthened*. One can read, therefore, in economists of the stamp of McCulloch, Ure, Senior and *tutti quanti*, on one page that *the labourer owes thanks to capital for developing productive forces, and on the next page that he must prove this gratitude by working 15 hours henceforth instead of 10.'*—I.L.H.]

237

workers, accustomed to traditional tools, as being incapable of yielding to new technological necessities. This education has been resolved without resorting to the more or less absurd methods devised by the utopians. The Fourierist theories which were fluttering about did not have to be taken into account in reaching the stage where a dozen calico weaving machines were operated by one worker.

Thus, capitalism has resolved the problems for which the utopians had looked in vain for solutions. It has created conditions which will permit the transition to a new social form. It cannot be demanded of reformers that they invent new scientific apparatus nor that they teach men how to produce at maximum capacity. Industrial capitalism resolves this problem every day, hesitantly and gradually. Marx, in disclosing the origin of this resolution, has rendered utopianism useless and even somewhat ridiculous.

However, socialism should not concern itself any longer with the means for aiding the progressive evolution of society. Marx energetically resists the attempt of the Lasalleans to demand the establishment of co-operatives subsidized by the State for the purpose of preparing the way for a solution of the social question. In the *Critique of the Gotha Programme* he noted that such an attitude is a deviation from socialism. Such a demand should be regarded as part of the class struggle. Socialism has only to concern itself with the revolutionary organization of *hands*, while utopianism wished only to advise the *head* of industry.

(c) The utopians were tremendously concerned with dividing wealth in a reasonable manner. In their time not only the financial aristocracy and the usurers seemed to take a disproportionate part, but the widespread existence of small industry tended to preserve situations of privilege for certain wage categories. Proudhon said in 1846: 'In Lyons it is a class of men who, thanks to the monopoly which the municipality permits them to enjoy, receive a higher salary than university professors or those in top ministerial positions: these are the petty thieves. . . . It is not unusual for a man to earn 12, 15 and up to 20 francs per day. . . . It is a matter of time. . . . The petty thieves of Lyons are today what they always were, drunkards, debauched, brutal, insolent, selfish and cowardly.'[1]

[1] Pierre-Joseph Proudhon, *Système des contradictions economique; ou philosophie de la misére* (Paris, 1846), Vol. I, pp. 131–2. (*System of economical contradictions: The Philosophy of Misery*. Translated by Benjamin R. Tucker, Boston, 1888.) He reproached them for their indifference to the silk workers' uprising. 'As long as they maintain their privileged position, they never get involved in politics.'

Capitalism causes the disappearance of most anomalies. It tends to produce a certain equalization of work among the various sections of the factory. But since it needs a considerable number of especially active, alert or experienced men, it contrives to give wage increases to those who render it the maximum service. It is not motivated by considerations of justice but solely by an empirical investigation of an *equilibrium determined by price*. Capitalism achieves a resolution of a problem which seemed insoluble. It resolves the question of the equality of workers while at the same time taking into account the natural or acquired inequalities which carry over into inequalities in work.[1]

It is known that Marx has formulated the principle: 'All the preceding classes that got the upper hand, sought to fortify their already acquired status by subjecting society at large to their conditions of appropriation.'[2]

He also employs the same principle at times in attempting to understand what happens to the world after a proletarian revolution. Thus, he announces the disappearance of the bourgeois family because the conditions of the proletariat do not permit it to practise the same type of sexual union. 'The proletariat has no fatherland.' The idea of patriotism must, then, disappear.[3]

In his communication of 1875 on *The Critique of the Gotha Programme*, Marx said that 'the principle that at present governs

[1] There are remarkable observations in *The Critique of the Gotha Programme* (New York, 1938) on this equality of law and the inequality of conditions.

[2] Karl Marx and Frederick Engels, *Manifesto of the Communist Party, loc. cit.*, p. 42. The (French) Revolution had based its law on the conditions of existence of the agricultural proprietors who formerly exploited land granted to them feudally. The descendants of the old grantees were considered to be without title, and total ownership was transferred to the commoner who cultivated the land. It is Paul Marie Viollet's estimate (cf. *Précis de l'histoire du droit Français, accompagné de nations de droit canonique et d'indications bibliographiques*, Paris, 1884–6, 2 volumes) that French feudal lands were turned into rented lands since everything subject to taxation became payable to the State. And in Napoleonic law, this involved the legal transference of land ownership. French general law in this way gradually becomes plebeian.

[The French Revolution did away with the system of giving the former serf, the emancipated peasant, the right to work the soil in return for a *cens*; i.e., a fee given to the landowner which usually carried hereditary rights. The monies transferred were known as the *cens*, while the lands worked by the tenant were known as the *censives*. A land leasing arrangement closely akin to this system was the *métayer* lease, or share-cropping system, which differed from the *censives* only in the mode of paying the landowner-rentier. For a fuller discussion of this, see Henri Pirenne, *Economic and Social History of Medieval Europe* (New York, 1937), especially Chapter III, 'Land and the Rural Classes.'—I.L.H.]

[3] Karl Marx and Frederick Engels, *ibid.*, Part II, pp. 44–51.

commodity exchange insofar as it concerns an exchange of identical value will apply to wages.' It is, he says, 'a bourgeois right' that makes for inequalities of content. 'It is, therefore, a right of inequality in its content, like every right.'[1]

Jules Guesde was very much within the Marxist tradition when he said to the Chamber of Deputies on June 24, 1896, that the problem of work could not present serious difficulties in collectivist society. In fact, one would be able by feeling one's way, by tentative procedures, to establish very short working hours for the least desirable occupations so as to attract precisely the number of men needed. 'The law of supply and demand will determine, without despotic or violent methods, this distribution which just now seems to you to be an insoluble problem.'[2] Others have thought that, instead of offering workers the enticement of greater leisure time, it would be more practical to continue offering them the enticement of higher wages.[3] This solution would seem to offer a stronger attraction. But it is essential to note herein that it is by a mechanism borrowed from the capitalist era that socialism can organize distribution.

Marxism is decidedly closer to Manchesterian political economy than to utopianism. It is important to emphasize this point. I have shown other thoroughgoing inter-relations between the two in my *Insegnamenti sociali della economia contemporanea*. Besides, the apostles of *social duty* have often pointed out the great danger that Manchesterianism presents to the capitalist system: it divides society into two classes between whom it establishes no bond and who, therefore, come to regard each other as enemies. The utopians, like the present apostles of *social duty*, did not wish to acknowledge the class struggle. It is not possible, then, to incorporate the concepts of the early socialists into Marxism without exposing oneself to very severe mistakes.

Now we shall examine what Bernstein calls Blanquism; we shall discover that divergence exists between Blanquism and Marxism.

[1] Karl Marx, *The Critique of the Gotha Programme, loc. cit.*, p. 9.

[2] Jules Guesde, *Quatre ans de lutte de classe à la chambre* (Paris, 1900), Vol. I, p. 96. Gabriel Deville wrote: 'A person will not work for pleasure. . . . The sole guide will be self-interest, a self-interest which is the point of departure for all human action, which controls all the relations of the individual with the environment. . . . No one will have either the direct obligation emanating from special legislation (to participate in dangerous or distasteful work) nor an indirect obligation resulting from the impossibility of managing to live by doing anything else' (Gabriel Pierre Deville, *L'évolution du capital*, Paris, 1883, p. 35).

[3] Gabriel Deville accepts both of these solutions.

V

The essentials of Marx's revolutionary ideas: the idea of class — Earlier theory of the destruction of the State — The Intellectuals — Analogy between Blanquist revolution and Hegelian theory, according to Bernstein; their differences — Social myths.

(*a*) BLANQUISM[1] is, in essence, nothing more than the revolt of the poor conducted by a revolutionary General Staff. Such a revolt can occur in any epoch whatsoever. It is independent of the system of production. Marx, on the contrary, considers that a revolution is made by a proletariat of producers who acquired economic capacity, intelligence in work, and juridical judgment under the very influence of conditions of production. The schematic description found in the next to the last chapter of the first volume of *Capital* states that the working class has been disciplined, united and organized in this manner.[2] I believe that Marx is describing here an advance toward rationality: from discipline one proceeds toward organization, that is to say, toward a juridical constitution. Without a juridical constitution it cannot be said that a class is fully developed.

The poor can appeal to the rich; the poor can remind the rich that they ought to fulfil a special duty toward them, the social duty that philanthropy and Christian charity impose on the upper classes. The poor can still rise up to impose their will and throw themselves upon the good things placed outside their reach. In either case, however, there is no juridical idea that society can acquire. The future depends on the good will of the leaders who will head the movement. They will lead their people: either to one of those bland, gentle societies that Renan regarded as being unfit to sustain the weight of a politically and nationally advanced society;[3] or to a society much like that

[1] I would remind the reader once again that it is not so much a question of Blanqui's ideas as of the Jacobin tradition which is implied in Bernstein's use of the term 'Blanquism.'

[2] Karl Marx, *Capital, op. cit.*, Vol. I, Chapter XXXII, 'Historical Tendency of Capitalist Accumulation,' pp. 834–7.

[3] Ernest Renan, *Histoire du peuple d'Israel* (Paris, 1887–93), Vol. III, p. 279. He gives as an example of this the Buddhist peoples. [Renan's *History of the People of Israel* is available in two English language editions. Volumes I, II and III were published in London (Chapman and Hall) between 1888 and 1891; while volumes I to V were published in Boston (Roberts Brothers) in 1896.—I.L.H.]

of the Middle Ages in which 'the thundering voice of the prophets as interpreted by Saint Jerome, terrifying the rich and powerful, hinders for the benefit of the poor, or so it is claimed, all industrial, scientific and worldly development';[1] or, finally, to a *Jacquerie*, as the utopians feared.

None of these hypotheses was acceptable to Marx. He had no sympathy for the morality of Buddhist renunciation. He saw the future in the shape of a prodigious industrial development. As for the *Jacquerie*, I recall with what horror Marx speaks of Russian revolutionaries who wanted to take the Cossack (Stenka) Razin, leader of an insurrection against Tsar Alexis, father of Peter the Great, as a model.[2] It is on the basis of technological progress, on science and on law that the new society will be constituted.

During the epoch when Marx wrote, there had not been enough observable working class experience to provide a perfectly clear picture of the means by which the proletariat could reach the degree of maturity he considered necessary for undertaking its emancipating revolution. He was generally content to provide concise and symbolic formulae which are usually very well chosen. But when he wanted, as a man of action, to pass on to everyday activity, he was considerably less inspired. It must not be forgotten that we hardly ever take action except when propelled by *memories often more vivid in our mind than immediate reality.* Marx revealed himself to be more backward as a man of action than he was as a philosopher. He was under the influence of the models bequeathed by the (French) Revolution, even when his economic doctrine should have led him to recognize the extreme difference that existed between the two epochs.

To look for the real meaning of Marxism in the advice given by Marx and Engels to their contemporaries would be self-deception. 'They had slipped into the most common errors of Blanquism,' said Bernstein.[3] This is true, although probably not to the extent that the German writer on Hegelian dialectic believed.

Marxism differs from Blanquism especially in its discounting of the *idea of party*, which was basic to the classic revolutionary conception;

[1] Ernest Renan, *op. cit.*, Vol. II, p. 540.
[2] *L'Alliance internationale de la démocratie socialiste et l'Association internationale des travailleurs* (International Working Men's Association) (London, 1873), pp. 62–3, 104.
[3] Eduard Bernstein, *op. cit.*, p. 63.

instead, Marxism returned to the *idea of class*.[1] But we no longer have the sociologist's vague and vulgar idea of a class as being an agglomeration of people in the same circumstances and situation. We have a society of producers who have acquired ideas fitting to their position and who consider themselves as having a unity entirely parallel to national bonds. It is no longer a question of directing the people but of leading the producers to think for themselves, without the help of a bourgeois tradition.

(*b*) The object of the party in all countries and at all times is to conquer State power and utilize it in the best interests of the party and its allies. Marxists, on the other hand, taught until recent years that they wished to suppress the State. This doctrine was presented with a wealth of detail, and sometimes of paradoxes, leaving no doubt as to its meaning. Naturally, the situation appeared in a different light when electoral success led socialist leaders to realize that the possession of power, even if it is only minimal, offers great advantages, such as can be obtained in municipal victories. The concept of the State which has replaced the original Marxian formulation was made on purely material grounds: the organization of socialist workers into a political party. In the *Aperçu sur le socialisme scientifique*, written by Gabriel Deville (in 1883), he has the following to say at the beginning of his analysis of *Capital*: 'The State is not—despite what is said by a certain bourgeois who has penetrated the socialist movement as a worm bores through a piece of fruit, in order to satisfy his unhealthy appetite by destroying it[2]—the ensemble of an already constituted public; that is to say, something which merely needs incidental alterations. The State is not to be perfected; it is to be abolished. It is poor strategy to begin by fortifying that which one wishes to

---

[1] The utopians were quite preoccupied with classes; but they did not understand this word in the modern sense. [This is clearly a debatable interpretation. Lenin firmly believed that the idea of party was a necessary part of any ideas about classes. Lenin's notion of the 'revolutionary vanguard' was primarily an attempt to avoid both the conspiratorial theory of Blanqui and the spontaneous theory of revolution held in common by anarchism and Russian Menshevism.—I.L.H.]

[2] This is a question raised by Paul Brousse, an old friend of Bakunin who had become the apostle of reformism. From this had come the name, *possibilistes*, a name assigned to his friends. He pursued a political line that eventually came to be turned into the modern socialist party; to seek and employ the power of administration to ameliorate the condition of certain groups of workers and to make, on occasion, revolutionary speeches. A very biting critique of this political line forms the preface of the first edition of the *Programme du parti ouvrier français* (Paris, 1883); this preface is absent in present editions.

destroy. It would increase the State's power to resist by aiding it to extend its control over the means of production; in other words, over the means of domination.'[1] Many other opinions from the same epoch could be cited on the danger to socialism arising from the extension of public services.

I believe that Engels wrote his book, *The Origin of the Family, Private Property and the State*, in order to show historically that the existence of the State is not as necessary as many people seem to think. For example, he draws the following conclusions: 'The State, then, has not existed from all eternity. There have been societies that existed without it, that had no idea of what the State and State power meant. At a certain stage of economic development, which was necessarily accompanied by the division of society into classes, the State became necessary as a result of this division. We are now rapidly approaching a stage in the development of production in which the existence of classes not only ceases to be a necessity, but becomes a positive fetter on production. They will fall as inevitably as they arose. With them the State will inevitably fall. The society that will reorganize production on the basis of the free and equal association of the producers will put the whole machinery of the State where it will then belong: into the Museum of Antiquities by the side of the spinning wheel and the bronze axe.'[2] In order to understand the transformation that socialist thought is undergoing, the composition of the modern state must be examined. It is a body of intellectuals invested with privileges and possessing so-called political means for defending itself against the attacks of other groups of intellectuals avid to acquire the profits of public offices. Parties are organized for the acquisition of these public posts which are imitative of the State. Marx's thesis is stated precisely in the *Communist Manifesto* in the following words: 'All previous historical movements were movements of minorities, or in the interest of minorities.'[3] We would say that all our political crises take the form of the replacement of intellectuals by other intellectuals. The result is to preserve the State and sometimes even to reinforce it, by increasing the number of interested partners.

Marx distinguished between the proletarian revolution and all pre-

[1] Gabriel Deville, *Aperçu sur le socialisme scientifique* (Paris, 1883), pp. 16–17.
[2] Frederick Engels, *The Origin of the Family, Private Property and the State (In the Light of the Researches of Lewis H. Morgan)* (Moscow, 1948), from the fourth German edition of 1891, pp. 246–7.
[3] Karl Marx and Frederick Engels, *Manifesto of the Communist Party, loc. cit.*, p. 42.

vious revolutions recorded in history. He conceived of this future revolution as bringing about the disappearance of 'the whole super-incumbent strata of official society being sprung into the air.'[1] Such a phenomenon admits of the disappearance of the fortress of the intellectuals, namely the State and the political parties. According to the Marxian conception the revolution is made by producers who, accustomed to the workshops of heavy industry, reduce intellectuals to being no more than clerks, performing as little work as possible. Indeed, everyone knows that a business is considered to be better managed if its administrative personnel is small.

There is a great deal of evidence relative to Marx's opinions on the revolutionary intellectuals in the International's circular of July 21, 1873. It matters little whether the deeds of which Bakunin's friends are accused are strictly accurate. All that matters is Marx's evaluation of those deeds. It is undistilled Blanquism, with its bourgeois chiefs of staff, that is censured with the utmost energy.[2]

[1] Karl Marx and Frederick Engels, *Manifesto of the Communist Party, loc cit.*, p. 43.

[2] [It should be noted that, while Sorel attributes the communication called *The Alliance of Socialist Democracy and the International Working Men's Association* to Marx, it is by no means certain that Marx had more than a cursory role in its preparation. In his authoritative biography Mehring had this to say about the preparation of the *Alliance* report, geared to solidify the expulsion of Bakunin from the International. 'The protocol commission of The Hague congress, consisting of Dupont, Engels, Frankel, le Moussu, Marx and Seraillier, therefore took over the task; a few weeks before the Geneva congress it issued a memorandum entitled: *The Alliance of Socialist Democracy and the International Working Men's Association.* This memorandum was drawn up by Engels and Lafargue, while Marx's share of the work was no more than the editing of one or two of the concluding pages, though naturally he is no less responsible for the whole than its actual authors.' Since Sorel bases much of his judgment on this pamphlet, it is interesting to read Mehring's comments on the *Alliance* pamphlet. He writes that it is 'below anything else Marx and Engels ever published. . . . It does not deal at all with the internal causes responsible for the decline of the International but merely continues the line adopted in the "Confidential Communication" and in the circular of the General Council on the alleged disruption in the International: Bakunin and his secret Alliance had destroyed the International by their intrigues and machinations. The Alliance pamphlet is not a historical document, but a one-sided indictment whose tendentious character is apparent on every page of it.' (*Karl Marx: The Story of his Life*, by Franz Mehring, London, 1936, pp. 496–7.) It is, furthermore, the case that Sorel confuses Marx's critique of the Blanqui–Bakunin élitist type of party with a general critique of the need for a proletarian political party. Marx does not, as Sorel maintains, replace the idea of a party with the idea of a class; but rather sees them in a complementary light. See Marx's *General Rules of the International Working Men's Association* in *Selected Works*, Vol. 1, pp. 350–3. Note particularly Article 7a, wherein Marx points out that 'the proletariat can act as a class only by constituting itself a distinct political party.'— I.L.H.]

He reproaches his adversary (Bakunin) with having formed a political association so strongly authoritarian that one might believe it inspired by a Bonapartist spirit.[1] 'We have, then, reconstituted, beautifully, all the elements of the authoritarian State. It matters very little if we call this machine a *Revolutionary commune organized from below*. Nevertheless Bakunin terms his State organization new and revolutionary.'[2] In the leadership of this organization were to be found bourgeois directors against whom Marx pours all his wrath: 'To say that the hundred leaders of the International should serve as intermediaries between the revolutionary idea and popular instincts is to create an insuperable abyss between the standpoint of revolutionary internationalism and the proletarian masses. It is to proclaim the impossibility of recruiting the vanguard anywhere else than among the privileged classes.' The outcome is a staff headquarters comprised of bourgeois revolutionaries which works with ideas and tells the people what to think, and a people's army which remains *cannon fodder*, to use Marx's words.[3]

The most violent reproaches are those made against the Italian 'alliancistes.' Bakunin, in a letter of April 5, 1872, is said to have found in Italy: 'a fervent, energetic youth, totally displaced,[4] without career and without outlet—a youth that threw itself headlong into revolutionary socialism.' Marx made the following remarks on this subject: 'All the so-called sections of the Italian International are led by advocates without a cause, doctors without treatments and without science, students of billiards, shopkeepers and others employed in commerce, and especially journalists of the petty press. By the seizure of all official positions in the sections, the Alliance sought to compel the Italian workers to enter into an arrangement whereby communication with the other sections of the International would pass through the hands of the déclassé supporters of the *alliancistes* who retrieved, in the International, a career and an issue.'[5]

It is difficult to express more repugnance at the invasion of proletarian organizations by intellectuals who bring with them the mores of the *political machines*. Marx clearly understands that such methods cannot lead to the emancipation of the producers' world. How could they possess the necessary ability for directing industry if,

---

[1] *L'Alliance internationale de la démocratie socialiste*, p. 11.
[2] *Ibid.*, p. 14.   [3] *Ibid.*, p. 15.
[4] Apparently we are to understand displaced as meaning declassed.
[5] *L'Alliance internationale de la démocratie socialiste*, pp. 48–9.

in order to organize themselves, they are obliged to subject themselves to the tutelage of politicians? There is an absurdity contained therein which could only disgust Marx.

(c) Bernstein is probably not mistaken in judging Marx to have been compelled to show sympathy with Blanquism due to the similarity he thought he perceived between the Blanquist revolution and the qualitative change which the Hegelian dialectic had led him to expect in the immediate historical future.[1]

But Bernstein deceives himself in his belief that there is a fundamental similarity between Blanquist ideas and Marx's concepts based on Hegelianism. It is more than likely an accidental similarity arising from the events of 1848. In this epoch they imitated the (French) Revolution as far as they could. Later, Marx described this imitation of the men of 1793 as farcical. The Blanquists, who suffered from an impoverishment of ideas, saw no reason not to act as in the times of the Terror: dictatorial measures for the benefit of the poor. Any counter-offensive by their adversaries evoked a condemnation of them as highly dangerous counter-revolutionaries, as a danger to the security of the new state of affairs. Blanquism realized that it had little influence throughout the country. It required a programme of concentrated revolution. And it wanted to make a leap into the new era with such audacity that it would go beyond the dialectical opposites of the Hegelian school.

Blanquism was not necessarily attached to the idea of absolute revolution. Like all parties, it had to assume a flexible attitude, in accordance with its political interests. At a time when they were sure that in France the support of a socialist deputy was useful,[2] the revolutionary party did not scorn the power of influence that it could draw from its relations with the government.

The way of conceiving the revolution, that Marx had been led to adopt by virtue of the Hegelian dialectic, makes impossible this evolution that Blanquism has undergone, or for that matter, that all political parties must undergo. Bernstein attacks this Hegelian dialectic because it concentrates the revolution on one sole act, which he considers to be incompatible with the necessities of political life in our advanced countries. If he had got to the bottom of the question, he would have known something still more important: that is, that his

---

[1] Eduard Bernstein, *op. cit.*, p. 49. Blanqui believed that forty-eight hours would be sufficient to change the orientation of a society.

[2] All journals have frequently cited it (Blanquism) as illustrative of this point.

master had always described revolution in mythical form and that therefore the agreement between Marxism and Blanquism was surface appearance. The first speaks of an ideal overthrow which is described imaginatively; whereas the second speaks of a change which is expected to be guided in terms of practical circumstances.

The penultimate chapter ('The Historical Tendency of Capitalist Accumulation') in Volume I of *Capital* leaves no doubt as to Marx's position. He describes the general direction of capitalism by way of hypotheses which would be suspect if they were applied literally to the historic events of the times, and even more so if applied to present day events. It could be said and it has been said that the revolutionary hopes of Marxism were fruitless because its description of society had lost its reality. Much ink has been spilled on the subject of the final catastrophe which is to occur following a workers' revolt. We must not take the text literally. We are in the realm of what I call a *social myth*. We have a vivid sketch that gives a clear idea of the change; but it is not possible to discuss details as historically verifiable facts.[1]

In exploring how minds are always prepared for revolutions, it is easy to see that there has always been recourse to social myths, the contents of which have varied according to the times. Our epoch requires more sober propaganda than was heretofore used; Marx can be credited with freeing his revolutionary myth from all the phantasmagoria which often led others to a search for the land of Cockaigne.

The myth does not lend itself to decomposing in changing and successive stages. It therefore becomes possible to construct in parts which, in showing results over a long period of time, can be considered as forming an evolved entity. This transformation (from myth to immediacy) is necessary in all action led by a political party and its functions particularly where socialists are members of parliaments. This is impossible with the myth which conceives of the revolution *en bloc*, as an indivisible whole.[2]

---

[1] I presented such an interpretation in the preface to the French edition of Napoleone Colajanni's *Socialisme* (Paris, 1900), p. xii. I have reproduced it at the end of the *Introduction à l'économie moderne*, and I have made great use of the social myths in the *Réflexions sur la violence*. An objection has been raised that Marx never seems to have recognized that he has employed mythical images; it is rather that he was sometimes so impassioned that this passion prevented him from viewing reality clearly. People sometimes forget that men of action would lose all power of initiative if they reasoned with the rigidity of a critical historian.

[2] Cf. 'Letter to Daniel Halévy' which forms the preface to the *Réflexions sur la violence*.

VI

Renaissance of the revolutionary idea: Fernand Pellou-
tier's role — The syndicalist reaction to the Marxists —
Purification of Marxism — The General Strike —
Democracy and sponsored trade unionism — Impossi-
bility of forecasting the future — The Renaissance.

THE preceding analysis leads us to realize that Marxism will not be
transformed in the way Bernstein had thought. It cannot be reconciled with a plan of industrial and political organization, any more
than it can be reconciled with a doctrine of justice, which would permit the heads of workshops and States to be the judges. Completely
dedicated to the preparation of proletarian revolution, it is not
worthwhile to argue with the rulers of society, something that the
utopians never ceased to do. They should be told that it is a *philo-*
sophy of hands and not a *philosophy of heads*, because it has but one
thing in sight: to lead the working class to an understanding that its
future hinges on the idea of class struggle; to lead it in a direction
where it will find the means to organize itself for the struggle, to reach
the point where it can dispense with its masters; to persuade the proletariat that it ought not to follow the examples set by the bourgeoisie.
Besides, Marxism is not in a position to submerge itself in other political parties, revolutionary as they may be, because the latter are
obliged to function like bourgeois parties, shifting their attitudes
according to the requirements of electoral circumstances and making
compromises, if needed, with other groups having similar electoral
ends. This is so because Marxism remains unalterably committed to
the idea of total revolution.

Several years ago one might have thought that the age of Marxism
had passed and that it was time for it to take its place, like many
other philosophical doctrines, in the necropolis of departed gods.
Only a historical accident was able to restore it to life. In order for
this to take place it was necessary that the proletariat organize itself
with distinct revolutionary goals; that is to say, the proletariat must
separate itself totally from the bourgeoisie.

Diverse circumstances have led some people, who observed the
tactics of politicians at close range, to make an effort in this direction. It is remarkable that their knowledge of Marxism was quite
superficial. They had undoubtedly read the Guesdist tracts and

journals, but they had found nothing that could satisfy them. The formulas in which Marxism was summed up in France seemed useless and false to them or given to a confusion of ideas.

Fernand Pelloutier, anti-politician and propagandist of revolutionary syndicalism, was a man whose worth cannot be exaggerated. 'Seized in his prime by a terrible illness, dying under conditions of severe poverty, as I have stated elsewhere,[1] Pelloutier in his writings has given only a hint of what he might have produced in the future. But when the hour of historic judgment comes, homage will be paid to the very important projects which he initiated. This great socialist will be famous when those who now hold first rank in our parliaments, and who represent socialism in the eyes of the admiring bourgeoisie, will have long been forgotten.'[2]

Pelloutier saw clearly the need for basing present-day socialism on an absolute separation of classes and on the abandonment of all hope for political reconstruction of the old order. He saw in the labour exchanges (*Bourses du Travail*)[3] the most complete organization of revolutionary tendencies of the proletariat. In 1900 he urged all people who did not want 'party regimentation' to 'pursue, more methodically and determinedly than ever before, the work of moral, administrative and technical education necessary to make a society of free men more viable.' In the same brochure he pointed to the need 'to prove to the working mass through experience, through their own institutions, that a government by itself and for itself is possible, and also to arm the working mass by instructing it in the need for revolution, in spite of the debilitating suggestions of capitalism.'[4]

In closely following this anti-political and revolutionary syndicalist organization, some of those who had given much thought to Marxism discovered that the new movement offered striking similarities to certain parts of their master's doctrine. They confirmed the fact that

[1] Georges Sorel, *Insegnamenti sociali*, pp. 53–4.

[2] Pelloutier has thus defined the role of the militants, such as it should be in practice. 'Devoid of all ambitions, unsparing of its forces, prepared to pay with their lives on the field of battle, after having thrashed the police, scoffed at the army, critical, uncompromising, the task of syndicalism is uncrystallized but *fruitful*'—Fernand Leonce Emile Pelloutier, *Le congrès général du parti socialiste français* (December 3–8, 1899) (Paris, 1900), p. vii.

[3] [*Les Bourses du travail*, sometimes referred to in syndicalist literature as the C.G.T., or *Union de Syndicats adhérentés à la Confédération générale du Travail*, was the central organ of syndicalist economic organization and 'anti-political' activity. Cf. Paul Delesalle, *Les Bourses du Travail et la C.G.T.*, Vol. IX of the *Bibliothèque du Mouvement Prolétarien* (Paris, circa 1900).—I.L.H.]

[4] Fernand Pelloutier, *op. cit.*, p. viii.

what the Socialist party had to say was desperately inadequate. Until the rise of syndicalism it had been claimed that Marxism had a true understanding of the need for preparing the proletariat for revolution.[1] But it was found that the doctors of Marxism were disoriented by an organization conceived according to the principles of class struggle in the strictest sense of the term. To extricate themselves from this difficulty these doctors indignantly denounced a counter-offensive of anarchism because many anarchists, on Pelloutier's advice, had entered the syndicates and labour exchanges. But words matter little to those who wish to get at the root of things. The cult of etiquette is for parliamentarians.

The *new school* could only slowly acquire a clear idea of its independence, compared with the old socialist parties. It did not attempt to form a new party which would compete with the other parties for working class membership. Its ambition was totally different: to understand the nature of the movement which seemed unintelligible to all others. It proceeded altogether differently from Bernstein's work. Little by little it rejected all the formulas that had proven to be utopianism or Blanquism. Thus it purged Marxism of all that was not specifically Marxist and it attempted to preserve what seemed to it to be the kernel of the doctrine. This assured the glory of Marx.

The writers who criticized Marx often reproached him with having spoken in symbolic language which they did not consider suitable for scientific investigation. On the contrary, it is those symbolic portions which were formerly regarded as being of dubious worth that constitute the definitive value of his work.

Apocalypse—which represented a scandalous ancestry to socialists who wished to make Marxism compatible with the practice of politicians in a democracy—in reality corresponds perfectly to the general strike which, for revolutionary syndicalists, represents the advent of the new world to come. They could not, however, be charged with having been deceived by the Hegelian dialectic; and since they reject the leadership of politicians, even the most advanced politicians, neither are they imitators of Blanquism. Thus we are led, by the observation of events among the proletariat to understand the value of the symbols employed by Marx, and they in turn permit us to appreciate the scope of the labour movement.

[1] Antonio Labriola, *Essais sur la conception matérialiste de l'histoire* (translated from the Italian by A. Bonnet) (Paris, 1902), pp. 40–1 (*Essays on the Materialistic Conception of History*, Chicago, 1904).

Even the idea of class struggle continued to remain quite vague, as long as there were no established workers' organizations along the lines outlined by Pelloutier; organizations of producers who conduct their own affairs without the necessity for resorting to the wisdom possessed by the representatives of bourgeois ideologies. In the work I have previously quoted Pelloutier explained the situation of his associates as follows: 'Outcasts from the Party because—while no less revolutionary than Vaillant or Guesde and while just as resolutely in favour of the abolition of private property—we are moreover that which they are not: unalterable rebels, without gods, master or fatherland; irreconcilable enemies of all despotism, moral or material, individual or collective, in other words, of law and dictatorship (including that of the proletariat) and passionate lovers of our own culture.'[1] The people who are motivated by such sentiments can do no less than put the doctrine of class struggle into practice in the most rigorous form.

The efforts made by the French government, after the Dreyfus affair, to gain the favour of the leading figures in working class circles have contributed much to the clarification of the nature of relations between society and democracy today. Admittedly the doctrine of progress is in vogue today. It became impossible not to consider democracy as a stage between the aristocratic society of the *ancien régime* and socialism. The nobility, the bourgeoisie, the petty bourgeoisie, the workers: the descending scale of wealth ought to correspond to a movement toward government of the poorest. Marx believed that a democratic system offers this advantage: once the attention of the workers is no longer drawn to the struggles against royalty and aristocracy, the idea of class struggle becomes much easier to understand. Experience teaches us, on the contrary, that democracy can work effectively to hinder the progress of socialism by orienting working class thought toward a government sponsored trade unionism. Ever since we have observed at close range two opposing forms of producers' organization, this danger in democracy has presented itself most sharply.

Thus one is led to look with suspicion on political revolutions. They are not possible unless the victorious party has the organized working masses behind it. A campaign against the rickety power of the old relations can make for the evolution of syndicalism toward sponsored trade unionism. Catholics make the greatest efforts to

---

[1] Fernand Pelloutier, *op. cit.*, p. vii.

group workers in syndicates, promising endless wonders in the hopes of frightening radical politicians and saving the Church. The Dreyfus affair can well be compared to a political revolution. For it would have resulted in a complete deformation of society if the entrance of many anarchists into the syndicates during that period had not oriented workers toward the path of revolutionary syndicalism and strengthened the idea of class struggle.

It must not be expected that the revolutionary movement can ever follow a pre-determined direction, that it can be conducted according to a master plan like the conquest of a country, that it can be scientifically studied other than in its own development. Everything about it is unpredictable.[1]

One must expect to encounter many deviations that seem to reopen every question. There will be times when all that seemed definitely achieved will appear to be lost. Trade unionism may even seem to triumph at certain moments. It is precisely because of this character of the new revolutionary movement that care must be taken to provide hypotheses other than mythical ones: discouragement could follow upon disillusionment arising from a discrepancy between the actual situation and the anticipated situation. Experience shows that many excellent socialists were thus led to the abandonment of their party.

When discouragement overtakes us, let us remember the history of the Church—an astonishing history which perplexed the minds of politicians, learned men and philosophers. At times one might have thought it to be guided by a mocking demon which took pleasure in amassing absurdities and in which the development of institutions has encountered a multiplicity of mishaps. The most reflective people have often remarked that the disappearance of the Church was merely a question of time. Nevertheless, the alleged death pangs were always followed by rejuvenation.

The apologists of Catholicism have been so impressed by the unrelated inconsistencies of its history that they can only explain it by

---

[1] One of the greatest illusions of the utopians has been the belief that one can deduce the pattern of the future by fully understanding the present. Against such an illusion, see Bergson's *Evolution Creatrice* (Paris, 1907), notably pp. 17, 57, 369 (cf. *Creative Evolution*, translated by Arthur Mitchell, New York, 1944, pp. 17–18, 57, 371). Bergson compares our personality to 'a sharp edge pressed against the future and cutting into it unceasingly' (p. 219 Fr. ed., p. 220 Eng. ed.). This beautiful image clearly shows how imagination offers a great deal for our intelligence.

claiming the intervention of providence, with its mysterious designs. I see it more simply. I see that the Church has endured despite the mistakes of its leaders, *thanks to spontaneous organization.* During each rejuvenation new religious orders are constituted which sustain the ruined edifice and even enhance it.[1] The role of the monks is analogous to that of the revolutionary syndicalists who save socialism. Deviations toward trade unionism, which is consistently the most formidable menace to socialism, recall the laxity of the monastic orders which brought about the disappearance of that separation between their members and the world which the founders of the orders had wished to establish.

The widespread experience that Church history makes available to us is of such a nature as to encourage those who have high hopes for revolutionary syndicalism, those who advise workers to conscientiously avoid any alliance with bourgeois parties. For it should be noted that the Church has profited more from efforts tending to separate it from the world rather than from alliances made between popes and princes.

[1] In an oft-cited passage, Machiavelli says that the Catholic religion would have disappeared if Saint Francis and Saint Dominic had not restored it to its principles in their mendicant orders (Décades, III, I). According to a well known legend, Innocent III had seen a vision in which Saint Francis (others say Saint Dominic) supported the Church of Latran which was threatened with destruction.

[There is, of course, no such work as *Décades.* What Sorel had in mind was Machiavelli's *Discorsi,* Book III, Section I, Paragraph 8; the full title of which is *The Discourses on the First Decade of Titus Livy.* The passage Sorel makes reference to reads as follows: 'As to religious institutions one sees here again how necessary these renovations are from the example of our own religion, which, if it had not been restored to its starting point by St. Francis and St. Dominic, would have become quite extinct.' Cf. *The Discourses of Niccolò Machiavelli,* translated from the Italian by Leslie J. Walker (London, 1950)—I.L.H.]

NAME INDEX

255

SUBJECT INDEX